From Marx
to Hegel

George Lichtheim

From Marx
to Hegel

Herder and Herder

1971
HERDER AND HERDER, NEW YORK
232 Madison Avenue, New York 10016

The author is grateful to the following for permission to reprint:

Triquarterly for "From Marx to Hegel" (number 12, Spring 1968);

Journal of the History of Philosophy for "The Origins of Marxism" (Volume III, number I, April 1965);

Survey for "On the Interpretation of Marx's Thought" (number 62, January 1967);

Problems of Communism for "Marxist Doctrine in Perspective" (November/December 1958);

Suhrkamp Verlag for "Sorel" (*Theorie*, I, 1969);

Times Literary Supplement for "Theodor Adorno" (September 28, 1967); "From Historicism to Marxist Humanism" (June 5, 1969); "Marx or Weber: Dialectical Methodology" (March 12, 1970);

New York Review of Books for "A New Twist in the Dialectic" (January 30, 1969); "Technocrats vs. Humanists" (October 9, 1969);

Commentary for "The Role of the Intellectuals" (April 1960).

Library of Congress Catalog Card Number: 70-167871

Printed in Great Britain

Contents

Introduction

The essays collected in this volume were mostly written in the 1960's, a time when the relationship of Marxism to its Hegelian origins was once more discussed at an intellectual level proper to the subject. During the preceding decade, all concerned had become obsessed with what was known as the Cold War. As a by-product of this concentration upon purely political issues, it was commonly supposed that Marx was of interest as a thinker mainly in so far as he prefigured the Russian Revolution and the rise of Communism or Marxism-Leninism. During the 1960's these certitudes gave way to the discovery that what was really of lasting importance in Marx's thought had more to do with the German intellectual tradition than with the use made of his ideas by Russian revolutionaries. In consequence, the topic was once again debated in the spirit in which it had been approached during the 1930's by the Central European group of scholars associated with the Frankfurt *Institut für Sozialforschung* and by outsiders such as the German philosophy professor Karl Korsch. The rise of the movement vaguely known as the New Left assisted this re-evaluation, at any rate in so far as it made possible an interest in German, French and Italian Marxists who from the Soviet viewpoint were unorthodox. The Roman Catholic *aggiornamento*, and the growing prominence of public debates between Catholic and Marxist spokesmen, likewise made a contribution to the spread of a new intellectual climate.

The present collection of essays must be read against this background. They were written for the purpose of clarifying theoretical problems quite independent of the political line-up which had resulted in the identification of Marxism with Leninism. In this respect the author of these lines stands in a tradition inaugurated by scholars such as Horkheimer, Adorno and Marcuse in the 1930's, and subsequently revived after the war by the successors of the original Frankfurt school— Professor Jürgen Habermas above all. The new problematic had to do with the relevance of Marxism to a society which in some respects no longer permitted a clear-cut distinction between "material base" and "ideological super-structure", both areas having been largely taken over by the state. The related problem of "technocracy" is the subject of a literature which assumed distinctive shape only during the 1960's. For the same reason, the controversy between the followers of the Hegelian-Marxist tradition and the positivist school founded by Max Weber gained new significance, notably in post-war Germany, but also in France and Italy. In Eastern Europe, political conditions inhibited the elucidation of these topics, although some Yugoslav writers joined the debate. The somewhat paradoxical title *From Marx to Hegel* has been chosen in order to suggest that the central problem now before us is not so much to change the world (that is being done independently), but to understand it. If the essays here presented to the public make a contribution to this aim, the author for his part will feel satisfied that his purpose has been achieved.

GEORGE LICHTHEIM

London, April 1971

From Marx to Hegel

The following observations are offered in an interpretative
and critical spirit. They contain no factual information of a
biographical or historical kind, and presuppose familiarity on
the part of the reader with the personalities and the work of the
writers under discussion. Anyone curious to discover more about
them must be referred to the sources or to the secondary literature cited in the course of the argument.[1]

A second cautionary remark may not be superfluous, since
we are dealing with one particular segment of a topic whose
ramifications are literally world-wide. Anyone concerned with
Marxist theory at the present time is likely to have his attention
directed to the discussions under way in France and Italy : these
being the only two Western European countries where the
Communist party has a mass following, and where Marxism—
or more precisely Marxism-Leninism—retains its hold over a
section of the intelligentsia. He will then discover that the
version of Marxist theorizing associated with the name of Louis
Althusser cannot be fully appreciated unless account is taken of
the post-war developments in French philosophy initiated by
Sartre and Merleau-Ponty, and of the more recent influence of
the "structuralist" school. In a certain fundamental sense all
these topics are related to the theme of the present essay, but
they cannot be pursued here. Whereas in France and Italy we
are dealing with a phenomenon best described as a "return to
Marx", the corresponding situation in Central Europe is rather

different, for what we have here is not so much a rediscovery of the authentic core of Marxism as a revival of a philosophical tradition which can properly be called Hegelian. It is understandable that this trend should manifest itself in areas where the Communist party has either failed to reach its goal (Western Germany and Austria), or has gained political power at the cost of sacrificing or compromising its humanist purpose (Poland, Czechoslovakia, Hungary). The East European "revisionists" confront a situation where the party is in power, but seemingly unable to satisfy the aims traditionally associated with the new form of social organization. They are thus driven back upon the romantic individualism of the young Marx. Meanwhile the West European Communists, having virtually abandoned the Leninist perspective of civil war and armed insurrection, are slowly reverting to the Social-Democratic pragmatism of their ancestors, or to a renewal of Syndicalism. It is only at the centre of the Old Continent, in the ancient geographical and spiritual heartland of Marxism, that one can speak of a return to philosophy : explicitly in the case of writers like Adorno and Marcuse, implicitly in Lukács' case, for all his outward assumption of the orthodox inheritance. In what follows, an attempt is made to draw out the theoretical and practical implications of this state of affairs.[2]

After these preliminaries, let us confront the evidence pointing to what has been tentatively described as a retreat from Marx to Hegel. This is a provisional manner of characterizing the outlook of our three representative thinkers. One might also name a fourth member of their generation : Karl Korsch, although (or because) his later development led away from the Hegelianized interpretation of Marx, and towards the conversion of Marxism into the theory of a revolutionary practice freed from all forms of philosophical speculation. This radical empiricism represents a critical counterpoint to our theme, which concerns the contrary phenomenon : namely the post-1945 revival of metaphysical idealism in the ancient Central European heartland of the Marxist tradition. Still, it does no harm to see how the situation presented itself thirty years ago to a theorist like Korsch, who in the 1920's had taken his share in defending the heritage of

German Idealism. And be it remembered that Korsch (although the lifelong friend and inspirer of Brecht) broke with the KPD and the Comintern in the 1920's because they seemed to him insufficiently revolutionary (as well as grotesquely servile to Moscow). Here is what the author of *Marxismus und Philosophie* (1923) had to say in 1938, at a time when disillusionment with the notion of "proletarian revolution" had not yet set in:

> Just as positivism could not move with freedom in the new field of social science, but remained tied to the specific concepts and methods of natural science, so Marx's historical materialism has not entirely freed itself from the spell of Hegel's philosophical method which in its day overshadowed all contemporary thought. This was not a materialistic science of society which had developed on its own basis. Rather it was a materialistic theory that had just emerged from idealist philosophy; a theory, therefore, which still showed in its contents, its methods, and its terminology the birthmarks of the old Hegelian philosophy from whose womb it sprang.[3]

A point worth stressing is that when one speaks of a "return to Hegel" one is *not* referring to the ontological system of "dialectical materialism" Engels sketched out in his writings of the 1870's and 1880's, and which subsequently became the cornerstone of the edifice known as "Marxism-Leninism". *This* kind of neo-Hegelianism has a long history. It began with Engels, was continued by the Russian Marxists, and eventually became the philosophy, or *Weltanschauung,* of Leninism : save where (as in Italy and France) the Communist movement produced indigenous theorists who were able to impose a corrective to the official line. To cite Korsch once more : "The critical principle of Marx's *social science* was during the subsequent development of Marxism converted into a general *social philosophy*. From this first misconception it was only one step further to the idea that the historical and economic science of Marx must be based on the broader foundation not only of a social philosophy, but even of an all-comprehensive 'materialistic philosophy' embracing both nature and society, or a general philosophical interpretation of the universe."[4] Korsch never attempted to explain how and why this misconception arose. Today, with the wisdom of hindsight, one is perhaps justified in saying that if "Marxism" was to function as the "integrative ideology" of a mass movement—be it Communist or Social-Democratic—such a development was inevitable.

Be that as it may, the topic concerns us here only insofar as Lukács can claim to be (or rather to have become) an "orthodox" Marxist-Leninist: a defender, that is to say, of the peculiar ontological system of metaphysical materialism invented by Engels and termed "dialectical materialism" by Plekhanov and Lenin. Clearly this orthodoxy is worlds removed from the neo-Hegelian idealism of Lukács' celebrated essay collection published in 1923 under the title *Geschichte und Klassenbewusstsein* and later repudiated by the author (but nonetheless included in the edition of his collected works prepared, with his active cooperation and consent, by a West German publisher). From about 1934 Lukács has appeared, in public anyhow, as a doctrinaire materialist for whom Lenin's treatment of the traditional themes of philosophy (in *Materialism and Empiriocriticism*, 1909) represents a satisfactory solution of problems which had troubled the youthful Lukács in his neo-Kantian phase around 1914. There is no need to inquire into the genuineness of this conversion. The purpose of these somewhat lengthy prefatory remarks will have been served if it is made clear that the whole area of dispute associated with Soviet philosophizing falls outside our purview. The topic which concerns us here is a different one, namely the revival of Hegelianism.

What is it about Hegel that renders his enduring influence crucial to an understanding of writers such as Lukács, Adorno, and Marcuse, who hold in common the notion that Marxism is to be understood as the legitimate heir of German Idealism? To put it differently: why is it that these writers—notwithstanding their adoption of widely divergent political standpoints— concur in believing that the theoretical and practical problems posed in Hegel's philosophy continue to be of importance for contem-

porary thought in general, and for Marxist theorizing in particular? To grasp what is involved one must disregard the trivial
notions still current about Hegel as the alleged inventor of a
universal *passepartout* labelled "the dialectic", possession of
which supposedly enables the initiate to predict, or control, the
future course of events. For even if it were the case that Hegel
had adhered to the triadic scheme usually cited in this connection (in fact he did nothing of the sort), this would not explain
why his legacy should concern the writers here under discussion.
The fact is that Hegel has continued to matter for a wholly
different reason : namely because his philosophy impinged upon
the central theme of political thought—the relation of theory
to practice.[5]

The issue had been posed by Hegel's predecessors, notably
by Kant, in terms appropriate to the Cartesian or Newtonian
doctrine that mathematical science alone provides adequate
insight into the laws governing material reality. This left uncertain the theoretical status of moral judgments, at any rate for
those who no longer accepted the guidance of theology. Kant's
solution of this problem was both simple and drastic. He
adopted the mathematical approach, but restricted it to the world
of appearances. Theoretical thinking thereby lost the standing it
had possessed for over two thousand years, that is to say since
Aristotle. It was limited to the phenomenal world which could
be described by (mathematical) science. The latter, as defined
in the *Critiques,* had nothing to say about morals. In Kant's
philosophy the moral life belongs to the noumenal realm of the
Ding-an-sich, along with God and the soul. Theory and practice
are thus torn asunder. Morality is approached through intros-
pection : by consulting the conscience whose inspired delive-
rances instruct us in our duties towards our fellow men. What
is morally obligatory or practical cannot be established by ratio-
cination, for while the natural world is analysable in scientific
terms, the moral world is not. Nature is subject to causality,
and thus follows unalterable laws, whereas the moral life is free,
in the sense of being self-determined. This freedom is "noumenal",
that is to say, transphenomenal. Hence the part of Kant's
philosophy which deals with ethics and politics is "practical"

in a sense wholly different from that intended by Aristotle (or by Thomist doctrine down to our own day). The dividing line runs not between theoretical contemplation and practical action, but between scientific understanding and ethical judgment. The distinction between theory and practice thus reflects the ontological difference between causality and freedom. Theory (science) has to do with appearances, moral judgment with supersensible reality. Kant's moral philosophy is "practical" not because (like any other moral philosophy) it deals with human practice, but because *morality cannot be grounded theoretically.* For Aristotle the difference between practice and theory corresponds to the distinction between physics and metaphysics. For Kant it runs parallel to the division between physics and ethics. There is a theory of nature : there is no theory of morals. What we *should* do, how we *ought* to behave, what sort of polity we *may* found, cannot be established by theoretical insight into the reality of things, for the "reality of things" is beyond our (theoretical) grasp. It is wholly a matter of conscience, of our free will. Freedom does not belong to the world of appearances and hence is not causally bound. If it were, morality could not tell us what we *ought* to do. Hence the subject matter of Kant's "practical" philosophy is the "ideal"—that which ought to be, but is not.[6]

But what if a follower of Kant—without explicitly going back to Aristotle, or to Spinoza—took the view that genuine theoretical insight into the ultimate ground of reality was possible? Then Kant's distinction between phenomena and noumena would go by the board, and the philosopher would once more derive his practical recommendations from his theoretical postulates. This is just what happened when Hegel refused to accept the Kantian noumenon, the *Ding-an-sich,* as a transphenomenal realm of being. There was (Hegel agreed) a distinction to be drawn between reality and appearance, *Wesen* and *Erscheinung.* But the noumenal realm of essence (*Wesen*) was accessible to reason! With this return to the metaphysical rationalism of the Greeks (and of Spinoza, whom Hegel was careful not to cite, since he counted as an "atheist"), the Kantian *ought* disappeared, or at any rate it ceased to be "practical" in the Kantian sense. There was once more a theory of ethics and consequently a theory of politics. Specifically, Hegel's *Philosophy of Right*—whose merits or demerits in terms of the factional quarrel between liberals and conservatives in the 1820's and 1830's need not concern us here—is "theoretical" although (or because) it deals with political "practice". In Hegel's philosophy, the relationship of theory to practice is not restricted by the Kantian notion of a supersensible realm accessible only to the will. There is a theory of politics, itself grounded in the understanding of history. Being a political conservative (and moreover temperamentally of a wholly contemplative bent) Hegel never caused the slightest apprehension to those in authority. No matter—he had taken the decisive step by restoring that union of theory and practice which Kant had torn apart. It was only necessary for the radicals among his followers, the Left Hegelians, to abandon his conservatism, and his philosophy could be turned into what Alexander Herzen called the "algebra of revolution".[7]

The gradual exfoliation of this theme in the writings of the Left Hegelians—from Arnold Ruge, Bruno Bauer, and Moses Hess to Marx himself—has been described countless times. For our purpose it is immaterial how one rates these thinkers in terms of the philosophical tradition of which Hegel was the last great representative.[8] What concerns us here is rather the degree of their success or failure in solving the problem Hegel had posed for them : how was (political) practice to be related to (philosophical) theory, once it was understood that speculative philosophy—i.e., Hegel's own system—had overcome the Kantian or Fichtean disjunction between the mere facticity of events and the *perennierendes Sollen* : the "perennial ought" so characteristic of these idealist thinkers and so uncongenial to Hegel. If the world was not to be confronted with subjective demands issuing from the "vanity" of the individual ego, then how could there be any kind of practice which did not result in conformity with whatever happened to be established? In his student days Hegel had cheered the fall of the Bastille; in later years he voiced a discreet admiration for Napoleon, who was not exactly inactive. Yet his seminal work, the *Phenomenology of Mind*, published at a time (1807) when he still looked hopefully to France, already struck the contemplative and conciliatory note dominant in his post-Napoleonic writings: the hidden essence of reality was seen to be in harmony both with itself and with the divinity. In less exalted language, the world was held to be precisely what it ought to be, namely reasonable. It is as well to bear in mind that Hegel had evolved this conviction long before, in the 1820's, he discovered the Prussian State to be a fairly close approximation to the rational State. This conclusion (which his more indignant critics in the 1840's attributed to his habitual conformism) was actually inherent in his method, though as a thinker he could equally well make room for a successful revolution—once it had occurred.

What he could never do was to supply a criterion for revolutionary practice here-and-now. Such a criterion had around 1800 been suggested by Fichte: the only one of Kant's pupils to adopt a Jacobin standpoint before turning into a German nationalist. But Fichte had been superseded: or so at least Hegel's followers believed (although some of them revived the Fichtean *ought* when in the 1840's they were confronted with an unsympathetic government which refused to appoint even moderate Hegelians to vacant positions in the universities). The problem, for those who had come to identify philosophy with absolute knowledge of reality, lay in discovering a principle which legitimized both the intellectual comprehension of the world and its (more or less radical) critique. From Cieszkowski and Bakunin to Hess and Marx, this was *the* great issue confronting Hegel's radical disciples. What is more, they were quite aware of it.[9]

On one point they were in agreement: if there was to be an intelligible ground of critical theorizing—let alone of revolutionary practice—it had to be discerned in the logic of the historical process itself. Otherwise they would be back with Kant's and Fichte's *Sollen*: with that disjunction between *is* and *ought* which Hegel had taught them to reject. The empirical reality had to be confronted with its own logic, not with moral commandments imported from a transphenomenal Beyond, or deduced from the "vanity" of the subjective consciousness, the ego. Of all the Left Hegelians, only Stirner in the end abandoned this approach—and thereby drew upon himself the thunders of Marx and Engels in the *German Ideology* (1846). All the others held fast to the original starting-point: practice was to be grounded in theory, action in thought, the revolution in the necessity of revolution. But if the revolution was "necessary" in the sense of being inevitable, then what reason was there for issuing a call to action? This was a puzzle. Marx solved it by discovering an inherently revolutionary class: the proletariat. But he also proclaimed (in the Feuerbach *Theses*, which he took care not to publish) that "the task" was to "change the world". This formulation, to anyone familiar with the literature of German Idealism, had a distinctly Fichtean ring. It was certainly not Hegelian. Yet it expressed Marx's innermost conviction.

The paradox could be resolved, even though the solution could (after the failure of the 1848 uprising) no longer be proclaimed to a public impressed by positivist scientism. Only if the proletariat possessed a universal mission—albeit one of which it was not conscious—could the philosopher identify himself with the revolution. This quasi-metaphysical assumption underlies the *Paris Manuscripts* of 1844, and is still discernible in the *Manifesto*. The proletariat is the "universal class" because it endures in the most concentrated form the suffering imposed by history upon the whole of humanity. Hence its self-emancipation is synonymous with the liberation of mankind from that bondage whose prehistorical origin is figured in the myth of Prometheus.[10]

But we have skipped one or two phases of the actual process whereby the greatest of the Left Hegelians made his escape from the metaphysical wonderland that in his youth had held him captive. The Promethean "wager" on the proletariat, as the force destined to "realize" the aims of philosophy, was the outcome of a particular spiritual crisis within one individual. But it was also an aspect of a more general crisis: the decomposition of the Hegelian school. The topic has become tediously familiar, notably with the growing popularity of a cult literature wherein Marx figures as a precursor of Existentialism, or even of Zen Buddhism. If it is still necessary to revert to it, the reason is that we are currently witnessing the rise of a neo-Hegelian movement. This development makes it necessary to inquire into the reasons that prompted Hegel's radical disciples to separate themselves from their master.

It is easy to see why they felt impelled to adopt a new *political* standpoint. After 1840, when the Prussian government officially embraced the most reactionary variant of the Romantic ideology to underpin the practice of royal absolutism, even the most moderate and long-suffering constitutionalists could no longer retain the illusion that Prussia represented the heritage of the eighteenth-century Enlightenment. Since it was this belief which had originally made possible Hegel's qualified support of enlightened authoritarianism in the 1820's, his followers had to seek fresh ground. But why did they have to invert the master's approach altogether? Simply because with Hegel the practical conclusion was already inherent in the theoretical assumption. If the intellectual comprehension of the world led to the discovery that the actual empirical state of affairs was irrational —i.e., contrary to Reason in the sense which the Enlightenment had given to this term—the system broke down. This notion was adopted with reluctance, and only after many initial hesitations. These took the form of differentiating the *method* from the particular affirmations made by Hegel in relation to Church and State : affirmations (it was explained) which were factually erroneous. Prussia was not, after all, a rational State, nor Lutheranism a rational faith. But liberals like D. F. Strauss, who contented themselves with this sort of criticism, were soon overtaken by radicals like Bauer, who proclaimed atheism; and Bauer in turn was shortly superseded by Feuerbach, who described religion as the "alienation" of man's innate powers to an imaginary Supreme Being. In relation to the Prussian State, even Arnold Ruge—no great radical—declared in the 1840's that the citizen could not become free and rational unless there was a political revolution. At this point there emerges the notion that *action* is grounded in *critical understanding*. Bruno Bauer drew no practical conclusions from this discovery, but the contemplative spell had been broken.

On the eve of 1848, when the radical doctrine was put to

the test, a "philosophy of action" (so described by Hess, who between 1842 and 1845 anticipated Marx in proclaiming the union of German theory and French practice) still presented itself as the extreme consequence drawn by the Left Hegelians from their master's understanding of history as a process unfolding towards a predetermined end. For Hegel this consummation had already been attained. The Left Hegelians (starting with Cieszkowski) transferred it to the future. At first it was merely asserted that the future could be *predicted;* later, that it could be brought about by action grounded in understanding —of what? Of the historical process that had carried mankind to the threshold of the promised land! Theory then had to become practice. It was the general conviction of Hegel's followers that there were no further philosophical problems to be solved, since Hegel had arrived at the standpoint of Absolute Knowledge. But precisely for this reason, philosophy could now be *applied* in practice. Cieszkowski, who was first with this announcement (thereby opening the way for Hess and Marx), was an aristocratic conservative, a believing Catholic, and an amiable philanthropist who toyed vaguely with Fourier's utopian socialism. Still, his *Prolegomena* made an immediate impact upon two Russian thinkers who stood on what was then the far Left—Alexander Herzen and Michael Bakunin : not accidentally, for Cieszkowski (perhaps inspired by Tocqueville) had hinted at the coming world role of the Slavs. One of the side-effects of the debate was in fact the growth of Panslavism : itself promoted by writers like Herzen and Bakunin, who for this reason later encountered the systematic hostility of Marx.[11]

The relationship of theory to practice was crucial for this generation of Hegelians, and one may say that its discussion provided the ferment which in the end resulted in the dissolution of the school. In the perspective of the left-wingers, the problem assumed a guise bewildering to orthodox Hegelians like Rosenkranz and Michelet, who felt that the radicals were reverting to a pre-Hegelian standpoint. As these philosophers saw the matter, it was absurd to transmute Hegel's mature thought into an instrument of consciously willed change. On this point at least they were in agreement with Marx, who in the end

abandoned speculative philosophy for precisely this reason. Yet
the fact remains that around 1840 something like a "philosophy
of action" was in fact worked out by rebellious Hegelians, some
of whom eventually (after the failure of the 1848 revolution)
transformed their earlier doctrine into a conservative and contemplative "philosophy of history". These were really two sides
of the same medal. For proof one may consider the case of
Bruno Bauer, once a prominent radical and Marx's first teacher.
Before 1848 Bauer had been foremost in trying to turn speculative *knowledge* into *critique*. In the 1850's, when faith in revolution (and in Europe's universal role) had been shaken, he was
among the first to proclaim the coming role of the Slavs and,
by implication, the dawn of an era of racial conflicts.[12]

  Geschichtsphilosophie (philosophy of history), in the sense of
Cieszkowski, Bauer, and Ruge, formed part of the intellectual
ferment associated with the disintegration of the Hegelian school.
It was the counterpart of the revolutionary "theory of action"
proclaimed in 1843 by Hess (who also tried his hand at the
philosophy of history, which as an ardent Francophile he interpreted in radically "Western" and "European" terms). Bauer—
the friend of Marx, later his opponent, and an important precursor of Burckhardt, Nietzsche, and Spengler—can be claimed
for both camps. What needs to be grasped is the enduring
relevance of Hegel for *all* these writers, even when they were
producing political journalism or speculating about the coming
decline of Europe. All of them had read Tocqueville, the first
volume of whose *Démocratie en Amérique* (1835) antedated
Cieszkowski's *Prolegomena* (1838) by exactly three years (the
second part, generally judged inferior, appeared in 1840). But
this alone would not have induced them to worry over the
coming role of America, just as Bakunin and Herzen would not
have arrived at Panslavism in the 1850's merely because Haxthausen (himself a Prussian official) had opened their eyes to the
importance of the agrarian commune as a potential source of
"communism" in the modern sense. All these notions, in themselves more or less commonsensible and grounded in the study
of actual social history, obtained an extra dimension in the light
of a philosophy of history derived from Hegel's thinking.[13]

This may seem farfetched; but one need only study the utterances of Hegel's more orthodox followers to see that they had taken to heart the master's message : only that which is fully comprehended has been overcome; conversely, intellectual comprehension is possible only in relation to that from which the spirit of life has already departed. "The owl of Minerva starts its flight when the shades of dusk have fallen." True understanding relates to the past, for the actual process "comes to itself" in the philosophy that sums up the sense of the epoch. Hence for an orthodox disciple of Hegel there could be no "philosophy of action", but there could and must be an effort to comprehend the necessity of the universal process as it unfolds through the ordinary vicissitudes of history. This in the end was Bauer's standpoint, and he was to have numerous successors, down to and including Spengler (who indeed sought an escape from determinism by appealing to Nietzsche's cult of "will", thereby landing himself in an inconsistency which has remained characteristic of all the ideologists of Fascism). Immediately, for those who shared Hegel's contemplative bent, the problem presented itself in the form of pessimistic reflections on the future of their own civilization : that of Europe. For if Hegel's philosophy represented the mature self-consciousness of the epoch, then plainly its appearance signified the approaching end of European history, and perhaps (according to Bauer) of Christianity as well. Hence the failure of the 1848 uprising made no deep impression on Bauer : it was (he said) a trivial incident in a process of disintegration which had gone too far to be reversed : "This whole revolution was an illusion. Originating in the general pauperism, it was merely a bloody intermezzo in the smooth, passive dissolution in which the whole hitherto existing culture withers away and passes into decay."[14]

What, it may be asked, is the relevance of all this to the work of three contemporary writers who represent the Hegelian strand within the Marxist tradition? The answer ought to be evident : on Hegelian principles, *Geistesgeschichte* records the dialectical movement of truth and reality, theory and practice, profane history and intellectual self-awareness. If then we find that contemporary thinking reproduces the problematic[15] of an earlier historical situation—namely that out of which Marxism arose—we are entitled to suppose that it does so because the relationship of theory to practice has once more become the sort of problem it was for Hegel's followers in the 1840's. The "overcoming" of philosophy in those days was intended to do away with the dualism of contemplative theorizing and empirical practicality. Specifically, the Hegelian system was perceived by its radical critics as a self-contradictory attempt to halt the historical process. Hegel's procedure implied the conclusion that world history, or at any rate European history, had been comprehended; by the same token it had to come to an end. In "going beyond" Hegel, his critics went beyond philosophy, just as Hegel had gone beyond theology when he suggested that the "truth" of religion was to be found in speculative metaphysics. His own synthesis collapsed when his followers went their separate ways, and they did so because the radicals among them operated with an activist concept of *Praxis* as the creation of man's collective existence in the historical present and future. The particular contribution of Marx was to transform this notion into a theory of action from which in later years there emerged a determinist sociology, conventionally described as "historical materialism" by Engels. This consensus in turn was disrupted in 1914–18. From 1918 onwards, the advent of a general crisis of European civilization became the common theme of revolutionaries who had gone back to the spirit of the 1848 *Manifesto* (the Communists), and of counter-revolutionaries who accepted the Hegelian premise, but opted for a different solution (the Fascists). As noted before, the growth of pessimism about Europe's future, and the eventual collapse into nihilism (Nietzsche-Spengler), grew from the same soil as did the world-transforming optimism of Marx and his friends. For Lenin's followers these themes were ultimately compatible, because the Bolsheviks (following the example set by Herzen and Bakunin) were able to bridge the traditional gulf between "Westernizers" and Slavophiles by arguing that Russia had turned out to possess the revolutionary potential Marx and Engels had vainly sought in Germany. In this perspective, 1917 was the fulfilment of 1789, the Russian Revolution the successor to the French. By implication, this notion also took care of Spengler's pessimistic outlook : what had "declined" was not "the West", but simply one particular social formation : bourgeois society.

This is still the official Leninist standpoint, and it also represents the settled conviction of Lukács. Yet for all his accommodations to the party line (whatever it might be at any moment) Lukács was never regarded as wholly orthodox from the Leninist-Stalinist viewpoint, and one can see why : once a Hegelian, always a Hegelian. Even after 1933 he did not really manage to shake off his conviction that there can be—indeed there must be—a privileged standpoint which permits access to permanent truths about the movement of history. This stand-point was supposed to coincide with the consciousness of the proletariat (or rather of "its" party) and Lukács never tired of proclaiming that only the Communist party possessed a "true" awareness of the world situation. Yet, by implication at least, the theorist reserved the right to certify the correctness of the party line, though for prudential reasons he might fall silent and busy himself with less explosive topics. He might even repudiate his earlier utterances, renounce the heritage of German Idealism (Kant included), subscribe to all the theoretical and practical monstrosities of Stalinism, and solemnly proclaim the East European police state the concrete realization of freedom. No matter : if the truth about history was independent of the findings available to empirical sociology, it was likewise (in principle anyhow) independent of politically motivated changes in the party line. When circumstances permitted, the philosopher would once more come forward and announce (albeit in muted language) that the real truth about the historical situation was such-and-such. Over the years, Lukács has in substance adhered to his conviction that a uniquely determined insight into the logic of history is available to the theorist. In this at least he has been consistent. When all is said and done, a Church cannot do without theologians, and who if not the theologian—he who has devoted his life to the study of the sacred texts—can judge the doctrinal correctness of the pronouncements made by authority?[16]

In fairness to Lukács it needs to be said that belief in the possibility of objective insight into reality is indeed part of the classical tradition from Aristotle to Marx.[17] The rejection of relativism and subjectivism links Lukács with thinkers otherwise antipathetic to him : some of them Marxists, others empiricists whose political standpoint is either liberal or socialist in the Western democratic sense. There is no need to identify "subjectivism" (i.e., disbelief in the possibility of valid statements about the world) with a generic "bourgeois class consciousness" which the Lukács of *History and Class Consciousness* (1923) had already hypostatized into an independent entity : three decades before the final (and quite explicitly Stalinist) condemnation pronounced by him in *The Destruction of Reason* (1953).[18]

Here it is worth remembering that the youthful Lukács before 1914 had been profoundly marked by the cleavage between the two philosophical trends then dominant in Germany : the neo-Kantian school (of which H. Rickert and E. Lask were the most distinguished representatives) and the historicism of W. Dilthey. The latter's tendency to identify *Gesellschaftswissenschaft* (sociology in the widest sense of the term) with *Geisteswissenschaft* (history of the spirit) seemed to open the door to an equivocation : if history was the record of the human spirit, then it was tempting to suppose that material (social) reality could be dissolved into ideology. In reacting against such notions—which in Italy were then being systematized, under Hegel's influence, by Benedetto Croce—the Marxists, from Gramsci to Lukács, revived Marx's "materialist" critique of Hegel : there was neither an ontological primacy of spirit over matter, nor a logical priority of the thinking subject vis-à-vis the material object. Yet if the equivocal terms *Geisteswissenschaft* was purged of its "idealist" and "subjectivist" overtones, it pointed to a circumstance already dimly perceived by Vico in the eighteenth century and revived by Hegel in the nineteenth : the fact that the world of history and society (unlike the realm of nature) is man-made, hence fully accessible to Reason. Hegel's critique of Kant's phenomenalism, after all, had taken for its starting-point the notion that the historical realm—being the work of man—is recognizable in its "noumenal" aspect, whatever might be said about the phenomenalism of the natural sciences. This epistemological realism formed part of the Hegelian legacy which Marx had inherited. It was not dependent on the "idealist" identification of subject-object, and quite compatible with empirical sociology. If this was all Lukács meant to convey, then there was no need to establish a Manichaean distinction between "bourgeois subjectivism" and "socialist realism".

But of course there was more to it. The Lukács of *History and Class Consciousness* (1923), for whose sake Westerners (and non-Leninist Easterners like Kolakowski) have patiently endured his later writings,[19] was not merely concerned to affirm that the truth about human history is cognizable. That would have been ordinary Hegelianism : doubtless a radical break with Lukács' neo-Kantian standpoint before 1914, when he shared the general conviction that the empirical world is the domain of the specialized sciences, but still no more than one philosophical construction among others. A total system of truth about the world is still a philosophical system, whether deduced from Hegel or from Husserl. If Lukács had remained at this level, he would simply have furnished a neo-Hegelian counterpoint to the Nietzscheanism of Spengler, or to the irrationalism of a *Lebensphilosophie* which held that an intuitive understanding of the self and of man is an ever-present possibility for certain privileged individuals. The originality of Lukács lay in the assertion that the totality of history could be apprehended by adopting a particular "class standpoint" : that of the proletariat. Class consciousness—not indeed the actual consciousness of the empirical proletariat, which is hopelessly entangled with the surface aspects of objective reality, but an "ideal-typical" consciousness proper to a class which radically "negates" the existing order of reality : this was the formula which had made it possible for the Lukács of 1923 to unify theory and practice. In this perspective, speculative philosophy had once more been "overcome" and the dimension of early Marxism had been recovered : not accidentally on the morrow of a revolution that temporarily revived the atmosphere of 1793 and 1848. At such a privileged historical moment it did not seem wholly extravagant to assert that Communism represented both the *theoretical* apprehension of the past and the *practical* construction of the future. But although Lukács hypostatized "the party" as the institutionalized will and consciousness of "the class" (a circumstance which did not shield him from orthodox indignation), he implicitly reserved the right to pronounce upon the correctness or otherwise of the party's *Weltanschauung*. What did this signify if not that the philosopher claimed the authority to systematize theory *and* practice? Gramsci, writing a few years later, at least affirmed that true insight and true *praxis* were conjoined in the empirically existing Communist party of his own country.[20]

It has been observed that the Lukács of 1923 was still under the spell of pre-1914 German *Geisteswissenschaft*.[21] So much indeed is obvious, as is the psychological overreaction apparent in his subsequent repudiation of his own past from 1933 onward: the Third Reich having (according to Lukács) discredited not only Nietzsche and Spengler—to say nothing of Hitler's philosophical clown, Heidegger—but the idealist tradition in general. But then what of Hegel? In his writings of the period (*Der junge Hegel* was actually completed in 1938, although published a decade later) Lukács was at pains to differentiate the "objective idealism" of Hegel from the irrationalism of Schelling and the "subjectivism" of Schopenhauer and Nietzsche. The Hegelian inheritance must *not* be repudiated, else Lukács' Hegelianized doctrine would lose its philosophical anchorage. Marxism, in Lukács' interpretation, certifies its own superiority over rival systems by "placing" them in a historical sequence corresponding to the decline of bourgeois civilization and the emergence of a higher type of society. This process is related to the West-East antagonism, so that the antithesis capitalism-socialism is made to correspond to the actual socio-political cleavage between Western and Eastern Europe, or between the USA and the USSR. However absurd, these assumptions are required for any Leninist, which is why Lukács' condemnation of modern art and literature as "decadent", so far from being an aberration, is a necessary consequence of his standpoint. If the West is identified with bourgeois society, and if this society is in decay, then its cultural manifestations must "reflect" this decay; whereas "socialist realism" represents the germ of a new and higher phase of human self awareness. That Lukács actually believes this is no more in doubt than that his approach to the topic reflects the traumatic shock he had suffered in 1933, when traditional bourgeois culture (the only culture he ever understood) crumbled under the onslaught of Fascism.[22]

But we fall short of the true significance of our theme if we retain only the apologetic character of Lukács' later writings; his accommodations to the party line; his tortured self-identification with a cause which was *also* the cause of the anti-Hitler struggle; his cultural pessimism, and the growing conservatism of old age. Lukács' role in the recent evolution of Marxism is an aspect of a wider phenomenon : the transformation of Marx's *critique* into a philosophy. In this perspective, the neo-Hegelianism of *History and Class Consciousness* supplies a key not only to its author's subsequent development, but to much else besides.[23]

The Lukács of 1923 had inaugurated the Hegelianized Marxism which arose in the West after 1945; and he had done so notwithstanding his own subsequent autocritique, his angry repudiation of his earlier views, and his increasingly rigid adherence to an "orthodoxy" whose descent from Engels and Kautsky was scarcely concealed by Lenin's polemics against the latter. For this orthodoxy, Marxism was the "science" of a "revolution" which followed with mechanical necessity from the operation of economic "laws". In rejecting this approach, the early Lukács revived the Left Hegelian attitude of the 1840's : philosophy could become "practical" only by transcending itself *qua* philosophy, and it could do so because a "total" revolution —carried forward by a class whose existence "negated" the status quo—was *ante portas*. A theory that "reflected" this situation thereby certified its own superiority to all other standpoints, for insight into the inner logic of the process partook of a higher order of reality than the empirical investigation of so-called facts. So much indeed might be conceded even by those who did not place their wager upon the advent of a proletarian revolution. If the crisis of Western society—or at any rate of Western European society—was indeed "total", then the familiar sociological relativization of different "standpoints" was out of place, as was the positivist belief in a science of society emancipated from philosophical speculation and consecrated to the "unprejudiced" study of objective data. The higher, or deeper, truth was attained by speculative reasoning. But what if theoretical insight into the actual march of events suggested conclusions unpalatable to the revolutionary?

Lukács in 1923 had subtitled his book "Studies in Marxist Dialectics" : in itself an affront to an orthodoxy committed to the metaphysical "materialism", or monism, of Engels and Lenin. If one abstracts from this not very fascinating quarrel, there remains the question whether Lukács was not in fact trying to combine incompatibles. The dialectic of the mature Marx (unlike that of Hegel and the Young Hegelians) was a dialectic of theory and practice, thought and action, generalization and experience. His *critique* was the intellectual side of a practical commitment whose success or failure could not be predetermined : whether or not the revolution will actually take place is a question to be answered by "scientific" study of the concrete social situation. It cannot be certified by a supposed insight into the logic of the historical process. In reverting to this mode of discourse, Lukács was in fact returning from Marx to Hegel.

A Hegelianized Marxism such as that of Lukács begins and ends of necessity with an attempt to portray the actual interplay of reality and ideality, logical categories and the "stuff" of experience, without yielding to Hegel's temptation—the construction of yet another metaphysical system. In 1923 Lukács for a moment believed he had solved the problem : it was only necessary to dispense with "vulgar materialism" so as to arrive at a dialectic in which "being" and "thinking" were reciprocally interdependent. One could then see that Hegel had in effect continued the Kantian enterprise, albeit with some modifications, and that Marx was in the tradition of classical (i.e. idealist) German philosophy, even though in his later writings he had permitted himself a few backslidings : not to mention Engels, whose naively realistic theory of cognition was clearly pre-Kantian.[24]

The later Lukács having reverted to the conception of the

mind as a mirror which "reflects" an external reality, the problem of formulating a "materialist dialectic" in terms that took account of Kant and Hegel presented itself anew to the group of scholars who in the early 1930's made up the inner circle of the Frankfurt *Institut für Sozialforschung* (subsequently transferred to the United States, where some of its members eventually settled down). After 1945 the discussion of this topic spread to France, primarily under the influence of Merleau-Ponty who had made his own the theme of Marx's early writings : *La seule manière de réaliser la philosophie est de la détruire*.[25] Here we are only concerned with the Central European debate, and specifically with the two writers who in recent years have systematized the Hegelianized Marxism of the original Frankfurt group : T. W. Adorno and Herbert Marcuse.[26]

The "Marxist-Leninist" approach starts from the "materialist inversion" of Hegel's philosophy which Marx is supposed to have effected. If this misunderstanding is avoided, as it should be,[27] a thinker who tries to operate with Hegel's method is confronted with the question what the dialectic signifies if it is not the movement of an absolute : be its label "Matter" or "Spirit". This is Adorno's problem. He has devoted a lifetime to its solution, and his work, taken as a whole, represents a counterpoint to that of Lukács, while Marcuse is best understood as the exponent of an intermediate position.

If this circumstance is borne in mind, a brief consideration of these two writers can afford to disregard their spectacular, and often very interesting, excursions into other fields, notably the interpretation of psychoanalytical theory. It is doubtless more than a biographical coincidence that both Adorno and Marcuse have felt the fascination of Freud, or that they have taken a prominent share in sponsoring the libertarian morality which differentiates Western from Eastern Europe. But these topics fall outside our theme, which is rather more narrowly defined than would be proper in a sketch of Central European intellectual history since the first world war. It is indeed useful to remember that all the writers in question have had to cope with a set of theoretical and practical problems which in the last resort stemmed from the collapse of traditional European society between the wars, and from the subsequent failure of Stalinism and Fascism to hold the allegiance of intellectuals brought up in the liberal tradition. But this having been said, the fact that Lukács, Adorno and Marcuse have arrived at different interpretations of the Hegelian inheritance constitutes a theoretical theme, not an invitation to spin biographical or psychological fantasies.

Adorno's work as a philosopher is refracted in a multitude of publications, of which only a few can enter into consideration here : principally his *Aspekte der Hegelschen Philosophie* (1957); *Zur Metakritik der Erkenntnistheorie* (originally composed in 1934–37, but given its final form in 1956); and *Negative Dialektik* (1966). Additionally, mention must be made of the selection of essays that appeared under the title *Prisms* in an English translation in 1966. Marcuse's study of Hegel, *Reason and Revolution* (London : 1941, 1955), established him in an unshakeable position, from which in later years he sallied out to deliver critical and polemical broadsides along a sector of the front usually associated with the New Left. It seems fair to say that, while politically further to the left, Marcuse shares Adorno's aversion to the type of dogmatic scholasticism institutionalized—with the help of Lukács—in the USSR and in Eastern Europe.[28]

What then is the enduring problem for a thinker who tries to operate with the Hegelian method, while retaining the Marxian critique of Hegel and of philosophy as such? We can approach the topic by citing what Adorno himself has to say about the inmost core of Hegel's logic : the notion of a subject-object relation which is *not* one of passive "reflection" of "the world" in something called "the mind" :

> In Hegel, idealism shows a tendency to pass beyond itself . . . the extreme idealist point of his thought, the construction of the subject-object, cannot be dismissed as the mere extravagance of logical absolutism. In Kant the hidden source of power already lies in the notion that a world divided into subject and object, in which we are, as it were, the prisoners of our own constitution—hence confined to

mere phenomena—is not the ultimate. To this [notion] Hegel adds something un-Kantian: [the idea] that in determining conceptually the block or frontier delimiting our subjectivity, in seeing through the latter as "mere" subjectivity, we have already passed beyond . . . Speculative idealism does not insanely disregard the limits of possible cognition, but [rather] seeks to formulate [the idea] that in every genuine act of cognition there inheres something like a relation toward truth as such; that cognition, if it is to be genuine and more than a simple duplication of the subject, must be more than subjective: Objectivity in the sense of Plato's objective Reason, whose heritage is chemically compounded in Hegel with the subjective philosophy of transcendentalism.[29]

But this qualified defence of Hegel's attempt to go beyond Kant and Fichte is crossed in Adorno's writings by a different line of thought. Hegel had tried to overcome the split between the world and the mind, but he had remained a prisoner of the fundamental vice inherent in the speculative enterprise from the very start: the attempt to define a self-consistent principle from which the world of appearances could be logically deduced. His dialectic presupposed what it was meant to prove: the identity of subject and object, and along with it the hidden primacy of spirit.[30] *Prima philosophia,* from Plato to Hegel and beyond, suffered from the same radical defect: it started from a first principle whose unfolding was supposed to encompass the totality of existence. No matter what was proclaimed as "the first" or "the absolute", the procedure as such constituted a kind of *hubris*: the philosopher identified himself with the world, subjected it to reasoning, and thus set up an implicit claim to total comprehension and domination of *what is*.[31] Hegel's dialectic did not escape this fate, whose subsequent implications Adorno has traced in a destructive analysis of Heidegger's ontology.[32] No matter from where he starts, the speculative thinker is obliged to lay down an irreducible principle whose generality safeguards him against the flux of ordinary experience. But in order to be general, the first principle must be abstract,

a creation of pure thought. In its origins an aspect of the metaphysical rationalism of antiquity, the problem recurs in its
modern form with the attempt to found a theory of cognition
upon self-evident axioms. Even Kant, who thought he had done
away with the *philosophia perennis,* could not elude this require-
ment. He "liquidated the quest for Being, and yet taught *prima
philosophia.*"[33] Thereafter, Hegel's "heroic effort" suffered the
same fate.[34] The Hegelian dialectic is not really what it purports
to be: an escape from the idealist cave in which the speculative
enterprise has been imprisoned since Plato. His procedure is
kept going by the operation of the sovereign intellect which
undertakes to render an adequate report of the world by reflecting up its own self-consciousness. There is a further problem:
the philosopher, as an empirical individual, is a contingent being
and as such cannot constitute an absolute starting-point. German
Idealism, culminating in Hegel, tries to escape from this
dilemma by treating the individual mind as the vehicle of Mind
or Spirit in the abstract: conceived as intersubjective and transphenomenal. But in making this assumption Hegel oversteps
the boundary of the idealist tradition, for what he calls Spirit
is no longer the subject of idealist metaphysics. Rather it is a
metaphor whose employment veils a particular kind of empirical
reality: the collective mind of society.

Here is the point where—always according to Adorno—
Hegel's thinking terminates in its own dialectical negation. *Geist*
(Spirit) does not merely manifest the world: it creates it. From
there it was only a step to the "materialist" inversion effected
by Marx in the *Paris Manuscripts* of 1844, where Hegel is
credited with the discovery that world history is the process of
man's self-creation. But the Hegelian dialectic, in transcending
itself, had already disclosed its paradoxical character, for Hegel
expressly affirms that the Truth about the Whole cannot be
compressed into a formula: the "system" is not reducible to a
first principle or to a set of abstractions. Rather, it is the totality
of the contradictions which keep the movement going. The
"subjectivism" of Kant and Fichte has been left behind: the
individual mind is seen by Hegel as a mere differentiation of the
universal Mind which is the common ground of being and

thinking. And yet the link with the idealist tradition remains unbroken, for in describing the logical form of the process, the mind (that of the thinker) affirms its own sovereignty: an attitude that reflects the traditional belief in the ontological primacy of "spirit" over "matter".[35]

This being admitted, wherein does Adorno differ from Lukács? Very simply in refusing to accept the "materialist" metaphysic which Engels and Lenin had read into Marx's critique of Hegel. This metaphysical materialism, in asserting the onto-logical priority of an absolute called "matter", does not trans-cend idealism : it merely inverts it, thereby once more sacrificing the dialectic on the altar of a "first principle" from which the world of appearances is deduced. At bottom the procedure remains metaphysical. A concept borrowed from the empirical world—mental activity in one case, material practice in the other—is invested with a supersensible dignity. Whereas the Marxian *praxis* signified an on-going activity encompassing both physical and mental labour, the dualism inherent in "dialectical materialism" revives the distinction between a "real" material world and a secondary realm of mental reflections or mirror-images. These images are either "correct" and "scientific", or distorted and "ideological", but in either case they have no independent existence : they translate what takes place in the "real" world. Matter is primary, spirit secondary (a metaphysi-cal statement in itself quite irrelevant to the transcript theory of cognition which Lenin superimposed upon this materialist ontology), and thus the task of a genuinely consistent and criti-cal dialectic—the destruction of *prima philosophia* as such, inclu-ding the very notion of an absolute beginning or foundation—has been abandoned.[36]

The distinction between the historical materialism of Marx and the dialectical materialism of Engels and his successors is crucial for Adorno, as it was crucial for the Lukács of *History and Class Consciousness*. Marx's "materialism" is "dialectical" in the sense that it seeks to portray the interaction between theory and practice, or between conscious activity and the "material" preconditions of existence : themselves the product of past history. It is *not* "materialist" in the sense of positing a particular substance (matter), or a particular sphere (material production) which is in some sense the determinant of the entire process. When Engels in his *Anti-Dühring* (1878) interpreted what he himself called the "materialist conception of history" as signifying that "the final causes of all social changes and political revolutions are to be sought . . . not in the *philosophy* but in the *economics* of each particular epoch",[37] he discarded dialectics in favour of positivism. Yet this abandonment of the original Marxian standpoint could (and did) draw some undeserved nourishment from Marx's equivocal employment of the terms "material base" and "ideological superstructure" in the *Preface* to his *Critique of Political Economy* (1859). In recovering the original dimension of Marx's thought, Adorno asserts the dialectical principle even against those ambiguous formulations whereby Marx had opened the door to the positivist misinterpretation of his doctrine. "Spirit can no more be split off from facticity than the latter can be divorced from spirit. Neither represents a prime datum. (*Beide sind kein Erstes.*) The fact that they are both essentially mediated by one another (*durcheinander vermittelt*) renders them equally useless as primary principles (*Urprinzipien*)."[38]

The detailed exposition of this theme takes up most of the 400 pages of Adorno's *Negative Dialektik* (1966): his major work, possibly also his intellectual testament. Here as elsewhere, he sides with Marx against Hegel on the issue which in the 1840's constituted the dividing line between speculative philosophy and revolutionary critique: that of human *praxis,* conceived as *labour* (and alienated labour at that), where Hegel had perceived only the "labour" of Mind "coming to itself". This radical vice of all speculative idealism Adorno had already denounced a decade earlier in terms echoing the Marx of the 1844 *Manuscripts*: "Idealism turns into untruth when it transforms the totality of labour into a being-in-itself, when it sublimates its principle in metaphysics, into the *actus purus* of Spirit, and thus by implication proclaims as eternal and right what is the work of men in all its contingency, along with the labour that represents (the element of) suffering."[39] Now, in a final summation, the "materialist dialectic" of Marx (though not its caricature: the "dialectical materialism" of Engels and his successors, down to Lenin and Lukács) is expounded and defended both against Hegel's idealist perversion and against the state-controlled optimism of Soviet "philosophy". Two other influential doctrines are likewise dismissed: the radical empiricism of contemporary logical positivism and the "pure" subjectivism of the existentialists (inheritors of Kierkegaard, whose critique of Hegel had already been brushed aside in the *Aspekte*). What then remains? Adorno emphatically does not believe that traditional metaphysics can be resurrected (he affirms the contrary),[40] but he does suggest that speculative thought conserves a dimension of the human spirit which must not be discarded, since it points toward a possible future when the discord between utopian dreams and a subhuman reality will at last be overcome:

> That metaphysical philosophy, historically in all essentials co-extensive with the great systems, has a splendour denied to empiricism and positivism, is not—as implied by the absurd term "conceptual poetry"—merely an aesthetic factum, nor is it a psychological wishfulfillment. The immanent quality of a thought: what it manifests in the way of power, resistance, imagination, union of criticism with its opposite, represents, if not an *index veri*, at any rate a signpost. That Carnap and Mises are truer than Kant and Hegel could not possibly be the truth even if it happened to be the case. The Kant of the *Critique of Pure Reason* had made it plain in his doctrine of ideas that theory is not possible without metaphysics. This possibility implies the *raison d'être* of a metaphysics to which Kant adhered in the very act of destroying it through the impact of his own work. The Kantian salvage of an intelligible sphere is not merely (as we all know) Protestant apologetics: it has an immanent tendency toward intervening at that point in the dialectic of the Enlightenment where it terminates in the abolition of Reason itself. . . .
>
> Metaphysics in relation to theology is not merely (as positivism would have it) an historically later stage, not simply the secularization of theology into logic. It preserves

theology in the act of criticizing it: by representing as a human possibility what theology imposes upon men and thereby degrades (*indem sie den Menschen als Möglichkeit freilegt, was die Theologie ihnen aufzwängt und damit schändet*) . . . The autonomous Beethoven is more metaphysical than Bach's *ordo*, hence truer. Subjectively liberated and metaphysical experience converge in humanity. Every expression of hope—more powerfully irradiated by the great works of art, even in the ages of silence, than by the traditional theological texts—is configurated with that of humanity. . . .[41]

If Adorno is Lukács' spiritual antipode—a critic of idealism for whom in the end Hegel remains relevant because speculative philosophy has *not* been superseded—[42] Herbert Marcuse (his senior by a few years, and like him a prominent representative of the original Frankfurt group) occupies an intermediate position: contemptuous of Soviet Marxism, yet unwilling to write the heritage of the October Revolution off as a total failure; Hegelian in the spirit of the early Lukács (and demonstratively silent about his later writings, which Adorno has made the target of withering critical comments),[43] yet close enough in spirit to the neo-Marxism of the present era to have become one of the philosophers of the New Left; a *grand bourgeois* intellectual of the Weimar Republic whose political loyalties (even in his self-chosen Californian exile) have remained frozen at the precise point in time at which they were formed—the murder in January 1919 of Karl Liebknecht and Rosa Luxemburg: the former a Kantian idealist and radical democrat, the latter a spiritual ally of the Mensheviks, reluctantly reconciled to the necessity of "temporary dictatorship". These options impose a mode of discourse whose inherent difficulties can be traced in Marcuse's finely balanced critique of Leninist theory and practice,[44] as well as in his more recent efforts to come to grips with the theory and practice of contemporary liberalism in Western Europe and the United States.[45]

These investigations have found their most recent (1967) summation in an essay bearing the title "The Obsolescence of Marxism", where we read: ". . . it appears that Marx's own idea of socialism was not radical enough and not utopian enough [sic]. He underrated the level which the productivity of labour under the capitalist system itself could attain and the possibilities suggested by the attainment of this level. The technical achievements of capitalism would make possible a socialist development which would surpass the Marxian distinction between socially necessary labour and creative work, between alienated labour and nonalienated work, between the realm of necessity and the realm of freedom . . ." Present-day industrial society has outgrown "the stage of the development of the productive forces that Marx considered as the inner limit of capitalism . . . For the Marxian concept implies the identity of the impoverished classes with the basic immediate producers, that is, with industrial labour." But the working class has been integrated into contemporary industrial society (capitalist or nominally socialist). In consequence Marcuse tends to identify the remaining chances of an uncorrupted "utopian" socialism with "the third world" of industrially backward areas. It is in the "militant underdeveloped countries" that in our time "at least one series of objective prerequisites for socialism prevails": principally the acute misery of the exploited, the patent inability of the ruling classes to develop the productive forces, and the presence of an "advanced militant leadership". The exploited classes, to be sure, are rural, not urban; agrarian, not industrial. But such as they are, they represent the "immediate producers" who by virtue of their economic function constitute the base of the established system, and "it is on these grounds that, according to Marxist theory, the proletariat becomes the historical agent of revolution."[46]

Marcuse's socialist critics have not been slow to point out that his analysis of advanced industrial society ignores the role of the labour movement in making possible what little socialization has actually been achieved: in other words, he ignores both democracy and the class struggle. However, on Marcuse's assumptions this criticism is less damaging than it must seem to a traditional socialist, since plainly the only form of class antagonism he takes seriously is one that pits the whole mass of the exploited (whoever they may be) against a ruling oligarchy. His position in this respect would be self-consistent and unchallengeable if he were not trying to relate it to the theorizing of the early Marx. The fact is that Marx assigned to the industrial proletariat a strategic role in the socialist transformation because he regarded it as the only class able and willing to abolish the capitalist mode of production. Whatever the importance of agrarian revolutionary movements in the pre-industrial hinterland of the modern world, they cannot have *this* particular role to play. If Marcuse holds that Marx was factually mistaken in expecting socialism to evolve from advanced industrial capitalism, he cannot at the same time assert that "according to Marxian theory, the pro-letariat becomes the historical agent of revolution", irrespective of whether the "revolution" is located in pre-capitalist or post-capitalist society; in the most highly advanced (and most demo-cratic) or in the most miserable and backward countries. What he is in fact saying is that (contrary to Marx's view) socialism can be built only where society has not been corrupted by bourgeois civilization and its offspring, the labour movement. This was substantially the anarchist standpoint, and indeed the current debate over the function of armed revolt by the exploited rural masses in the *tiers monde* tends to reproduce the ancient quarrel between socialism and anarchism.[47]

Prior to the political upsurge of the 1960's, Marcuse's thinking had gravitated between the two poles of a relatively optimistic critique oriented on Marx and Freud (see his *Eros and Civiliza-tion,* 1955), and a pessimistic philosophy of history derived from Hegel. In his former role he treated the Marxian view of human "alienation" as a forerunner, or counterpart, of Freud's critique of instinctual repression. The link was constituted by the image of a repressive society which denies to the individual the grati-fication of his natural spontaneity, at the same time that it subjects the exploited class (the immediate producers) to the tyranny of authoritarian rule. The "materialist" critique of both forms of oppression had indeed been an important element in the writings of the early Marx, notably in the *Holy Family* (1845). It is not easily reconciled with Freud's stoical acceptance of repression as unalterable.[48]

The two strands of the argument are pulled together in Marcuse's indictment of rationalism in its specifically liberal-bourgeois guise. The supplementary epilogue (written in 1954) to the second edition of *Reason and Revolution* already strikes a melancholy chord whose echoes vibrate a decade later through the stately lament intoned in *One-Dimensional Man* : Logos and Eros are in conflict (and have been antagonistic from the very start). The 1954 passage must be quoted in full :

> The defeat of Facism and National Socialism has not arrested the trend toward totalitarianism. Freedom is on the retreat—in the realm of thought as well as in that of society. Neither the Hegelian nor the Marxian idea of Reason have come closer to realization; neither the development of the Spirit nor that of the Revolution took the form envisaged by dialectical theory. Still, the deviations were inherent in the very structure which this theory had discovered—they did not occur from outside; they were not unexpected.
>
> From the beginning, the idea and the reality of Reason in the modern period contained the elements which endangered its promise of a free and fulfilled existence : the enslavement of man by his own productivity; the glorification of delayed satisfaction; the repressive mastery of nature in man and outside; the development of human potentialities within the framework of domination. In Hegel's philosophy, the triumph of the Spirit leaves the State behind in the reality—unconquered by the Spirit and oppressive in spite of its commitment to Right and Freedom . . . At the beginning and at the end, Western philosophy's answer to the quest for Reason and Freedom is the same. The deification of the Spirit implies acknowledgement of its defeat in the reality . . .[49]

Written in 1954, these lines anticipate the subsequent judgement on the failure of Soviet socialism to transcend the authoritarian ethos of a repressive culture which sacrifices the present to the past, the individual to the real or supposed needs of the collectivity :

In the Soviet system, the "general interest" is hypostatized in the state—an entity separate from the individual interests. To the extent that the latter are still unfulfilled and repelled by reality, they strive for ideological expression; and their force is the more explosive to the regime the more the new economic basis is propagandized as ensuring the total liberation of man under communism. The fight against ideological transcendence thus becomes a life-and-death struggle for the regime. Within the ideological sphere, the centre of gravity shifts from philosophy to literature and art. The danger zone of *philosophical* transcendence has been brought under control through the absorption of philosophy into official theory. Metaphysics, traditionally the chief refuge for the still unrealized ideas of human freedom and fulfillment, is declared to be totally superseded by dialectical materialism and by the emergence of a rational society in socialism. Ethical philosophy, transformed into a pragmatic system of rules and standards, has become an integral part of state policy.[50]

The link between freedom and reason is the oldest theme of German Idealism, going back beyond Hegel to Kant and Fichte: whose impact upon the youthful Marx (evident enough from the spiritual turmoil of his student years) is perhaps understressed by Marcuse. In the 1954 epilogue to *Reason and Revolution* it was the Hegelian stress on the "power of negativity" that served as a bridge from theoretical comprehension to practical negation :

> Hegel saw in the "power of *negativity*" the life element of the Spirit and thereby of Reason. This power of Negativity was in the last analysis the power to comprehend and alter the given facts in accordance with the developing potentialities, by rejecting the "positive" once it had become a barrier to progress in freedom.[51]

There is a certain ambiguity here—Marcuse slides too easily from "the power to comprehend" to the notion of "altering" the given actuality, once it has become "a barrier to progress in

freedom". Hegel (as we saw earlier) never approved of a revolution until its victory had certified the historical necessity and
reasonableness of the "power of negativity" : which was just why
Marx in the end despaired of him. Marcuse—in this respect a
genuine Hegelian of the Left—would like to have it both ways :
Hegel's dialectic is for him the true algebra of revolution :

> Reason is in its very essence [sic] contra-diction, opposition,
> negation, as long as freedom is not yet real. If the contra-
> dictory, oppositional, negative power of Reason is broken,
> reality moves under its own positive law and, unhampered
> by the Spirit, unfolds its repressive force.[52]

How "reality" manages to dissociate itself so entirely from
"Reason" is not easily understood. In defence of Marcuse's
position it can be said that his condemnation of the *status quo*
in East and West is impartial, although this very circumstance
introduces a certain imbalance, inasmuch as he equates the
manipulation of what passes for "public opinion" in the West
with the total *suppression of freedom* by the omnipotent and
omnicompetent East European police state. At any rate he has
no illusions as to the functional significance of "socialist realism":
a doctrine which (it is too often forgotten) Lukács helped to
elaborate, and was still busy defending in his writings of the
1960's. In *Soviet Marxism* (1958) this theme is unmistakably
spelled out :

> Realism can be—and has been—a highly critical and pro-
> gessive form of art; confronting reality "as it is" with its
> ideological and idealized representations . . . In this sense
> realism shows the ideal of human freedom in its actual nega-
> tion and betrayal, and thus preserves the transcendence
> without which art itself is cancelled. In contrast, Soviet
> realism conforms to the pattern of a repressive state . . .
> The future is said to be nonantagonistic to the present;
> repression will gradually and through obedient effort
> engender freedom and happiness—no catastrophe separates
> history from pre-history, the negation from its negation.
> But it is precisely the catastrophic element inherent in the

conflict between man's essence and his existence that has been the centre toward which art has gravitated since its secession from ritual. The artistic images have preserved the determinate negation of the established reality—ultimate freedom. When Soviet aesthetics attacks the notion of the "insurmountable antagonism between essence and existence" as the theoretical principle of "formalism", it thereby attacks the principle of art itself.[53]

The Soviet philosophers (had any existed) might have replied that the notion of an insurmountable conflict between man's essence and his existence is incompatible with the mature Marx, although quite concordant with Schopenhauer, Nietzsche, and Freud. It is true that immediately following the passage just cited Marcuse writes: "In Marxian theory, this antagonism is an *historical* fact, and is to be resolved in a society which reconciles the existence of man with his essence by providing the material conditions for the free development of all humane faculties. If and when this has been achieved, the traditional basis of art would have been undermined—through the realization of the content of art. Prior to this historical event, art retains its critical cognitive function : to represent the still transcendental truth, to sustain the image of freedom against a denying reality. With the realization of freedom, art would no longer be a vessel of the truth."[54] One may readily agree that Soviet society shows no disposition to fulfil these desiderata, although the bare possibility of such an outcome is at any rate not excluded (by Marcuse) on grounds of principle, as long as the fundamental antagonism between essence and existence is described as "a historical fact". A good deal depends here on what is meant by "historical". If (as the more pessimistic philosophers and psychologists seem to think) the "antagonism" is embedded in the very circumstances which set human "history" going, then a socio-political upheaval, however radical, is unlikely to remove it. Marcuse seems undecided as between these conflicting and ultimately incompatible standpoints, although on balance inclined toward the disillusioned attitude of the later Hegel.[55]

In *One-Dimensional Man* the balance has shifted further toward metaphysics, and by implication away from the "historical" approach in the narrow (political or practical) sense. It is the human condition as such that supplies the philosopher with his theme : as indeed it must, except that we are then no longer in the area of the post-Hegelian unification of theory and practice. Man once more confronts a hostile universe. Marcuse cites some pessimistic utterances about the state of the modern world (e.g., "Nothing remains of ideology but the recognition of that which is—model of a behaviour which submits to the overwhelming power of the established state of affairs")[56] as a justification for the frank utopianism of that consistently romantic neo-Marxist, Ernst Bloch : "Against this ideological empiricism, the plain contradiction reasserts its rights : '. . . that which is cannot be true.' "[57]

To make quite sure that the point is not missed, Marcuse proceeds to ram it home. A statement such as " . . . that which is cannot be true" may sound outrageous and absurd (he writes), as well as being at the opposite pole from the Hegelian "What is real is rational." "And yet, in the tradition of Western thought, both reveal, in provocatively abridged formulation, the idea of Reason which has guided its logic. Moreover, both express the same notion, namely the antagonistic structure of reality, and of thought trying to understand reality. The world of immediate experience—the world in which we find ourselves living—must be comprehended, transformed, even subverted in order to become what it really is."[58]

What Marcuse calls "the tradition of Western thought" is here identified with the heritage of a particular type of metaphysical speculation. He is of course quite right in saying that German Idealism as a whole represented an attempt to reconstitute the ancient unity of logic and ethic within the bounds of a supersensible cognition of reality. "In classical Greek philosophy, Reason is the cognitive power to distinguish what is true and what is false insofar as truth (and falsehood) is primarily a condition of Being, of Reality . . . True discourse, logic, reveals and expresses that which really *is*—as distinguished from that which *appears* to be [real] . . . Epistemology is in itself ethics, and ethics is epistemology."[59] But somehow Marcuse does not make it clear to the reader (or to himself) that Hegel accomplished this return to the metaphysical rationalism of the Greeks (and of Spinoza) by jettisoning the Kantian safeguard (the distinction between noumena and phenomena). The outcome was a system whose intellectual self-consistency was purchased at the cost of renouncing that "practical", critical function of Reason which Marcuse cannot do without. His solution is to credit Reason with an inherently critical "power of negativity" which only awaits the proper historical moment to manifest itself. "Dialectical thought understands the critical tension between 'is' and 'ought' first as an ontological condition pertaining to the structure of Being itself. However, the recognition of this state of Being—its theory—intends from the beginning a concrete *practice*."[60] In the light of two and a half millennia of traditional philosophy (not to mention nineteen centuries of a Christianity infused from the very hour of its Pauline birth with the speculative concepts of Greek metaphysics), this assertion appears questionable, to say the least. If "theory" can really be said to have possessed a "practical" orientation "from the beginning", the history of thought will have to be rewritten.[61]

So far as it is possible to summarize in a few pages a somewhat compressed investigation into an intellectual process that took half a century to work itself out, the following brief conclusions may perhaps be ventured :

1. The revolutionary Marxism of the 1920's and 1930's was everywhere a response to the Russian Revolution, but in Central Europe it represented additionally a revival of certain issues which had originally made their impact upon German society in the age of the French Revolution. Since classical German philosophy had come into being very largely as a theoretical reflection of (or reaction to) the events in France, it was inevitable that the role of Marxism in promoting the subsequent upheaval in Russia should from the start have found a deeper resonance in Central Europe than elsewhere.

2. The Russian upheaval having coincided with an internal

crisis of German society consequent upon the 1914–18 war and the disintegration of liberalism, the traditional (Social-Democratic) version of "orthodox" Marxism fell into disrepute : not merely for political reasons having to do with the failure of the Weimar Republic, but because this version of Marxism formed the counterpart of the official academic neo-Kantianism in the universities. This school—in its most eminent represen-tatives, e.g., Max Weber, Heinrich Rickert, and Emil Lask (Lukács' teacher)—had introduced a systematic distinction bet-ween philosophy and empirical science on the one hand, between the natural sciences and the humanities on the other. The Hegelianized Marxism of Lukács and Korsch in the 1920's was both an attempt to close this gap and a critique of the then prevailing positivist version of "orthodox Marxism".

3. The rise of Stalinism and Fascism, and the growing realiza-tion that these phenomena were interconnected, produced a further differentiation among the Central European neo-Marxists. While Lukács identified himself with Stalinism so completely as to be unable to shake off the permanent imprint of this experience even when it had become permissible and indeed advantageous to do so, the other representatives of the school either retained the Marxian approach while repudiating the Bolshevik experience (Korsch), or else retreated into an essentially critical, contemplative, and—in the traditional sense —philosophical attitude (Horkheimer, Adorno, Bloch). In this perspective, Marcuse's attempt to establish a link between the critique of contemporary society and the political aims of the New Left appears both logical and utopian : logical because his writings resume the central theme of the theory-practice debate among the Left Hegelians in the aftermath of the French Revolution; utopian because he proclaims simultaneously the failure of Marxism and the coming attainment of its ultimate aims (which are also those of classical German philosophy) in areas of the world currently engaged in reproducing all the more catastrophic experiences of the bourgeois revolution, minus its liberating features. His interpretation of the recent past, moreover, takes no account of the dialectical interdependence of Stalinism and Fascism. He views the former as an unfortunate

accident, the latter as an extreme form of "repressive" authoritarianism : whereas in reality the Fascist movement was pseudo-revolutionary (not least in the erotic sphere, where it challenged all the bourgeois conventions) and owed its temporary success precisely to this circumstance, and to its anti-bourgeois character in general.

4. In the course of the prolonged crisis in Central Europe, from the 1920's to the 1940's, the neo-Marxism of Georg Lukács, Bertolt Brecht, Karl Korsch, Walter Benjamin, Ernst Bloch, Max Horkheimer, Theodor Adorno, Herbert Marcuse, and the other representatives of the school, was sustained by the idea that in asserting the continuity of classical German philosophy with Marxism they were also defending the liberal heritage. In this respect their efforts paralleled those of another Hegelian Marxist : Antonio Gramsci. Unlike Gramsci, most of them failed to grasp that Fascism was trading on the failure of the national-democratic movements in their respective countries. In Italy this situation for a while led so many disillusioned ex-Socialists and ex-Syndicalists into the Fascist camp as to induce one of the more intelligent Comintern theorists to describe Fascism as "the bourgeois revolution in the age of the bourgeois counter-revolution" : a paradoxical formulation which nonetheless provided some insight into the *problematic* of a nationalist movement in a situation where liberalism had failed to unify the country (or to get the industrial revolution going). In Germany, where the Fascist movement in the 1930's could exploit the exacerbation of national sentiment (not to mention the collapse of liberalism in the face of mass unemployment and economic catastrophe), it was likewise difficult for Marxists to assume the defence of the liberal heritage : either because (like Lukács) they had compromised themselves with Stalinism, or because (like Bloch) they shared the romantic and anti-liberal attitude of Nietzsche's heirs : notably Spengler and the other ideologists of the "conservative counter-revolution" against the "ideas of 1789".

5. In the perspective of the comparatively peaceful (though distinctly philistine) Germany of the 1950's and 1960's the neo-Hegelianism of T. W. Adorno and Herbert Marcuse—for all

the political differences separating the critic of the Establishment from the philosopher of the New Left—appears as the final chapter in a story which opened with the disintegration of the Hegelian school in the 1840's. That the relationship of theory to practice should from the start have furnished a major topic is hardly surprising when it is remembered that the Marxian critique of Hegel centred upon the latter's political philosophy. What appears to be required at the present stage is an understanding of Marxism as the theory of *the bourgeois revolution* in its European setting. This done, the further problem of elaborating concepts appropriate to the post-bourgeois stage of modern society should become more manageable.

6. Trivial though it may sound in the present context of world affairs, the statement that the cultural pessimism of Bruno Bauer and his heirs—down to Nietzsche and Spengler—has been validated by the course of events since the first world war bears repeating. To the significance of the European catastrophe, Adorno at least has borne witness in a perceptive essay on Spengler, which does not spare the precursor of Hitler, yet concedes the relative truth of what for brevity's sake one may call "the reactionary critique of liberalism". This critique ultimately drew whatever force it possessed from themes which had already been sounded in the 1840's and 1850's. It was then that the notion of an approaching "end of European history" first suggested itself to thinkers as disparate as Cieszkowski, Bauer, and Hess: contemporaries of Marx, who for his part repeatedly displayed an awareness of the dangers threatening European civilization unless it was regenerated by socialism.

The revival of these fears after 1918, while for obvious reasons more strident in Germany than in Western Europe, provided the hidden dynamic behind the rival claims of Communism and Fascism. At the ideological level, both movements could and did operate with concepts derived from Hegel's philosophy, and they could do so because Hegel had integrated the theory of history with the traditional themes of philosophy. In this perspective, the return from Marx to Hegel currently observable among the disillusioned heirs of Marxism in Central Europe forms the counterpart of that rival stream of conservative pessimism which—from Bruno Bauer via Jacob Burckhardt to Karl Löwith —has accompanied the decline of religion and the dissolution of traditional European society. The political rift that runs through the geographical centre of the Continent is the outward symbol of a catastrophe of whose possibility Hegel's followers were already conscious. Even though this division may gradually lose its acuteness, it stands as a reminder that the two European wars of this century have had their prime locus in an area whose representative thinkers had for a century made the understanding of history the first of their concerns. *Geschichtsphilosophie* has been a German preoccupation ever since Hegel set the minds of his countrymen working on the theme. There is a case for saying that in its more fatalistic aspects this orientation has been a misfortune for Germany and the world alike : notably in predisposing the intellectual elites of Central Europe to adopt a resigned attitude in the face of what (both in 1914 and in 1939) they regarded as the inevitability of war.

It can also be argued that in so doing they displayed a deeper understanding of the real situation than did their liberal contemporaries in the West. This is not a party matter : Marx's socialism too bears the traces of its origin. Conceived in response to questions Hegel had posed, it retained the metaphysical dimension which positivism had extruded from the socialist movements of Western Europe. If this is the secret of its appeal, it is also the source of its inner tensions and unsolved problems : nowhere more palpable than in the centre of Europe whence it derives the hidden sources of its power.

NOTES

1. A good critical introduction to Lukács is to be found in Morris Watnick's essay, "Relativism and Class Consciousness: Georg Lukács", in *Revisionism: Essays on the History of Marxist Ideas* (London-New York: 1962), 142 ff.; this also provides some brief bibliographical data. For a more detailed treatment see Peter Ludz's introduction to his edition of Lukács' *Schriften zur Literatursoziologie* (Neuwied: 1961). For Adorno see the 1963 *Festschrift* published on the occasion of his sixtieth birthday by the Frankfurt *Institut für Sozialforschung,* and the critical appraisal of his work in the London *Times Literary Supplement* of September 28,

1967. A brief critical study of Marcuse's more recent work is to be found in Peter Sedgwick, "Natural Science and Human Theory", in *The Socialist Register* (London: 1966), 163 ff. For the rest, the author is obliged to refer the reader to his own articles on the related topics of "Alienation", "Hegel", and "Lukács", in the revised (1968) edition of the *International Encyclopaedia of the Social Sciences*.

2. Needless to say this approach involves a certain degree of arbitrariness in compartmentalizing an interconnected whole of politico-theoretical debates. Communism happens to be a universalist movement. Even the "philosophical" inanities of Stalin or Mao are somehow part of it, as is the related practice. At a higher level, the internal stresses of Marxism-Leninism appear in writings such as Lukács' polemic against Sartre; cf. *Existentialisme ou Marxisme?* (Paris: 1961), 133 ff.; or—to take a more topical example—in Louis Althusser's critical reflections on the Hegelian heritage. An earlier stage of the debate is reflected in Gramsci's cautiously critical observations on Lukács' heresies (reprinted in *The Modern Prince and other writings* [London: 1957, 1967], 109). But all this, however interesting, is somewhat external to our topic.

3. Karl Korsch, *Karl Marx* (London: 1938, New York: 1963), 231. A similar argument had already been advanced, in a different context, by Sidney Hook in his important study, *From Hegel to Marx* (New York: 1936, 1950), and the topic was to receive even sharper emphasis in the same author's trenchant critique of Engels's philosophical writings: cf. "Dialectic and Nature", in Hook, *Reason, Social Myths and Democracy* (New York: 1940, 1950). In recent years the distinction between the "historical materialism" of Marx and the "dialectical materialism" of Engels has, if anything, been overstressed. For a scholarly dissection of this topic cf. Z. A. Jordan, *The Evolution of Dialectical Materialism* (London-New York: 1967), *passim*.

4. *Op. cit.*, 168. Notwithstanding its positivist ring, this criticism was in 1938 voiced by a writer who then still considered himself an oppositional Communist. Thirty years later this type of argument was more commonly advanced by Socialists who combined empiricism with a democratic position in politics. But the case of Louis Althusser shows that by now it has become possible to combine a prominent role in the Communist movement of an important West European country with a critical attitude to "dialectical materialism"; cf. Althusser, "Contradiction et surdétermination", in *Pour Marx* (Paris: 1966).

5. Cf. Nicholas Lobkowicz, *Theory and Practice: History of a Concept from Aristotle to Marx* (University of Notre Dame Press: 1967), 123 ff. and *passim*. For Marcuse's view of the subject see his *Reason and Revolution* (2nd ed., London: 1955), *passim*. For a critical restatement of the Hegelian-Marxian position, in terms adapted to the contemporary situation in Western society, see Jürgen Habermas, *Theorie und Praxis* (Neuwied: 1963), *passim*.

6. Cf. Lobkowicz, *op cit.,* esp. 129: "Nature has to be studied in terms of *Naturbegriffe,* natural concepts, and to be dealt with in terms of deterministic natural causality; morality, on the contrary, has to be analysed in terms of the *Freiheitsbegriff,* the concept of freedom, and the causality involved is a totally different causality of free will, a causality of auto-determination."

7. For the Thomist view of the matter cf. Lobkowicz, *op. cit.,* 193 ff. For a Marxist interpretation see Marcuse, *passim.* For Hegel's impact on the youthful Herzen see Martin Malia, *Alexander Herzen* (Harvard: 1961), 228.

8. Lobkowicz, *op. cit.,* 207 ff., is struck by what he describes as their overweening self-confidence (216), in which respect, however, they hardly differed from Fichte and the Romantics who preceded them. Karl Löwith, writing from the standpoint of a moderate Protestant conservative, likewise has no use for their inflammatory utterances; cf. his *From Hegel to Nietzsche* (London-New York: 1964), 65ff. The force of these complaints is rather diminished by the circumstance that some of the more notorious of these firebrands (notably Bruno Bauer and Arnold Ruge) ended their days as admirers of Bismarck, while D. F. Strauss—in the 1830's the terror of the Lutheran theologians—evolved into a harmless liberal and a butt for Nietzsche's destructive scorn in the 1870's. The simple fact is that Marx was the only genuine revolutionary of the lot, and he had to emigrate to Western Europe (first Paris, then London) in order to escape the all-enveloping fog of German philistinism—not to mention the Prussian censorship.

9. For August von Cieszkowski see Lobkowicz, 193 ff.; H. Stuke, *Philosophie der Tat* (Stuttgart: 1963), *passim;* D. Chizhevski ed., *Hegel bei den Slawen* (Darmstadt: 1961), *passim;* Dieter Groh, *Russland und das Selbstverständnis Europas* (Neuwied: 1961), 244 ff. Marx was personally acquainted with this aristocratic Polish Hegelian (who was also a Catholic mystic), though it is uncertain whether he read his *Prolegomena zur Historiosophie* (1838). What is certain is that Moses Hess knew and admired the book, and Hess in the early 1840's was Marx's teacher. For Cieszkowski's influence on Herzen, who had read the *Prolegomena* soon after the book's publication, see Malia, *op. cit.,* 197.

10. In the later Victorian age this perspective was replaced by the rather less dramatic notion that labour's gradual emancipation would transform both its own condition and that of society. This became the faith of democratic socialism in the era of the First International (1864–76) of which Marx, after all, was the prime mover. There is no warrant for Lobkowicz's assertion that Marx "never made the slightest effort to help the proletariat" (371), and that he positively welcomed the prospect of "increasing misery", or pauperization, as being likely to hasten the advent of revolution. Such notions were characteristic of Bakunin, and indeed formed the principal obstacle to cooperation between Socia-

lists and Anarchists after the International had split in 1872. Moreover, belief in "progressive pauperization" is incompatible with the logic of Marx's argument in *Capital,* though he seldom bothered to spell it out.

11. See Groh, 244 ff., for the attitude of the Left Hegelians to the Slav peoples, and the simultaneous impact of Tocqueville upon those among them (notably Bruno Bauer) who began to toy with the notion that Europe's historic role was drawing to a close, and that the future belonged to America and Russia.

12. See his *Russland und das Germanenthum* (1853). But already in 1842, when he contributed to the *Rheinische Zeitung* (then edited by his friend Marx), Bauer had spelled out the meaning of Tocqueville's recent warning for the benefit of his German readers: "In considering the future of Europe and Germany, one must not leave North America out of account, for the conflicts among the European States will shortly give way to a greater conflict, to a struggle between Continents *(dem Kampf der Welttheile)*." See Groh, 264. Bauer is among the direct precursors of Nietzsche (who thought highly of his devastating critique of Christianity) and Spengler.

13. Groh, 206 ff. It is common knowledge that A. v. Haxthausen's studies on Russian agriculture and the communal structure of the Russian village were taken up by Herzen and Chernyshevski, and even found a cautious echo in some of Marx's later utterances. The topic played its part in the dispute between Marx and Bakunin in the 1870's, and its echoes are still traceable in the later development of Russian Marxism, down to and beyond Lenin.

14. D. Hert-Eichenrode, *Der Junghegelianer Bruno Bauer im Vormärz* (Berlin: 1959), 111; see Lobkowicz, 224. Similar sentiments were voiced by Jacob Burckhardt: not accidentally Nietzsche's first teacher and master (cf. Löwith, *op. cit., passim*). Löwith is himself in the same tradition, although he looks back to Goethe rather than to Hegel. In the 1850's the underlying assumption of decline was shared by some contemporary Catholic writers, who made their contribution to the philosophy of history, notably E. v. Lasaulx, another precursor of Spengler. Cf. Hans Joachim Schoeps, *Vorläufer Spenglers: Studien zum Geschichtspessimismus im 19. Jahrhundert* (Leiden: 1955). By contrast, Nietzsche subsequently adopted a different solution: history was "abolished" and replaced by the "will to power"—a biological metaphor which served to conceal the fundamental nihilism of a writer who (unlike Hegel's pupils) had abandoned the notion that rational thinking can yield valid conclusions. Bauer's pessimism about Europe is still compatible with the belief that world history will continue. Nietzsche has stopped thinking about it.

15. There appears to be no precise equivalent of the German term *Problematik,* in the sense of an interlocking set of issues held together by a central theme. The term is used here to signify that there is a particular unsolved problem (theoretical *or* practical) which keeps the

debate going, and that the disputants are more or less conscious of this situation.

16. Cf. G. Lukács, *Mein Weg zu Marx*, in *Georg Lukács zum 70. Geburtstag* (Berlin: 1955), 227 ff. See also the massive *Festschrift zum 80. Geburtstag von Georg Lukács*, ed. F. Benseler (Neuwied: 1965), *passim*. This volume includes a number of contributions by Western scholars on topics only very tenuously linked to the ostensible subject, and at least one essay by a Polish "revisionist" (L. Kolakowski) who takes issue, politely but relentlessly, with the metaphysical "materialism" Lukács shares with Soviet orthodoxy. Kolakowski is an empiricist, and his heresies strike at the root not merely of Lenin's doctrine, but at Lukács' interpretation of Marx. For a restatement of Lukács' position see the article by István Mészáros.

17. See Lobkowicz, *passim*. For a penetrating analysis of the Hegelian-Marxian heritage, which retains the classical approach without closing the door to empirical sociology, see Habermas, *Theorie und Praxis*, notably 261 ff.; also S. Avineri, *The Social and Political Thought of Karl Marx* (Cambridge: 1968).

18. Cf. Lukács, *Die Zerstörung der Vernunft*, in *Werke*, vol. 9 (Neuwied: 1961). The preface to the second edition, dated "Budapest, December 1960", explicitly reaffirms the thesis that positivism and irrationalism have become and remained ideological twins in promoting "the apologetic of the capitalist system." According to G. K. Freyer, one of the contributors to the 1965 *Festschrift* (l.c., 211), Lukács' monstrous 700-page pamphlet of 1953 is to be regarded as his "principal work". But then even Mészáros (no Stalinist himself) appears to see nothing wrong with it.

19. It is safe to say that but for the author's early distinction no one would have paid any attention to his dull tome on Hegel *(Der junge Hegel: Über die Beziehungen von Dialektik und Ökonomie)*, originally published in 1948, and reprinted in 1967 as vol. 8 of the *Werke* issued by Luchterhand in West Germany. The most that can be said in its favour is that it is manifestly superior to a monstrosity such as *Die Zerstörung der Vernunft:* a work of which T. W. Adorno pertinently observed that it reflected the destruction of Lukács' own reasoning power (cf. Adorno, *Noten zur Literatur*, II, 153).

20. Cf. Antonio Gramsci, in *The Modern Prince and other writings* (London: 1957, 1967), 137: "The modern prince, the myth-prince, cannot be a real person, a concrete individual; it can only be an organism; a complex element of society in which the cementing of a collective will, recognized and partially asserted in action, has already begun. This organism is already provided by historical development and it is the political party: the first cell containing the germs of collective will which are striving to become universal and total." This formulation, for all its Sorelian overtones (Gramsci had moved from Syndicalism to

Communism under the impact of the October Revolution which he misinterpreted as a proletarian seizure of power, on the model of the North Italian factory occupations in 1919–20), was still compatible with Marx. But then Gramsci was an authentic labour leader, not a disillusioned elitist reflecting upon the "mission" of a proletariat whose empirical condition only supplied a theme for speculative constructions.

21. Cf. M. Watnick, in *op. cit.*, 155: "The idea that a system of thought might be conceived as an ideal type and then imputed to a social group, likewise thought of as an ideal type, was an inspiration Lukács borrowed from his teacher, Max Weber, and by grafting it onto Marx's sociology of classes, he was able to derive a doctrine of proletarian class consciousness distinctly his own." Weber's neo-Kantian standpoint, though, was not really compatible with Hegel's (and Lukács') metaphysical confidence as to the possibility of supra-historical knowledge. The "ideal type", after all, is "ideal" just because it is our construction which was certainly not Lukács' view in 1923 (or indeed in later years, when he had settled for the epistemological realism of Engels and Lenin).

22. For a critical analysis of Lukács' extremely odd and idiosyncratic notions on the topic of modernism, see Harold Rosenberg, "The Third Dimension of Georg Lukács", in *Dissent,* Autumn 1964. The occasion was provided by the publication in 1963 of an English-language version of Lukács' 1957 work, *The Meaning of Contemporary Realism.* Of this extraordinary pamphlet against modernism (post-Stalin, and thus all the more significant) Rosenberg observes with justice that it represents both a return to the nineteenth century (when bourgeois civilization was still intact) and a demand "that conditions be cured in literature before they are changed in life." For a qualified defence of Lukács' writings on aesthetics see Mészáros.

23. For this aspect of the contemporary situation see Habermas, *op. cit.*, pp 269 ff.; Iring Fetscher, "Von der Philosophie des Proletariats zur proletarischen Weltanschauung", in *Marxismusstudien,* vol II (Tübingen: 1957), 26 ff., Günther Hillmann, *Marx und Hegel* (Frankfurt: 1966), *passim.*

24. *Geschichte und Klassenbewusstsein,* 220; see also 218: "Wenn es aber keine Dinge gibt—was wird im Denken 'abgebildet'"? (If there are no things, what is being "pictured" in thought?) Lukács at this point specifically dissociated himself from Engels, whose philosophy he linked with a "bourgeois materialism" which in its time had been "the ideological form of the bourgeois revolution." (*Ibid.,* 221n.) This of course was heresy and not to be endured, for in 1923 Soviet Communism was already committed to "the ideological form of the bourgeois revolution" which Russia had recently undergone (under "Marxist" leadership, it is true).

25. Merleau-Ponty, *Sens et non-Sens* (Paris: 1948), *passim.* In the then prevailing fashion, Marx's critique of philosophy was described by

Merleau-Ponty as "existential"; cf. *op. cit.*, 137: " Ici se rejoignent les deux moitiés de la postérité hégélienne: Kierkegaard et Marx." This could also be asserted from a conservative standpoint, e.g. by Löwith; not to mention Heidegger, who in 1947 tried to get on the bandwagon with his *Letter on Humanism*.

26. For a critical analysis see Habermas, *op. cit.*, 290 ff., where account is also taken of the theological echoes of this debate, and specifically of Ernst Bloch. The latter's work falls outside our context, being a species of gnosticism or pantheism whose Schellingian origins do not concern us here. Neither need we trouble ourselves about Lucien Goldmann's fruitless efforts to acclimatize Lukács in France.

27. On this point see Z. A. Jordan, *The Evolution of Dialectical Materialism* (London: 1967), especially 151 ff.

28. See Marcuse, *Soviet Marxism: A Critical Analysis* (New York-London: 1958), with its somewhat muted but still distinctly heretical, critique of Soviet ideology, especially 120 ff. For his subsequent, and better known, assault on the official ideology of the American liberal consensus, see his *One-Dimensional Man* (Boston: 1964): a critical and polemical tract to which we shall return. In a differently organized context one would also have to consider Marcuse's *Eros and Civilization* (1955), where Freud's analysis of repression is placed in a Marxian perspective. But the subject, however fascinating, is only very distantly related to the "materialist dialectic" as these writers conceive it.

29. *Aspekte der Hegelschen Philosophie*, 12–13. In the same passage, Hegel's *Phenomenology of Mind* is explicitly linked to Husserl's phenomenological method: described as "thoroughly Hegelian" *(Hegelisch durch und durch)*, albeit not confined (as with Hegel) to one particular type or stage of consciousness.

30. *Zur Metakritik*, 12.

31. *Ibid.,* 17.

32. *Ibid.,* 23 ff.

33. *Ibid.,* 30.

34. *Ibid. "Noch das Subjekt-Objekt ist verkapptes Subjekt"*: (Even the subject-object is concealed subject). Adorno's critique of Husserl (*ibid.,* 50 ff.) falls outside the range of our theme, as does his assault on Heidegger; for the latter cf. *Negative Dialektik,* 114 ff.

35. *Adorno, Negative Dialektik,* 123–25, 137 ff.

36. *Ibid.,* 195 ff. Matter as a single primal substance, of which all things in the world are modifications, is not essential to a doctrine which merely asserts the objectivity of thought, in the sense that cognition "reflects" an external reality. Viewed in ordinary logical terms, the metaphysical materialism of Engels is not required from Lenin's standpoint, nor from that of Lukács. But it *is* required for a totalitarian state-party which has to provide an answer to all questions that may be bothering its adherents. Lukács is of course aware of this circumstance,

whence his addiction to a distinctly Jesuitical mode of discourse: there are different levels of comprehension suited to the ordinary believer and to the theorist, who in his private capacity may smile at certain naiveties, but in public must keep a straight face, so as not to shock his audience. These are, one might say, the inherent problems of every totalitarian movement: it must operate with the concept of two truths. But no amount of apologetic talk about the need for accommodation can justify this procedure if the existential commitment to "truth" (in the sense of truthfulness) is taken seriously. In this respect the personal and intellectual cleavage between Lukács and Adorno reproduces a situation that is as old as philosophy itself.

37. *Herr Eugen Dühring's Revolution in Science* (London: 1955), 369.

38. *Zur Metakritik*, 33.

39. *Aspekte der Hegelschen Philosophie*, 28.

40. *Negative Dialektik*, 394.

41. *Negative Dialektik*, 375–76, 387.

42. Cf. *Negative Dialektik*, 13: "Philosophy, which at one time appeared to have been overtaken, remains in being because the moment for its actualization has been missed. The summary judgment that, in merely interpreting the world, philosophy suffered a crippling resignation before reality, turns into the defeatism of reason, now that the transformation of the world has failed . . . The [temporal] moment on which the critique of theory hinged cannot be prolonged theoretically."

43. Cf. "Erpresste Versöhnung", in *Noten zur Literatur* II (1961).

44. *Soviet Marxism: A Critical Analysis, passim.*

45. Cf. *One-Dimensional Man, passim.* For a critique—delivered from a Marxist standpoint influenced by logical positivism—see Peter Sedgwick, "Natural Science and Human Theory", in *The Socialist Register* (London: 1966). For an assessment of Marcuse's philosophical procedure see Alasdair MacIntyre, in *Dissent* (New York, Spring 1965), and in *Survey* (London, January 1967). The critical points made by these authors —which *inter alia* also relate to Marcuse's interpretation of Freud—will here be taken for granted. For further light on Marcuse's rather personal interpretation of the Freudian (or Reichian) heritage, see his debate with Erich Fromm in *Voices of Dissent* (New York: 1954), 293 ff.

46. Marcuse, l.c. All these citations are taken from the essay as reprinted in the volume titled *Marx and the Western World,* ed. Lobkowicz (University of Notre Dame Press: 1967), 413–15. For a critical analysis of the dichotomic view of class structure which underlies Marcuse's social philosophy see Stanislaw Ossowski, *Class Structure in the Social Consciousness* (London: 1963), 19 ff.

47. So far as the advanced countries are concerned, Marcuse places his hopes upon the current "conspicuous radicalization of the youth and the intelligentsia" (*ibid.*, 416), as a movement which "in spite of all its limitations, tends toward a fundamental transvaluation of values." The

choice of a Nietzschean terminology is scarcely accidental: the youthful Lukács, too, had accepted Nietzsche's critique of bourgeois values before he made the transition to Marxism. The effective link between advanced and backward societies was thus (in 1967) envisioned in terms of a simultaneous rejection of "the oppressive power of the affluent society." (Marcuse, *ibid.*) But what if "affluence" should turn out to be precisely the goal of those impoverished masses in whom the philosopher of libertarian socialism has come to invest his hopes?

48. See Fromm's rejoinder to Marcuse, in *Voices of Dissent*, 313 ff. In a sense, Freud's critique of society is more "radical" than that of Marx, since he holds that men will always have to forgo those satisfactions which, if they could be attained, would remove the blockage of spontaneous instinctual gratification by an ethic of self-denial. This hardly fits in with Marcuse's rather Rousseauist vision of a society in which cultural sublimation will cease to be repressive. Once more the anarchist strain that runs through Marcuse's thinking is at variance with his desire to hold the capitalist form of society responsible for repressions which, being historically conditioned, can be overcome by political action.

49. *Reason and Revolution* (2nd ed., 1955), 433.

50. *Soviet Marxism* (1958), 127–28.

51. *Reason and Revolution*, 433–34.

52. *Ibid.*, 434.

53. *Op. cit.*, 129–30.

54. *Ibid.*, 130.

55. He does say: "Marxian theory retained the historical link between social progress and the obsolescence of art: the development of the productive forces renders possible the fulfilment of the *promesse du bonheur* expressed in art." (*Ibid.*, 130.) But the naturalism of the French "materialists", which Marx adopted after his repudiation of the "German Ideology", is just the element of Marxism which separates it from the "tragic" view of the human condition.

56. *Op. cit.*, 120. The reference is to Adorno's essay in Kurt Lenk, ed., *Ideologie* (Neuwied: 1961), although the actual formulation cited by Marcuse appears to be Horkheimer's. Cf. M. Horkheimer and T. W. Adorno, *Sociologica II* (Frankfurt: 1962), 256 ff.

57. *Ibid.*; the reference is to Bloch's *Philosophische Grundfragen* I (Frankfurt: 1961), 65.

58. *One-Dimensional Man*, 123.

59. *Ibid.*, 124–25.

60. *Ibid.*, 133.

61. It is a good deal easier to show that Marcuse is in tune with the unbroken tradition of German Idealism. Specifically, his defence of the "transcendental" element in art is quite in accord with the Kantian and Fichtean idealism of Schiller: cf. the latter's *On the Aesthetic Education*

of Man, now available in an authoritative new edition (with the original text on facing pages), introduced by E. M. Wilkinson and L. A. Willoughby (Oxford: 1967). Hegel's debt to Schiller in the domain of aesthetics is notorious, as is Schiller's admiration for classical antiquity and his implicit critique of the human condition in the modern age (i.e., the late eighteenth century). Cf. the *Sixth Letter:* "It was civilization itself which inflicted this wound upon modern man . . . the inner unity of human nature was severed . . . and a disastrous conflict set its harmonious powers at variance. The intuitive and the speculative understanding now withdrew in hostility to take up positions in their respective fields . . . Everlastingly chained to a single little fragment of the Whole, man himself develops into nothing but a fragment; everlastingly in his ear the monotonous sound of the wheel that he turns, he never develops the harmony of his being, and instead of putting the stamp of humanity upon his own nature, he becomes nothing more than the imprint of his occupation or of his specialized knowledge." (*Op. cit.,* 33–35.) This complaint was uttered in 1794: half a century before Marx's *Paris Manuscripts.*

The Origins of Marxism

Interest in the philosophical origins of Marxism is currently so widespread as to constitute something of an intellectual phenomenon in its own right. That it denotes a shift of attention away from Marx's own emphasis on human *praxis* as the cure for useless metaphysical agonies, the authors here under review would not deny. A tendency to see Marxism as an historical phenomenon—thus applying to it the criterion of judgment inherent in Marx's own critique of his predecessors—is common to them all. Such an approach is proper to a post-revolutionary age, though this description may seem oddly chosen in view of the continuing turmoil that surrounds us. To describe the present age as post-revolutionary is after all to say no more than was implied by those nineteenth-century writers who looked back upon the French Revolution. If our situation today is similar, it does not follow that we are about to enter calmer waters, though for all one knows the East-West antagonism may gradually come to resemble the rather undramatic tension which characterized Anglo-French relations during the earlier part of the Victorian era. The Russian Revolution might then at last appear as a closed chapter, and Marx himself as its Rousseau: the philosopher of one particular historic upheaval whose consequences have now been absorbed.

Such an attitude presupposes that one is not unduly concerned with the intellectual claims of Soviet Marxism but treats it as the ideology of a society which has not yet acquired a self-critical understanding of its own myths. This would be quite in tune with Marx's own approach, though hardly with the Leninist belief that the Russian Revolution represents the start of a new epoch : that of consciousness raised to the level of global reconstruction. For to say that the Bolsheviks, like the Jacobins before them, unwittingly prepared the way for a new exploitative society is to say that the enterprise was a failure. At the same time, recognition of this fact validates the Marxian insight into the peculiar mechanism whereby history has hitherto managed to accomplish its real aims. Thus the critical, or "revisionist", Marxist is able to have it both ways.

What prevents the writers under review from taking this easy way out is their concern with the philosophical origins of Marxism. If Marx had been content, like Weber and Pareto, to analyse the mechanism whereby society renews itself from time to time, his position would be unassailable, but by the same token he would simply be another scholar. The perennial interest of Marxism springs from that "union of theory and practice" of which Marx himself was the first and greatest exemplar. No one who has felt the spell of the *Theses on Feuerbach* or the *Economic and Philosophic Manuscripts* can fail to inquire whether these writings may not outlast the dissolution of the scholastic system constructed by Engels and the epigoni. To say this is not to range oneself on the side of romanticism in its current quasi-anarchist form, which plainly corresponds to a loss of interest in politics. It is simply to acknowledge that thinking people will go on asking the same questions about the fate of the individual in an increasingly mechanized and centralized society. If these questions lead back to the perennial themes of philosophy, they may also help us to grope our way forward. It cannot be an accident that every movement of revolt in the Soviet orbit, whether political or merely literary, emphasizes the libertarian origins of the official creed. The idealist motives of Marx's own early thought carry over into the spontaneous urge to have done with constraint and lies. If the whole movement is necessarily confined to the intelligentsia, that is no reason for not treating it with seriousness.

Dr. Eugene Kamenka's work (*The Ethical Foundations of Marxism* [London : Routledge and Kegan Paul, 1962], 208 pp.) has affinities with this libertarian trend, though the author is in every sense a Westerner, having acquired his philosophical training in Australia. His book reflects the influence of the late Professor John Anderson, a distinguished and original thinker insufficiently known outside Australia, where his position in some respects corresponded to that of Dewey. The application of democratic theory to the wide open spaces of a frontier society is a topic familiar to Americans, as is the tension between an earlier individualism and the growing pressures of a centralized industrial milieu. A European may be forgiven for doubting whether a model derived from a society of free and equal citizens can be applied to the circumstances of our own day, but Anderson's rugged faith in liberty and democracy has its value beyond the particular context to which his social-democratic creed seems most apposite. His pupil's sympathies—at any rate in the work under review—lie with the libertarian current generally labelled anarcho-syndicalist, though he is too sophisticated to accept without qualification the Sorelian myth. The link between this theme and the more technical sections of his interesting study of Marxist ethics is furnished by the now familiar contrast between the libertarian Marx of the *Paris Manuscripts* and the determinist of *Capital*.

Unlike some well-known popularizers, Kamenka approaches this subject with a sense of responsibility which does honour to his teacher. The reader who imagines that nothing further is to be said about the Marx of 1843–45 will discover from his work that it is possible to sustain a considerable degree of logical rigour in dissecting this well-worn topic; also that it is possible to dispense both with modish talk about Zen, and with the theological blinkers worn by writers for whom Kant and Hegel are "neurotics". Kamenka in fact directs his critique at Marx "from the left" so to speak : he deplores his vestigial Hegelianism because it gets in the way of his sound naturalistic rejection of universal laws. For him, Marx is not quite naturalistic and libertarian enough. Whether one accepts this is perhaps less important than whether one appreciates the relevance of an intellectual position which combines empiricism with faith in freedom as the human essence. Kamenka's study provides the most incisive discussion of Marxian ethics known to the reviewer, though some of his statements seem questionable. In his later sections he turns his critical searchlight on the inanities of Soviet philosophy: a topic which, for linguistic and other reasons, he is particularly well qualified to discuss.

Language can be a barrier also to the understanding of what might be called "classical Marxism", as distinct from Soviet Marxism-Leninism. For obvious reasons most of the literature associated with the pre-1917 phase was in German. It is less clear why this state of affairs should continue so far as the philosophic origins of Marxism are concerned, though there is now a growing literature in France. But French philosophers, however hard they try to assimilate the Hegelian viewpoint, always end by sounding like Cartesians. There appears to be a deep mental cleavage between these two civilizations, going back perhaps to the Reformation. One cannot read German authors brought up on the tradition of Kant and Hegal without becoming aware that much of this idealist metaphysic is secularized Protestantism of a kind that has no precise counterpart in the Anglo-American world, let alone in France—save for the handful of contemporary French philosophers and theologians who have grasped what a term like *Geist* means to Germans. Most Frenchmen (including would-be Marxists like Sartre) are hopelessly at sea in this strange gnostic universe, and yet Marxian socialism goes back to Saint-Simon as well as to Hegel, and Marx acquired his political education in Paris. French socialists have never had any difficulty with the *Manifesto:* it is the *German Ideology* that stumps them. As for the British and Americans, they are perfectly at home with *Capital,* less so with Marx's political writings, and wholly lost in trying to disentangle his relationship to the German idealist tradition.

Dr. Werner Hofmann's tightly packed and closely reasoned little paperback (*Ideengeschichte der Sozialen Bewegung des 10.*

und 20. Jahrhunderts [Berlin: Walter de Gruyter, 1962], Sammlung Göschen, 236 pp.) is an excellent introduction to this three-fold theme: a lucid essay in *haute vulgarisation* which performs the feat of condensing a great deal of factual information and superior theorizing into an economically printed textbook. He is particularly good on Marxian economics and on the various modifications of Marxist theory since the opening years of the twentieth century. Proper due is given to the Austro-Marxists, while Leninism is treated with a critical fairness which its exponents have never yet displayed in dealing with the various brands of "revisionism". The author's own standpoint clearly is that of the postwar school of German sociology as represented, e.g., by R. Dahrendorf; that is, he takes it for granted that the problems of present-day industrial society should be discussed in socialist terms, but not necessarily in terms of Marxism, save insofar as Marx anticipated Weber, Pareto, and others in analysing certain structural changes inherent in the gradual transformation of the market economy. This kind of approach is not altogether common in West Germany, notwithstanding the political strength of the Social Democratic party; it is, however, on the increase and may soon be as academically respectable as it has already become in Scandinavia.

With Dr. Alfred Schmidt (*Der Begriff der Natur in der Lehre von Marx*, Frankfurter Beiträge zur Soziologie [Frankfurt: Europäische Verlagsanstalt, 1962], 182 pp.) we are in a different and more complex world: that of classical German philosophy and its transformation into the historical and dialectical materialism of Marx and Engels. But the familiarity is more apparent than real. Dr. Schmidt's essay, a subtle and learned investigation into the philosophic origins of Marxism, is sustained not only by wide reading, but by a level of intellectual sophistication unequalled on the Eastern side of the Curtain, and not often matched on our side, for all the growing familiarity with the existentialist vocabulary of "alienation". The book is sponsored by the Frankfurt *Institut für Sozialforschung* and prefaced by Max Horkheimer and Theodor W. Adorno—names familiar on both sides of the Atlantic. Its contemporary points of reference are Herbert Marcuse, Ernst Bloch, Arnold Hauser, and Walter

Benjamin, rather than the familiar representatives or orthodoxy, or even Lukács, whose unmerited reputation for intellectual daring cannot survive closer acquaintance with his output in recent years. With Schmidt—as with Adorno from whom he has clearly learned a great deal—we are in a different universe. This is not to say that he has written a polemical tract. Even his critique of Engels—which should put the final quietus on the notion that Marx and Engels meant the same thing when they talked about nature and history—manages to avoid polemical overtones. It is none the less effective for being conducted in the most courteous of tones. This is an admirable work. One can only hope that it will be made accessible to students unable to read German.

What Schmidt has to say relates to an order of ideas which is not the less important for having been almost submerged under a flood of modish writing about the soul-pains of people who can find no solace in Kierkegaard. Those students of the *Paris Manuscripts* who have wrestled in vain with the metaphysical and psychoanalytic interpretations they have been offered will find in Schmidt a useful companion-piece to what is still the best German-language work on the early Marx: Heinrich Popitz's *Der Entfremdete Mensch* (1953). Unlike Popitz, whose masterly study "places" Marx in the context of the eighteenth-century Enlightenment and the German Idealist movement, Schmidt is concerned with the inner cohesion of the Marxian world-view, as it gradually unfolds from the earliest fragments down to the final volumes of *Capital* and Engels' commentaries. Though his special theme is the concept of nature, he also clarifies a number of topics usually subsumed under the heading of historical materialism—such as the significance of the labour process—which have puzzled a good many exegetes. Where he criticizes, he does so after explaining what Marx meant, e.g., in saying that nature exists for man only as it is mediated by history. The whole subject has suffered so many confusions—not least at the hands of Marx's followers, beginning with Engels—that it was time a monograph was devoted to it.

This point necessarily leads to a consideration of Engels' place in the history of Marxism. It is evident that a critical examination of this theme cannot be undertaken by Soviet Marxists (nor, for that matter, could it have been undertaken by Lukács after his apostasy in 1924, when he retreated from the position tentatively adopted in *History and Class-consciousness*). The movement in this direction, inaugurated by independent Marxists like Karl Korsch in the early 1930's, has now come to fruition under the auspices of the Frankfurt group, which for two decades was almost alone in preserving an awareness that Marx was not just a materialist. Today this requires no emphasis, but it still needs to be understood just what it is that separates Marx from Engels. Everyone instinctively knows what is signified by the statement that Marx is an important thinker in a sense in which Engels is not, but the difference has to be clarified in relation to the basic Hegelian and Marxian concepts: man, nature, history. This was the topic Lukács cautiously approached in 1923, and then promptly abandoned when the storm broke over his head. Ever since then, Soviet Marxism has lost contact with philosophy, and in the end has become sterile and boring even to its own would-be adherents. Why this is so the reader can discover from Schmidt, where he will also find that a sympathetic understanding of Brecht's poetry—as a protest against "alienation"—can coexist quite peacefully with a decidedly "Western" and sceptical view of the contemporary situation. One gathers that this has also, since his flight to the West, become the standpoint of Ernst Bloch.

The two volumes of texts from the writings of Hegel's followers (*Die Hegelsche Rechte,* ausgewählt und eingeleitet von Hermann Lübbe [Stuttgart: Frommann Verlag, 1962], 330 pp.; *Die Hegelsche Linke,* ausgewählt und eingeleitet von Karl Löwith [Stuttgart: Frommann Verlag, 1962], 288 pp.) furnish the indispensable background to this theme. They are of unequal interest, though this is not wholly the fault of their editors. The conservative wing of Hegelianism inevitably attracts less interest than do the radicals, its representatives leaning heavily in the direction of *status quo* apologetics. With the best will, Kuno Fischer, Karl Rosenkranz, and Carl Ludwig Michelet are no match for Heine, Stirner, Bruno Bauer, Feuerbach, and Marx. Unfortunately, the editors have not tried to compensate this inherent unbalance by letting some of the Hegelian theologians speak up for conservatism : on the contrary, the only theologian of the lot, Kierkegaard, has been included in the volume on the Hegelian Left edited by Professor Löwith! It is true that this absurdity is balanced by the inclusion of the liberal Carové, and the equally liberal Gans, in the companion volume devoted to Hegel's right-wing followers! On the other hand, the great Tübingen school of Biblical criticisms founded by the Hegelian F. C. Baur is not represented at all. These oddities are presumably explicable in terms of the editorial purpose of providing the student, and the general reader, with a handy selection of texts relevant to the philosophy of history; they are nonetheless regrettable.

Such as they are, these two volumes have to be welcomed. The texts are well chosen (though in some cases lamentably truncated) and when read in succession they do convey something of the atmosphere of Germany's greatest intellectual period. Once again it becomes evident how crucial was the political failure of 1848–49 which discredited liberal democracy and drove the middle class back upon an arid constitutionalism. In this the more conservative of Hegel's followers were in the true succession, as evidenced by Hegel's own uneasy reaction to the not very drastic British Reform Bill of 1831. The writings collected by Professor Lübbe in *Die Hegelsche Rechte* are proof that continuity was maintained. Some of them also strike a patriotic note which Hegel would have thought odd, the more so since he had been distinctly lukewarm about the so-called "war of liberation" against Napoleon in 1813–15. For a right-wing Hegelian like Hinrichs, writing thirty years after this event, "German philosophy" was a new spiritual principle already manifest in the wars of Frederick of Prussia and brought to fruition in the romantic nationalism of the 1813 rising (*op. cit.*, p. 89). With the last of these conservative Hegelians, Constantin Rössler, we are already on the threshold of Bismarckian "realism".

Rössler's *System der Staatslehre* (1857) anticipates the entire subsequent development of National Liberalism, down to Max Weber. He is neither a democrat nor a romantic reactionary, but an advocate of that uniquely German creation, the authoritarian *Rechtsstaat,* with its ruling bureaucracy barely controlled by its own legislation. The inmost principle of his thinking is the exaltation of the State as the concrete realization of the moral purpose animating the body politic. Rössler's (and Hegel's) ideal is the *polis,* with its near-total claim upon the allegiance of its citizens. His synthesis of nationalism and liberalism subordinates the individual to the community, and the nation to the state, which latter is imperceptibly equated with the ruling authorities. At one point he himself notes (p. 297) as a possible objection that in this construction the nation appears to have been confused with the state, but he quickly recovers his confidence : "The nation is the concrete expression of the state." Its essence is sovereignty, i.e., the will to maintain itself by all means and against all comers. War, the *ultima ratio* of politics, is the test of a nation's will to exist. Pacifism is contemptible, the idea of universal peace an absurd chimera typical of the Enlightenment. "War is the greatest necessity of all (*das Nothwendigste von Allen*), great and beneficial" (p. 305). Rössler has been unduly ignored. He was important in furnishing the educated upper strata of Bismarck's *Reich* with a sophisticated apology of *Realpolitik.* A civil servant himself, he helped to mould the outlook of the Prussian-German bureaucracy which employed him. In an important sense this stratum may be said to have survived the catastrophe of the *Reich,* for what educated German conservatives today call *Staatsgesinnung* is still in all essentials the creed of Rössler.

The State is likewise the central theme of the Young Hegelians whose writings have been excerpted by Karl Löwith for the companion volume, *Die Hegelsche Linke.* This is true even of Kierkegaard, here represented by some characteristically hysterical comments on the 1848 revolution, which—like his spiritual *confrère* Donoso Cortes—he saw as a demonic revolt against religion. The oddity of this choice in a selection of texts from the Hegelian Left has already been noted. Readers familiar with Löwith's *Von Hegel zu Nietzsche*—a major work, whatever may be thought of its central thesis—will be aware that he ranks Kierkegaard with Marx among the critics of what for some

reason he calls "the bourgeois-Christian world," i.e., the civilization of the nineteenth century. Given this somewhat eccentric
starting point (hardly a compliment to Christianity, one would
have thought), it is perhaps justifiable to include Kierkegaard, on
the strength of his remarks about Communism as a religious
phenomenon. The choice of the others—Heine, Ruge, Hess,
Stirner, Bauer, Feuerbach, Marx—requires no justification,
though one misses the Polish Hegelian August von Cieszkowski,
whose *Prolegomena zur Historiosophie* (1838) on some points
anticipated Marx (who may have read him). On the other
hand, it is a relief not to have Cieszkowski's fellow-student (and
fellow-believer in the historic mission of the Slavs), Bakunin,
served up as a "thinker". Heine perhaps does not quite deserve
this honorific either, but his essay on German philosophy (1834)
has claims beyond its obvious entertainment value: it culminates
in the often cited vision of a coming Germanic assault on civilization. The question has been asked how Heine was able to make
such an accurate prediction. Trivial though it sounds, the
answer seems to be that as a Jew he was just sufficiently
"alienated" from his German contemporaries to be struck by
peculiarities which to them seemed quite normal. (The same
may be said of Moses Hess, who likewise had few illusions
about his fellow-Germans.)

Before turning to Lademacher's selection from Hess, it may
be worth noting that only a decade separates Cieszkowski's semi-
mystical *Prolegomena* from the *Communist Manifesto*. At our
present distance from the scene it is easy to see that the same
spirit animates both documents, even though Marx had cast
metaphysics overboard, and moreover substituted the proletariat
for the Slavs. Hess, with his demand for a "philosophy of action"
(*Philosophie der Tat*) is an important link between the two men,
though the text excerpted by Löwith—from *Die letzten Philo-
sophen* (1845)—lacks the revolutionary edge of his political
pamphleteering. Among the others, Ruge, Stirner, and Bauer are
now widely regarded as stations on a journey leading to Marx.
In fact they represent three different variations on a common
theme: liberalism, anarchism, and cultural pessimism. Of the
three, Bruno Bauer is the most interesting. His *Russland und das*

Germanenthum (1853), with its vision of an ageing Europe over-run by the Slavs, anticipates Spengler, while his hints about a coming post-Christian epoch entitle him to be called a precursor of Nietzsche. (An interesting and suggestive discussion of this topic is to be found in Dieter Groh, *Russland und das Selbstver-ständnis Europas* [1961].)

What all these writers had in common was a sense of imminent crisis—a crisis affecting European history as such, i.e., one that raised the question whether Europe was going to have any sort of future worth being called "history". In this context, Marx's well-known dislike of Panslav authors like Herzen and Bakunin cannot be divorced from the fact that, during his formative years in Berlin, Bruno Bauer was his spiritual mentor. (Hess, who replaced Bauer in this role for some years, was like-wise critical of Panslavism, though personally on friendly terms with Herzen.)

Löwith's introduction not surprisingly lays all the stress on the dissolution of the Hegelian system. In this connection Feuerbach necessarily looms larger than Bauer, since he supplied some of the philosophical categories of the post-Christian and post-Hegelian *Weltbild*. What needs to be remembered, though, is that Feuerbach's critique of religion created the mental climate which subsequently enabled Nietzsche to state as a matter of plain fact that "God" was "dead", i.e., that educated people had ceased to take Christianity seriously. The peculiar atmos-phere of Germany in the later nineteenth century cannot be properly understood unless it is realized that the Hegelians of 1830–1848 had already envisioned the spiritual and political crises of the coming age and tried to prescribe remedies for them. A pessimistic historian like Bruno Bauer would not have been in the least surprised by the insanities of the Third Reich and its dénouement: the Russian Army's entry into Berlin. That Europe was drifting toward catastrophe was common ground among these thinkers. If Marx refused to join the pessi-mists, the reason was that he regarded the coming social revolu-tion as a means of regenerating Europe (though there were moments when he too wondered whether it might not be too late).

In a curious manner all this intellectual turbulence came to a head in a writer who is today remembered, if at all, mainly as a precursor of Zionism: Moses Hess (*Moses Hess: Ausgewählte Schriften,* ausgewählt und eingeleitet von Horst Lademacher [Cologne: Joseph Melzer Verlag, 1962], 467pp.). Just because he was not a systematic thinker, Hess was ideally suited for the role of mediator. For some years he was indeed the single most important link between the burgeoning socialist sects in France and the nascent radical movement in Germany. This aspect of his career is familiar from the various accounts of his relationship with Marx, which came to an end when Marx repudiated him, though Hess for his part continued to have a high opinion of his former associate. (*Vide* his correspondence with Herzen, *op. cit.*, esp. p. 397.) But there was more to Hess than a gift for interpreting French and German thinkers to each other. He was one of those utopians with a talent for prophecy who are ineffective in their own lifetime because they are ahead of their age. His 1841 pamphlet, *Die europäische Triarchie* (*op. cit.*, pp. 83 ff.), anticipates practically all the Pan-European themes of our own day, though in an idiom that has become unfamiliar. Hess was a Romantic who saw in the unification of Western Europe a cure for mankind's spiritual ills. When one subtracts his more extravagant flights of fancy, there remains a solid core of good sense. He had a political vision which transcended national patriotism in the direction of a European confederation: with France, Germany, and England working together and complementing one another. He was a tireless advocate both of the "liberal alliance" between France and England (which eventually materialized in the Crimean War of 1854–56), and of Franco-German reconciliation. The latter indeed to this born Rhinelander had a quasi-metaphysical significance. It was his root conviction that Germany could be regenerated only by absorbing the lessons of the French Revolution: that true opening of the modern age. At this point Hess joined Heine, but also Marx; in fact he was the link between them, just as in 1842–46 he became the chief mediator between the Left Hegelians and the French socialists and communists.

All this, and a great deal more, was done by a gifted but

largely self-taught polymath who never held an academic post, and who to the end combined literary hack-work with a kind of learned pamphleteering that has gone out of fashion. In this respect he resembled Herzen, with whom he also shared the characteristic synthesis of utopian socialism and romantic nationalism. His originality lay in the manner in which he combined these elements with a purely personal streak of religious mysticism—rooted in his orthodox Jewish upbringing—which became more pronounced as the year passed. *Rom und Jerusalem* (1862) is the best-known product of this mature thought. Interest in this astonishing pamphlet has been revived in our days, for reasons which require no emphasis; but long before the rise of Israel, Zionists in Germany and elsewhere had found in it a philosophic basis for their belief that Jewry was destined to go on, even though faith in Judaism declined. Hesss was a true visionary in that he was able to anticipate events inherent in the logic of those spiritual processes which for him were the essence of history. In matters historical he had an eye for essentials, as witness his uncomfortable reflections on German history and the reason why Germany's national development had been aborted (*op. cit.*, pp. 318–20). He even foresaw, correctly, that if the Germany of Bismarck achieved national unity in a reactionary war against France, it would pay for this short-lived triumph with a repetition of its previous failures to become a nation in the Western sense, and thus lay the ground for further catastrophes. To have seen this : to have said in 1862 that German nationalism was rooted in medievalism and *therefore* doomed to disaster, testifies to an uncommon talent for distinguishing the wood from the trees. Hess, who died in 1875—after having worked with both Lassalle and Marx and helped to get the German socialist movement under way—is a key figure in the transition from romanticism to "realism" which accompanied the great economic and political gearshift of those years.

On the Interpretation
of Marx's Thought

A consideration of the phenomenon called "Marxism" has
an obvious starting-point in Marx's own reflections on the subject
of intellectual systematizations. According to him, they were either
"scientific" (in which case they entered into the general inheritance of mankind), or "ideological", and then fundamentally
irrelevant, for every ideology necessarily misconceived the real
world, of which science (*Wissenschaft*) was the theoretical
reflection. Yet it is a truism that Marxism has itself in some
respects acquired an ideological function. How has this trans-
mutation come about, and what does it tell us about the
theoretical breakthrough which Marx effected and which his
followers for many years regarded as a guarantee against the
revival of "ideological" thinking within the movement he had
helped to create?

Regarded from the Marxian viewpoint, which is that of the
"union of theory and practice", the transformation of a revolutionary *theory* into the *ideology* of a post-revolutionary, or
pseudo-revolutionary, movement is a familiar phenomenon. In
modern European history—to go back no further—it has
furnished a theme for historical and sociological reflections at
least since the aftermath of the French Revolution. Indeed,
there is a sense in which Marx's own thought (like that of Comte
and others) took this experience as its starting-point. In the

subsequent socialist critique of liberalism, the latter's association with the fortunes of the newly triumphant bourgeoisie furnished a topic not only for Marxists. But it was the latter who drew the conclusion that the "emancipation of the working-class" had been placed upon the historical agenda by the very success of the liberal bourgeoisie in creating the new world of industrial capitalism. In so far as "Marxism", during the later nineteenth century, differed from the other socialist schools, it signified just this : the conviction that the "proletarian revolution" was *an historical necessity*. If then we are obliged to note that the universal aims of the Marxist school, and the actual tendencies of the empirical workers' movement, have become discontinuous (to put it mildly), we shall have to characterize Marxism as the "ideology" of that movement during a relatively brief historical phase which now appears to be closed. The phase itself was linked to the climax of the "bourgeois revolution" in those European countries where the labour movement stood in the forefront of the political struggle for democracy, at the same time that it groped for a socialist theory of the coming post-bourgeois order. Historically, Marxism fulfilled itself when it brought about the upheaval of 1917–18 in Central and Eastern Europe. Its subsequent evolution into the ideology of the world Communist movement, for all the latter's evident political significance, has added little to its theoretical content. Moreover, so far as Soviet Marxism and its various derivations are concerned, the original "union of theory and practice" has now fallen apart.

This approach to the subject is not arbitrary, but follows from the logic of the original Marxian conception of the *practical* function of *theory*. It was no part of Marx's intention to found yet another political movement, or another "school of thought". His prime purpose as a socialist was to articulate the practical requirements of the labour movement in its struggle for emancipation. His theoretical work was intended as a "guide to action". If it has ceased to serve as such, the conclusion imposes itself that the actual course of events has diverged from the theoretical model which Marx had extrapolated from the political struggles of the nineteenth century. In fact it is today generally agreed among Western socialists that the model is inappropriate to the post-bourgeois industrial society in which we live, while its relevance to the belated revolutions in backward pre-industrial societies is purchased at the cost of growing divergence between the utopian aims and the actual practices of the Communist movement. From a different viewpoint the situation may be summed up by saying that while the bourgeois revolution is over in the West, the proletarian revolution has turned out to be an impossibility : at any rate in the form in which Marx conceived it in the last century, for the notion of such a revolution giving rise to a classless society has now acquired a distinctly utopian ring. Conversely, the association of socialism with some form of technocracy—understood as the key role of a new social stratum in part drawn from the industrial working class, which latter continues to occupy a subordinate function—has turned out to be much closer than the Marxist school had expected. In short, the "union of theory and practice" has dissolved because the working class has not in fact performed the historic role assigned to it in Marx's theory, and because the gradual socialization of the economic sphere in advanced industrial society has gone parallel with the emergence of a new type of social stratification. On both counts, the "revisionist" interpretation of Marxism —originally a response to the cleavage between the doctrine and the actual practice of a reformist labour movement—has resulted in the evolution of a distinctively "post-Marxian" form of socialist theorizing, while the full doctrinal content of the original systematization is retained, in a debased and caricatured form, only in the so-called "world view" of Marxism-Leninism : itself the ideology of a totalitarian state-party which has long cut its connections with the democratic labour movement. While the Leninist variant continues to have operational value for the Communist movement—notably in societies where that movement has taken over the traditional functions of the bourgeois revolution—the classical Marxian position has been undercut by the development of Western society. In this sense, Marxism (like liberalism) has become "historical". Marx's current academic status as a major thinker in the familiar succession from Hegel (or indeed from Descartes-Hobbes-Spinoza) is simply another manifestation of this state of affairs.[1]

While the inter-relation of theory and practice is crucial for the evaluation of Marx—far more so than for Comte who never specified an historical agent for the transition to the "positive stage"—it does not by itself supply a criterion for judging the permanent value of Marx's theorizing in the domains of philosophy, history, sociology, or economics. In principle there is no reason why his theoretical discoveries should not survive the termination of the attempt to construct a "world view" which would at the same time serve as the instrument of a revolutionary movement. This consideration is reinforced by the further thought that the systematization was after all undertaken by others—principally by Engels, Kautsky, Plekhanov and Lenin —and that Marx cannot be held responsible for their departures from his original purpose, which was primarily critical. While this is true, the history of Marxism as an intellectual and political phenomenon is itself a topic of major importance, irrespective of Marx's personal intentions. Moreover, it is arguable that both the "orthodox" codification undertaken by Engels, and the various subsequent "revisions", have their source in Marx's own ambiguities as a thinker.

So far as Engels is concerned, the prime difficulty arises paradoxically from his life-long association with Marx. This, combined with his editorial and exegetical labours after Marx's death, conferred a privileged status upon his own writings, even where his private interests diverged from those of Marx, e.g. in his increasing absorption in problems peculiar to the natural sciences. While Engels was scrupulous in emphasizing his secondary role in the evolution of their common viewpoint,[2] he allowed it to be understood that the "materialist" metaphysic developed in such writings as the *Anti-Dühring* was in some sense the philosophical counterpart of Marx's own investigations into history and economics. Indeed his very modesty was a factor in causing his quasi-philosophical writings to be accepted as the joint legacy of Marx and himself. The long-run consequences were all the more serious in that Engels, unlike Marx, lacked proper training in philosophy and had no secure hold upon any part of the philosophical tradition, save for the Hegelian system, of which in a sense he remained a life-long prisoner. The "dialectical" materialism, or monism, put forward in the *Anti-Dühring,* and in the essays on natural philosophy eventually published in 1925 under the title *Dialectics of Nature,* has only the remotest connection with Marx's own viewpoint, though it is a biographical fact of some importance that Marx raised no objection to Engels' exposition of the theme in the *Anti-Dühring.* The reasons for this seeming indifference must remain a matter for conjecture. What cannot be doubted is that it was Engels who was responsible for the subsequent interpretation of "Marxism" as a unified system of thought destined to take the place of Hegelianism, and indeed of classical German philosophy in general. That it did so only for German Social-Democracy, and only for one generation, is likewise an historical factum. The subsequent emergence of Soviet Marxism was mediated by Plekhanov and Lenin, and differs in some respects from Engels' version, e.g. in the injection of even larger doses of Hegelianism, but also in the introduction by Lenin of a species of voluntarism which had more in common with Bergson and Nietzsche than with Engels's own rather deterministic manner of treating historical topics. In this sense Leninism has to be regarded as a "revision" of the orthodox Marxism of Engels, Plekhanov, and Kautsky. The whole development has obvious political, as well as intellectual, significance. I have dealt with it at some length elsewhere, and must here confine myself to the observation that Soviet Marxism is to be understood as a monistic system *sui generis,* rooted in Engels' interpretation of Marx, but likewise linked to the pre-Marxian traditions of the Russian revolutionary intelligentsia. Unlike "orthodox" Marxism, which in Central Europe functioned for a generation as the "integrative ideology" of a genuine workers' movement, Soviet Marxism was a pure intelligentsia creation, wholly divorced from the concerns of the working class. Its unconscious role has been to equip the Soviet intelligentsia (notably the technical intelligentsia) with a cohesive world-view adequate to its task in promoting the industrialization and modernization of a backward country. Of the subsequent dissemination and vulgarization of this ideology in China and elsewhere, it is unnecessary to speak.[3]

In the light of what was said above about the transformation
of Marxism from a revolutionary critique of bourgeois society
into the systematic ideology of a non-revolutionary, or post-
revolutionary, labour movement in Western Europe and elsewhere, this contrasting, though parallel, development in the
Soviet orbit presents itself as additional confirmation of our
thesis. The latter assigns to Marxism a particular historical
status not dissimilar from that of liberalism : another universal
creed which has evolved from the philosophical assumptions and
hypotheses of the eighteenth-century Enlightenment. The universal content is, however, differently distributed. Liberalism was
from the start markedly reluctant to disclose its social origins
and sympathies, whereas Marxism came into being as the self-
proclaimed doctrine of a revolutionary class movement. The
humanist approach was retained in both cases, but whereas
liberal philosophy in principle denies any logical relation between the social origin of a doctrine and its ethico-political
content, Marxism approached the problem by constituting the
proletariat as the "universal" class, and itself as the theoretical
expression of the latter's struggle for emancipation : conceived
as synonymous with mankind's effort to raise itself to a higher
level. Hence while for contemporary liberalism the unsolved
problem resides in the unacknowledged social content of its
supposedly universal doctrine, the difficulty for Marxism arises
from the failure of the proletariat to fulfil the role assigned to
it in the original "critical theory" of 1843–48, as formulated in
Marx's early writings and in the *Communist Manifesto*. Whereas
liberalism cannot shake off the death-grip of "classical", i.e.
bourgeois economics—for which the market economy remains
the centre of reference—Marxism (at any rate in its Communist
form) is confronted with the awkward dissonance between its
universal aims and the actual record of the class upon whose
political maturity the promised deliverance from exploitation and
alienation is held to depend. There is the further difference
that the Marxian "wager" on the proletariat represents an
"existential" option (at any rate for intellectuals stemming
from another class), whereas liberalism—in principle anyhow—
claims to be in tune with the commonsense outlook of educated

"public opinion". This divergence leads back to a consideration
of the philosophical issues inherent in the original codification
of "orthodox Marxism".

Marx's early theoretical standpoint, as set out in the *Holy
Family* (1845) and the *German Ideology* (1845–46), was a development of French eighteenth-century materialism, minus its
Cartesian physics and the related epistemological problem in
which he took no interest. The basic orientation of this materialism was practical, and its application to social life led in the
direction of socialism, once it was admitted that between man
and his environment there was an interaction which left room
for a conscious effort to remodel his existence. As Marx put it in
the *Holy Family,* "If man is shaped by his surroundings, his
surroundings must be made human. If man is social by nature
he will develop his true nature only in society. . . ."[4] Materialism
or naturalism (the terms are employed interchangeably by Marx)
is the foundation of communism. This conclusion follows *necessarily*, once it is grasped that the material conditions of human
existence can and must be altered if man is to reach his full
stature. Materialism is revolutionary because when applied to
society it discloses what the idealist hypostatization of "spirit"
obscures : that man's history is a constant struggle with his
material environment, a struggle in which man's "nature" is
formed and re-formed. The historicity of human nature, which
is a necessary consequence of this anthropological naturalism,
raises the question what criterion we possess for judging the
activities of men in their effort to subdue the non-human environment : an effort mediated by social intercourse with other men,
since it is only in and through society that men become conscious of themselves.[5] The answer Marx gives is open to criticism
on the grounds of circularity, since it amounts to saying that
man's "nature" is constituted by his *Praxis,* i.e. his capacity for
constituting a man-made world around him. However this may
be, it is plain that for Marx the only "nature" that enters into
consideration is man's own, plus his surroundings which he transforms by his "practical activity". The external world, as it exists
in and for itself, is irrelevant to a materialism which approaches

history with a view to establishing what men have made of themselves. It is doubly irrelevant because, on the Marxian assumption, the world is never simply "given" to consciousness any more than man himself is the passive receptacle of sense impressions. An external environment true knowledge of which is possible in abstraction from man's active role in moulding the object of perception, is a fantasy. The only world we know is the one we have constituted—that which appears in our experience. The "subjective" nature of this experience is checked by its social character, which in turn is rooted in the permanent constituents of man as a "species being" (*Gattungswesen*) who "comes to himself" in society. There is, in the strict sense, no epistemological problem for Marx. The dialectic of perception and natural environment cannot, in his view, be compressed into a formula, for "reason" is itself historical and its interaction with nature is just what appears in history. Man has before him a "historical nature", and his own "natural history" culminates in his conscious attempt to reshape the world of which he forms part.

The notion that this anthropological naturalism is anchored in a general theory of the universe finds no support in Marx's own writings. There is no logical link between it and the "dialectical materialism" of Engels and Plekhanov, any more than there is a necessary connection between Marx's pragmatic view of conscious mental activity as an aspect of *Praxis* and the epistemological realism of Lenin. Indeed, in the latter case there is positive incongruity. Perception as a mirror-image of an external reality which acts upon the mind through physical stimuli has no place in Marx's theory of consciousness. The copy theory of perception set out in *Materialism and Empiriocriticism* (apart from being inadequate and self-contradictory in the way Lenin presents it) is incompatible with the Marxian standpoint. Its formulation arose from the accidental problem of working out a new theoretical basis for the natural sciences—a problem in which Marx had taken no interest. It also involved a divergence from Engels' approach, since materialism for Engels was not the same as epistemological realism. In Engels' quasi-Hegelian treatment of this theme, "matter" conserved some of the attributes of a primary substance which was somehow involved in the constitution of the universe. The difference between idealism and materialism was seen by Engels to lie in the former's claim to the ontological pre-eminence of mind or spirit, whereas natural science was supposed by him to have established the materiality of the world in an absolute or ultimate sense. The resulting medley of metaphysical materialism and Hegelian dialectics (first described as "dialectical materialism" by Plekhanov) was conserved by Lenin, but his own theory of cognition—which was what mattered to him—was not strictly speaking dependent on it. Matter as an absolute substance, or constitutive element of the universe, is not required for a doctrine which merely postulates that the mind is able to arrive at universally true conclusions about the external world given to the senses. Lenin's standpoint in fact is compatible with any approach which retains the ontological priority of the external world (however constituted) over the reflecting mind. Belief in the existence of an objective reality is not peculiar to materialists. It is, moreover, only very tenuously connected with the doctrine of nature's ontological primacy over spirit, which Lenin had inherited from Engels and which was important to him as a defence against "fideism".

The whole confusion becomes comprehensible only when it is borne in mind that the transformation of Marx's own naturalism into a metaphysical materialism was a practical necessity for Engels and his followers, without being a logical one. It was required to turn "Marxism" into a coherent *Weltanschauung,* first for the German labour movement and later for the Soviet intelligentsia. As such it has continued to function, notwithstanding its philosophical inadequacies, but it has also suffered the fate of other systematizations undertaken for non-scientific reasons. At the same time it has paradoxically served to weaken the appeal of Marx's own historical materialism, since the latter was supposedly derived from a metaphysical doctrine of the universe—or an indefensible theory of cognitive perception—with which in reality it had no connection whatever.

To grasp the full extent of this intellectual disaster it is necessary to see what Marx intended when he applied his realistic mode of thought to the understanding of history. The doctrine sketched out in his early writings (notably in the first section of the *German Ideology*), and subsequently given a succinct formulation in the well-known *Preface* to the 1859 *Critique of Political Economy,* was "materialist" in that it broke with the traditional "idealist" procedure wherein ordinary material history was treated as the unfolding of principles laid up in the speculative heavens. The primary datum for Marx was the "real life-process" in which men are engaged, the "production and reproduction of material existence", as he put it on some occasions. In this context, the so-called higher cultural activities appeared as the "ideological reflex" of the primary process whereby men organize their relationship to nature and to each other. Whatever may be said in criticism of this approach, it is quite independent of any metaphysical assumptions about the ontological priority of an absolute substance called "matter", though for evident psychological reasons it was easy to slide from "historical" to "philosophical" materialism. Even so, the grounding of the former in the latter does not necessarily entail the further step of suggesting that human history is set in motion and kept going by a "dialectical" process of contradiction within the "material basis". Such a conclusion follows neither from the materialist principle nor from the quasi-Hegelian picture Marx drew in the 1859 *Preface,* where he referred briefly to the succession of stages from "Asiatic society", via Antiquity and the Middle Ages, to the modern (European) epoch. Marx's own historical research (notably in the *Grundrisse* of 1857–58) stressed the radical discontinuity of these "historical formations". It is by no means the case that the emergence of European feudalism from the wreck of ancient society was treated by him as a matter of logical necessity. Even in relation to the rise of capitalism he was careful to specify the unique historical preconditions which made possible the "unfolding" of the new mode of production. The notion of a dialectical "law" linking primitive communism, via slavery, feudalism, and capitalism, with the mature communism of the future, was once more the contribution of Engels, who in this as in other matters bore witness to the unshakeable hold of Hegel's philosophy upon his own cast of mind.

The reverse side of this medal is the ambiguous relationship of Marx and Engels to Comte, and of Marxism to Positivism. The point has occasionally been made[6] that in dealing with the rise of the "historical school" in nineteenth-century Europe, one has to go back to the intermingling of Hegelian and Comtean strands in the 1830s—mediated in some cases by writers who had actually studied under both Comte and Hegel.[7] It is also arguable that Marx may have been more deeply influenced by Comte than he was himself aware, since some of Saint-Simon's later writings are now known to have been in part drafted by his then secretary. However this may be, it is undeniable that the general effect of Engels' popularization of Marx ran parallel to the more direct influence of Positivism properly so called. With only a slight exaggeration it may be said that "Marxism" (as interpreted by Engels) eventually came to do for Central and Eastern Europe what Positivism had done for the West: it acquainted the public with a manner of viewing the world which was "materialist" and "scientific", in the precise sense which these terms possessed for writers who believed in extending to history and society the methods of the natural sciences. Marx had taken some tentative steps in this direction, but it was Engels who committed German socialism wholeheartedly to the new viewpoint.

At first sight it is not apparent why a Hegelian training in philosophy should predispose anyone in favour of the Comtean approach, which in some respects stands at the opposite pole. Moreover, Marx owed more to the French materialists than did Engels, so that there appears to be a certain paradox in the notion that the fusion of Hegelian and Comtean modes of thought was mediated by the latter. It must, however, be borne in mind that the *philosophie positive* had two aspects. In so far as it stressed the purely empirical character of science and dispensed with metaphysical explanations, it belonged to the tradition of the Enlightenment, in its specifically French "materialist" form (which was the only one Marx took seriously). In so far as it aimed at a universal history of mankind, its influence ran parallel to that of Hegelianism. Now the peculiarity of Marx's "historical materialism" is that it combines universalism and empiricism. For Marx (e.g. in the *Preface* to the 1859 *Critique*), the historical process has an internal logic, but investigation into the actual sequence of socio-economic formations is a matter for empirical research. The link between the two levels of generality is to be found in the interaction between technology ("forces of production") and society ("relations of production"). This interaction, however, is not uniform, i.e. not of such a kind that the historical outcome can be predicted in each case with reference to a general law abstracted from the principle of interaction. Unlike Hegel, Marx does not treat history as the unfolding of a metaphysical substance, and unlike Comte he does not claim to be in possession of an operational key which will unlock every door. Even the statement that "mankind always sets itself only such tasks as it can solve"[8] is simply an extrapolation from the empirically observable circumstance that in every sphere of life (including that of art) problems and solutions have a way of emerging jointly. A formulation of this kind is at once too general and too flexible to be termed a "law". It is a working hypothesis to be confirmed or refuted by historical experience. Similarly, the statement that socialism grows "necessarily" out of capitalism is simply a way of saying that economic conflict poses an institutional problem to which socialism supplies the only rational answer. Whether one accepts or rejects this, Marx is not here laying down a "law", let alone a universal law. On his general assumptions about history, the failure to solve this particular problem (or any other) remained an open possibility. In such a case there would doubtless be regress, perhaps even a catastrophe. The "relentless onward march of civilization" is a Comtean, not a Marxian, postulate. If the first generation of his followers understood Marx to have expounded a kind of universal optimism, they thoroughly misunderstood the meaning and temper of his message.[9]

In relation to bourgeois society the Marxian approach may be summarised by saying that this formation contains within itself the germs of a higher form of social organization. Whether these latent possibilities are utilized depends upon historical circumstances which have to be investigated in their concreteness. One cannot deduce from a general law of social evolution the alleged necessity for one type of society to give birth to a more developed one—otherwise it would be incomprehensible why classical Antiquity regressed and made room for a primitive type of feudalism, instead of evolving to a higher level. In fact Marx held that the collapse had been brought about by the institution of slavery, which was both the basis of that particular civilization and the organic limit of its further development.[10] In principle the same might happen again. If Marx makes the assumption that the industrial working class is the potential bearer of a higher form of social organization, he is saying no more than that no other class appears capable of transcending the *status quo*. What might be called the existential commitment of Marxism to the labour movement follows from this assumption. Like every commitment it carries with it the implied possibility of failure. Were it otherwise, there would be no sense in speaking of "tasks" confronting the movement: it would be enough to lay down a "law" of evolution in the Comtean or Spencerian manner. Belief in an evolutionary "law" determining the procession of historical stages was the mark of "orthodox" Marxism, as formulated by Kautsky and Plekhanov under the influence of Spencer and other evolutionists, but also of Engels, whose synthesis of Hegelian and Comtean modes of thought made possible this fateful misunderstanding.

In justice to all concerned it has to be borne in mind that Marxism and Positivism did have in common their descent from the Saint-Simonian school. It was in the latter that the notion of history as a developmental process subject to "invariable laws" was first adumbrated in confused fashion, later to be given a more adequate formulation by Comte and Marx. The justification for treating these two very disproportionately gifted thinkers under the same heading arises from the evident circumstance that their contemporaries were affected by them in roughly similar ways. In general it might be said that Marx did for the Germans—notably for German sociology and the "historical school" (Schmoller, Weber, Sombart, Troeltsch, etc.)

—what Comte had earlier done for Durkheim and his school in France. And this assimilation of Comtean and Marxian modes of thought into the canon of academic sociology was evidently rendered possible by their commitment to the idea of history as the special mode of societal evolution. In saying this one is simply stating the obvious, but on occasion this does no harm. It was Saint-Simon who first laid it down that the proper business of social science is the discovery of laws of development governing the course of human history. To say that Marx, no less than Comte, remained true to this perspective is simply to say that he remained faithful to his intellectual origins (which in this case antedated the Hegelianism of his student days, since we know that he had come across Saint-Simonism while still a schoolboy). That human history represents a self-activating whole —in Hegelian terms a "concrete universal"—was a certainty he never surrendered. There is the same attachment to the original vision in his oft-repeated statement that knowledge of the "laws" underlying historical development will enable society to lessen the "birthpangs" inseparable from the growth of a new social formation. Insight into the regularities of history is, by a seeming paradox, seen as the means of controlling the future course of development.

In all these respects Comte and Marx appeared to be saying the same thing, and it was this similarity which led so many Positivists to describe themselves as Marxists : notably in France, where indeed this identification became a factor in the evolution of the socialist movement. Yet the differences are as important as the similarities. Comte's sociology dispensed with the notion of class conflict, which for Marx was the central motor of historical progress. The Comtean view of society not only posited the latter as the basic reality—over against the state on the one hand, and the individual on the other—but also elevated it to a plane where the "science of society" was seen to consist in the elucidation of an harmonious interdependence of all its parts. From the Marxian viewpoint this is sheer fantasy, a wilful disregard of the reality of conflict whereby alone social progress takes place. In the subsequent evolution of the two systems, this difference in approach translated itself *inter alia* into the conflicting doctrines of Russian Populism (heavily impregnated by Comte) and its Marxist rival. There is a sense in which the defeat of *Narodnichestvo* represented the triumph of the Marxian over the Comtean school. The Russian Marxists were aware of this situation, and down to Lenin's polemics in the 1890's, the need to differentiate themselves from the Positivist belief in the organic unity of society played an important role in the development of their thinking.[11]

The last-mentioned consideration, however, also serves to define the historical context within which the Marxian doctrine could expect to play a role in the formation of a revolutionary movement. When in the 1880's some former Populists turned from *Narodnichestvo* to Marxism, they did so because they found in Marx a convincing statement of the thesis that the economic process would slowly but unavoidably undermine the old regime, so that the Russian proletariat, in an historical development proceeding just as inexorably as the development of capitalism itself, would thereby be enabled to "deal the deathblow to Russian absolutism".[12] In other words, what they found was a *theory of the bourgeois revolution*. The latter being a "necessary" process—in the sense that the political "superstructure" was bound, sooner or later, to be transformed by the autonomous evolution of the socio-economic realm—it was possible to interpret Marx's doctrine in the determinist sense. In *Capital* Marx had indeed done so himself, to the extent that he had treated the "unfolding" of the new mode of production—once it had come into being—as a process independent of the conscious desires and illusions of its individual "agents". Hence the link between the "materialist conception of history" and the notion of "ideology" as "false consciousness".

What his contemporaries, and the first generation of his followers, failed to see was that the entire construction was strictly appropriate only to the evolution of bourgeois society, which in Western Europe was coming to an end, while in Russia the "bourgeois revolution" was about to be carried through by a movement hostile to the traditional aims of the middle class. Marxism as a theory of the bourgeois revolution was destined to celebrate its triumph on Russian soil at the very moment when it began to falter in the post-bourgeois environment of Western industrial society. This discontinuity was later to be mirrored in the cleavage between the determinist character of "orthodox Marxism" and the voluntarist strain which came to the fore in the theory and practice of the Communist movement. The latter, faced with the evident exhaustion of the revolutionary impulse which had accompanied the great economic gearshift of the nineteenth century, was increasingly obliged to seek fresh sources of popular spontaneity in areas of the world not yet subjected to industrialism (whether capitalist or socialist). At the theoretical level, the need to locate a substitute for the revolutionary proletariat of early capitalism—an aspect of the bourgeois revolution, for it was only the latter that roused the working class to political consciousness—found its expression in the doctrine of the vanguard : an elite which substitutes itself for the class it is supposed to represent. This development signifies the dissolution of the Marxian "union of theory and practice" : a union originally built upon the faith that the working class can and will emancipate itself, and the whole of mankind, from political and economic bondage.

(This essay was originally written for a "Marx-Symposium" held at the University of Notre Dame in April 1966. It was later included in Marx and the Western World, *edited by Nicholas Lobkowicz, University of Notre Dame Press.)*

NOTES

1. Cf. *inter alia* the treatment of the subject in *Karl Marx—Selected Writings in Sociology and Social Philosophy,* ed. T. B. Bottomore and M. Rubel (London: 1956), and the recent spate of editions of Marx's early writings. Historically, the interpretation of Marxism as the theory of a revolutionary movement which has now come to an end, goes back to the writings of Karl Korsch; cf. in particular his *Karl Marx* (London-New York: 1938, 1963).

2. Cf. in particular his letter to F. Mehring of July 14, 1893, and the *Preface* to the English edition of *The Condition of the Working Class in England.*

3. It is impossible here to document the links in the historical chain leading from Engels to Lenin and beyond, but reference should be made to Plekhanov's essay "Zu Hegels sechzigstem Todestag", originally published in *Neue Zeit,* November 1891, and reprinted in G. Plekhanov, *Selected Philosophical Works* (Moscow: 1961), vol. I, p. 455 ff. Lenin's contribution to the "philosophical" debate in his *Materialism and Empiriocriticism* (1909) is well-known, as is his belated discovery of Hegel; cf. his *Philosophical Notebooks* of 1914–16, now reprinted in vol. 38 of the *Collected Works.* The embarrassment caused to his editors by the evident incompatibility of the rather simple-minded epistemological realism expounded in the earlier work with the more "dialectical" approach of the *Notebooks* is among the minor charms of Soviet philosophical theorizing.

4. *Marx-Engels Gesamtausgabe* (hereafter MEGA), I/3, pp. 307–8.

5. "Language, like consciousness, . . . arises . . . from the necessity of intercourse with other men . . . Hence consciousness from the very start is a social product and remains one as long as men exist at all." *The German Ideology* (MEGA, I/5, p. 19.)

6. e.g. by F. A. Hayek, in *The Counter-Revolution of Science* (Glencoe: 1955), especially p. 191 ff.

7. *Ibid.,* 193.

8. *Op. cit.*; cf. *Selected Works* (London: 1968), p. 183.

9. On this point cf. Korsch, *op. cit.,* p. 51 ff.

10. *Grundrisse der Kritik der politischen Oekonomie* (Berlin: 1953), p. 380 ff.

11. Cf. *inter alia* Plekhanov's writings of the 1880's (now reproduced in vol. I of his *Selected Works*). See also Ryazanov's preface to the 1929 German edition of Plekhanov's *Fundamental Problems of Marxism* (1908).

12. Cf Plekhanov's pamphlet, *Socialism and the Political Struggle* (1883).

Marxist Doctrine in Perspective

The principal difficulty in dealing with Marxism is that it is both a theory and a movement. As a theory it calls for the kind of critical detachment with which it is customary to approach theoretical constructs whatever their subject-matter; as a movement it evokes loyalties and passions which cut across mere theorizing, and more important it demands an *historical* approach.

The significance of the latter point appears more clearly when one contrasts Marxism with Darwinism (incidentally a practice inaugurated by Engels). Darwin and Marx can with some justice be bracketed as Great Victorians who did much to shatter the Victorian frame of mind; but although the theory of evolution has had its own history since it was formulated, Darwinism never became a "movement", while what is called "social Darwinism" (i.e., the more or less legitimate confusion of Darwinian and Malthusian concepts in relation to the social world) is best regarded as a passing intellectual fashion.

There is not, that is to say, any compelling reason for discussing Darwinian (or for that matter Freudian) doctrine in terms of contemporary history. Neither the original formulation of the theory, nor its subsequent modification under the stress of criticism and experience, require more than a passing glance at the socio-historical matrix out of which this particular form of thinking arose. This is not to deny the importance and fascination of biography, for we cannot know enough about the thinkers who have shaped our intellectual world. But biography, even at its fullest and most extensive, is not to be confused with *Geistesgeschichte*; its subject is the individual, not the passage of the historical process through the medium of the uniquely determined personality.

The introduction of such quasi-Hegelian termini no doubt indicates a kind of methodological *parti-pris,* and indeed it must be conceded at the outset that the standpoint from which it is proposed here to review the development of Marxism is itself historical, i.e., directed toward an understanding of the subject-matter as a phenomenon whose meaning cannot be grasped apart from its unfolding in history. Marxism is not to be conceived *either* as a set of formulas *or* as the ideology of a movement, but as the interaction between a certain theory and a certain practice.

Once this is accepted, various pseudo-problems fall by the wayside, e.g., the question of "what Marx really meant". For if it can be shown that in "meaning" different things at different times (and contradicting himself in the process) he was nonetheless consistent in struggling with a particular set of (theoretical and practical) problems, it becomes unnecessary to try to divide the orthodox sheep from the heretical goats. Orthodoxy and heresy both have their roots in the mind of the revolutionary theorist who in 1848 stood for a species of Jacobin dictatorship, and a generation later had become the patron saint of West European Social Democracy. As in politics, so in philosophy : the young Hegelian of the Berlin salons, and the ageing scholar in the British Museum reading-room, represent different terms of an intellectual development which in its totality nonetheless discloses a remarkable cohesion—as did nineteenth-century culture in general.

If the subject is approached in this manner, it becomes easier to account for the discrepancy between the current status of Marxism as a doctrine and the political influence wielded by the movement which has appropriated its symbols. The existence of such a gap has been evident since the sterilization of Soviet

Marxism in the 1930's, and possibly even before that date.[1] The point at issue in this particular context is the theoretical status of "Marxism-Leninism", i.e., the Leninist version of Marxism which has become official doctrine in the USSR. This question involves a proper appreciation of the role played by Marxism in Central European history since 1848, and of the imprint which the 1848 and 1918 revolutions left on Marxist theory. If this interrelation is not always clearly perceived, the cause lies in the political collapse of Central Europe during and after World War II. In 1918 it was perfectly obvious that the socio-political cleavage between Russia and Central Europe corresponded to the emerging split between Russian Communism and Central European (then largely German) Social Democracy. The political situation in 1945–48 was very different, but the old cultural cleavage was still sufficiently powerful to give rise, after a few years of complete exhaustion, to the current struggle between "orthodox" and heretical (i.e., autonomous) tendencies within the Communist parties themselves (and this although the Jewish intelligentsia and the Jewish labour movement could no longer be counted on to lend support to such un-Russian phenomena as Trotskyism, Luxemburgism, or Austro-Marxism—not to mention Menshevism, which in its origins and in its subsequent development can hardly be understood save in relation to the role played by westernizing Jewish intellectuals in the Russian revolutionary movement).

The starting-point for any serious consideration of Marxism as a "system" (which Marx never intended it to be) is the recognition of its *historical* locus. In the words of one of the few serious writers on the subject :

> Marx is best understood as a classically rooted western European who functioned in a time when his area was the centre of the whole world in a far greater degree than it is now; when Great Britain was the economic and political model . . . when France was a reliable catalyst of revolution; and when a predominantly agrarian society was emerging into the phase of early industrialism.[2]

Although this succinct statement omits to stress the Central European context, it does give due weight to the role which French political, and English economic thinking played for Marx, as indeed for almost all his German contemporaries. France as the laboratory of revolution, and England as the cradle of the modern world—these overwhelming realities had impressed themselves upon the minds of the generation which in 1848 confronted a dramatic political test. It has been said of Marx that to the end of his life he always remained the man of 1848; but the same can be said of his contemporaries, including Bismarck. For all of them 1848 was the moment of decision when the distinctively modern age impinged with shattering violence upon the world in which they had grown up.

What is at issue here is *German* thinking, *German* political experience, the first great upheaval of modern *German* society. A British writer, Mr. John Plamenatz, has remarked, a little unkindly, that in turning from the German to the Russian Marxists "we leave the horses and come to the mules". Insofar as this judgement is true, it reflects a circumstance of which the early Russian Marxists were painfully aware, namely their dependence on the more advanced political thinking which reached them from Germany. It is a fact of the first importance that the Russian radicals in the 1880's and 1890's turned to Marx and away from their earlier infatuation with French socialism; but to realize the significance of this event it has to be added that the French were simultaneously doing the same! Proudhon was not more discredited in Petersburg than in Paris, where his remaining disciples had to account for the failure of the Commune in 1871. Marxism triumped in the French as well as in the Russian socialist movement (though not across the Channel) for roughly the reason that German academic scholarship was then being introduced in American universities, or German research methods in the British chemical industry (not to mention the introduction of Prussian military drill in Japan). For Germany was then nearing the pinnacle of her power and prestige, and behind this sudden rise to world status there lay that sudden expansion of the national mind on which the Germans have lived ever since. In progress since the second half of the eighteenth century, this belated cultural renaissance—the first true intellectual awakening to reach the country since the Reformation—for a while gave the Germans a head start in almost every domain. What happened when the impetus had exhausted itself is another story. Here the point is that Marxism came in just when this national expansion was nearing its zenith, between 1848 and 1918; indeed it was an important part of it. If Russian and Chinese students are today brought up on Hegel and Feuerbach (however absurdly interpreted by doctrinaire and often barely literate schoolmasters), the reason is that there was a brief moment in European intellectual history when Germany headed the procession. If England has been responsible for the westernization of India and much of Southeast Asia, Germany may in the long perspective appear to have performed a similar service for China—not that anyone ever plans these results beforehand.

Such reflections are not irrelevant to a consideration of Marx's theoretical heritage. On the contrary, they take one straight to the heart of the current controversy over Marxism as a body of doctrine. The trouble is that the argument tends to be conducted (on all sides) in the manner of medieval scholasticism. Texts are cited to confirm antecedent positions which would not be one whit affected if the evidence were read differently. Astonishment is voiced at the apparent invulnerability of a body of thought which today appears at best oldfashioned, and in some respects incompatible with modern scholarship. Again and again it is pointed out that Marxism is a nineteenth-century doctrine, as though the same were not true of liberalism; that Marx had mid-Victorian England in mind when he wrote (what about Mill?); that his theories are not applicable to modern industrial societies (it used to be maintained that they made no sense in agrarian countries, but the Bolsheviks thought otherwise); that dialectical materialism represents an unstable compound of philosophy and science (is it therefore inferior to pragmatism?); that the labour theory of value is useless as a tool of economic analysis (it may however be important to economic sociology); and finally that the class struggle is a myth.

Some of the more fashionable utterances on this well-worn subject serve to display a degree of misplaced polemical zeal on the part of their authors, e.g., the frequently heard complaint about Marx's warmongering in 1848–49—a trait he shared with all the German radicals of his day, not to mention the French republicans under Napoleon III, the Italian liberals of the Cavour-Mazzini period, or the Polish nationalists, who were the greatest warmongers of all! Other strictures betray a curious lack of historical sense—for example, the assertion that the frequent talk of imminent revolution in the Marx-Engels correspondence suggests that the fathers of German Social Democracy believed the socialist world revolution to be around the corner. An unbiased study of the evidence (including both their correspondence and their published writings) discloses that "the revolution" to which they constantly referred was the European democratic uprising against the old regime—a movement which had been aborted in 1848, stayed underground after 1871, and finally broke through in 1918. In this respect, at any rate, they proved better prophets than the majority of their contemporaries. For the rest, the labour movement was assigned the task of exploiting the democratic revolution to advance its own aims. It is true that the *Communist Manifesto* makes a sweeping attempt to telescope democracy and "proletarian revolution"; but then the *Manifesto* was published a few months before the failure of the June 1848 rising in Paris disclosed the political immaturity of the working class in the most advanced country of continental Europe. The effect on Marx was profound; it is not too much to say that after 1848–49 he became what is nowadays called an ex-Communist. At any rate, he and Engels helped to bring the democratic labour movement into being, and even the Paris Commune of 1871 did not seriously dislodge them from the theoretical and practical position of their middle years. That the residual ambiguities in Marx's thought were subsequently utilized by Lenin to justify his own strategy is a different matter.[3]

The current academic fashion is to distinguish between

orthodox Marxism (supposedly represented by Russian Communism) and various forms of quasi-liberal "revisionism", starting with Eduard Bernstein. This curious manner of approaching the subject ignores the fact that Bernstein regarded himself (and was regarded by others) as a Marxist, though a somewhat unusual one, and that the real "revision" was subsequently introduced by Lenin, when he substituted the centralized vanguard of "professional revolutionaries" for the political self-determination of organized labour. It also ignores the important fact that some of Bernstein's subsequent heresies have their source in Engels,[4] who must be regarded as the real founder of German Social Democracy and of Social Democratic orthodoxy as it existed between the death of Marx (1883) and the revolutionary upheaval of 1917–18.

Lastly, the proponents of this viewpoint seem to have forgotten Lassalle (1825–64), who has a much better claim than Bernstein to represent a non-Marxian form of socialism. A Ricardian socialist in economics, an old-fashioned idealist Hegelian in philosophy, and an unashamed nationalist in politics, Lassalle stood for a synthesis of patriotism and radicalism which was immensely attractive to many Germans of his generation, though plainly quite incompatible with international socialism as Marx and Engels understood it. At any rate the experiment of marrying nationalism and socialism was stillborn. When Lassalle threw away the life of which he had grown weary, German democracy lost its ablest leader, and the German labour movement quite conceivably missed its chance to take the lead in the national movement. This issue was then regarded as relatively unimportant. It is so no longer, now that we have had the experience of Fascist "national socialism" filling the vacuum left by its rivals, not to mention the spectacle of national movements in Latin America, Asia, and Africa claiming simultaneous descent from the American, French and Russian revolutions. How much of all this is already implied in the differences between Marx and Lassalle remains a largely unexplored subject.

The reason all this has been forgotten is that Social-Democratic Marxism has since 1918 lost ground on the left and on the right, to Leninist Communism on the one hand, and Fabian socialism on the other. Whether or not one welcomes this development—which was certainly inevitable once the 1917–18 revolution had done away simultaneously with the Tsarist, Hohenzollern and Habsburg regimes—the historian is obliged to relate his interpretation of Marx as a thinker to his understanding of the epoch in which Marx's thinking took form. Failing this, it is impossible to make sense of what "orthodox Marxism" meant to an age which lived in the lively (and, as it turned out, justifiable) expectation of wholesale political and social collapse.

Of course people always mistake the revolution they are witnessing for "the revolution" of the social utopians—the golden age of classless and stateless harmony; it is arguable that the socialists of this particular generation were led astray by the more radical aspects of Marx's own thinking, though in fact he was a good deal more hard-headed than one would gather from his latter-day critics. What needs to be understood is that the character of his political thinking struck the Germans, and *a fortiori* the Russians and other East Europeans, as rather more utopian than it did contemporary English or American audiences. The latter were used to attacks on governmental authority, and even to the suggestion that the state was parasitical on society, whereas in Central and Eastern Europe such assertions smacked of anarchism. Marx and Engels of course looked forward to the replacement of "the government of men" by "the administration of things"[5]; but as an interim measure they were reconciled to (and hopeful of) a substantial diminution of state power in the Germany of their day. This was precisely what Social Democracy stood for, though with some vacillations which Marx was not slow to detect when they manifested themselves in the draft of the German Social Democrats' 1875 "Gotha Programme". The drafting committee had proclaimed "the free state" as one of the party's aims, on which Marx commented:

> In the German Empire the "state" is almost as "free" as in Russia. Freedom consists in converting the state from an

organ superimposed upon society into one completely subordinated to it, and today, too, the forms of state are more
free or less free to the extent that they restrict the "freedom
of the state".[6]

Leaving aside the textual quibble, these remarks disclose a
pretty shrewd estimate of what was, and what was not, politically possible in the Germany of 1875. Twenty-five years earlier,
after the failure of the 1848-49 movement, Marx had already
made his position clear in a review of Emile de Girardin's *Le
socialisme et l'impôt* (Paris, 1850), which urged the virtual
abolition of taxes and centralized administration :

> Behind the abolition of taxes there is concealed the aboli-
> tion of the state. The abolition of the state has meaning only
> for Communists, as the necessary result of the abolition of
> classes, with which the necessity of the organized force of
> one class for the suppression of other classes falls away of
> itself. In bourgeois countries the abolition of the state
> signifies the reduction of state power to the level it has in
> North America. . . . In feudal countries, the abolition of
> the state means the abolition of feudalism and the establish-
> ment of the familiar bourgeois state.[7]

To Marx the democratic state (on the North American model)
is still a state, and therefore destined to disappear under full
socialism, but meanwhile the labour movement must do what
it can to approximate political conditions in continental Europe
as closely as possible to the American (or English, or Swiss)
model. This aim would hardly have seemed outrageously radical
to Gladstone or Grover Cleveland, but in Germany even the
wretched "Gotha Programme" alarmed the government—so
much so that in 1878 Bismarck banned the Social Democrats as
a menace to his empire. (Partly in consequence, Marx's *Critique
of the Gotha Programme* had to await publication until 1891;
even then the full text was withheld for another twenty years.)

Against such a background the assertion that Marx and
Engels were utopians, who lived in daily expectation of some
nameless cataclysm, loses much of its force. They were in fact

leaders of the radical wing of the German democratic movement who saw their aims travestied and aborted by Bismarck, and rightly did not expect his empire to stand up under the double stress of democracy and industrialism. Their political thinking was shaped by the experience of the 1848–71 period, when the conservative forces in state and society tried to bring the revolutionary movement under control by adopting some of its aims. Unlike their liberal contemporaries they expected the attempt to fail, as it did; it even occurred to them that this failure might manifest itself in the most ramshackle of the three Eastern Empires, that of the Romanovs. After 1890, when the Russian revolutionary movement began to display its latent energies, Engels occasionally referred to Russia as "the new France". No one familiar with the antecedents of the 1789 revolution could miss the point.

If this perspective is kept in mind, 1848 appears as the connecting link between 1789 and 1917–18, which is another way of saying that Marxism is the bridge between the French and the Russian revolution. This point can be made in a number of different ways, e.g., by tracing the development of nineteenth-century Russian thought in relation to French and German philosophy; but whatever approach one chooses to adopt, some familiarity with European history is required for a proper understanding of Marx's role in synthesizing the radical thinking of his epoch. As a political philosopher he stood close to his liberal contemporaries, though he differed from them on the issue of social regulation and private property. As a theorist of the democratic revolution he was concerned with the specific issue which the 1848 movement had bequeathed to its successor. The prelude of 1848–49 pointed straight to the greater upheaval of 1917–18. In between these two crucial dates the ancient political structure was once more propped up, force being employed to keep democracy and the labour movement at bay: it was not only in Russia that an attempt was made to refloat the old regime by harnessing the new energies let loose by industrialism.

The experiment failed. The revolution resumed its course, with a violence proportionate to the degree of repression it had suffered, and at the same time with a "new look". When it rose to the surface once more, it was still democratic, but no longer "bourgeois". Social Democracy—so patriotic in 1914, to all appearances so completely won over to reform and constitutionalism—was about to reveal its Janus head.

Every political doctrine implies a philosophy of history. In the case of Marxism, which as a theory of society centres upon the understanding of the historical process, the relationship becomes explicit : if the theory is adequate, its truth can and must be demonstrated by political practice acting upon the raw material of history. Conversely, if history does not take shape along the lines intended by political action, the theoretical assumptions must be at fault. The "union of theory and practice" is fundamental to Marxism. Theorems which cannot be demonstrated in social reality have no place in it. At the same time practice embodies the purposeful aims of men in society; hence the material environment can be reorganized—on condition that the historical limitations of human freedom are properly understood. There is a realm of "necessity", of "musts", chiefly represented by economics, i.e., by the "production and reproduction of material life". In order to maintain life, man, whether civilized or savage, must wrestle with nature, "and he must do it in all forms of society and under all possible modes of production". The true realm of (personal) freedom lies outside this sphere of economic necessity and social order, which is also the sphere of political authority, regulation, the state.

In its essentials this outlook does not differ from the traditional liberal emphasis upon the gradual enlargement of human freedom. It is derived from the same eighteenth century sources, makes similar assumptions about human nature, and departs from classical liberalism only at the point where all socialists have found it necessary to signify dissent : in rejecting the liberal claim that private property and the market economy embody the only possible institutional guarantees of personal freedom. On the contrary, according to Marx (and to socialists generally) the "anarchy of production" needs to be brought under purposive control if the individual is to be freed for the pursuit of "the true realm of freedom, which however can flourish only upon the realm of necessity as its basis".[8]

The meaning of this theme for an understanding of Marxism has recently obtained greater emphasis.[9] It is indeed high time for its relevance to be more generally recognized in the English-speaking world, following the example already set in Western Europe. We shall never begin to understand the significance of Marx for the socialist movement generally until we free ourselves from the habit of identifying Marxism with Leninism. There is even less excuse for paying special attention to the "theoretical" utterances that reach us from Peking.

If one abandons scholasticism in favour of history, Marxism stands out as a socialist system which has successfully combined a certain kind of theory with a certain type of practical activity, under circumstances determined by the historical evolution of continental Europe and the regions under its control. As an "orthodoxy" it lasted for exactly one generation, between the death of Marx in 1883 and the cataclysm of 1918; as the starting point and common source of virtually every major socialist school in the modern world with the exception of Fabianism, it remains central to the understanding of what socialism is about (and even Fabianism contains a large though unacknowledged infusion of Marxian ideas). It is thus quite useless to proclaim that the development of a new class society in the USSR has invalidated interest in Marxism as a body of thought. The fact that everyone surreptitiously employs Marxian categories in analyzing Soviet society rather suggests that sociology and political science are still busy trying to catch up with Marx.

At the same time there can be little doubt that the "system" has increasingly come to wear the look of one of those grandiose but abortive attempts at universal synthesis of which nineteenth-century European (and notably German) history furnishes corresponding examples. The point made here is simply that in the critical contemplation of Marxism's theoretical structure, the historical approach must not be left out of sight. Liberalism and Marxism have a great deal more in common than polemicists on either side are willing to concede; unfortunately this judgement also implies that both movements (or doctrines) may be somewhat outdated—e.g., in regard to the issue of large-scale organization and social planning. Where they happen to concur—as in their hostility to the state and their stress on the enlargement of the realm of freedom—we do well to remember the similarities as well as the differences. The intellectual and political orientation of socialism in the modern world is perhaps the greatest single issue that confronts us. Its clarification represents among others a problem of political theory—and modern political theory is incomplete without Marx.

NOTES

1. See Herbert Marcuse, *Soviet Marxism, A Critical Analysis* (Columbia University Press, New York: 1958), *passim.*

2. Solomon F. Bloom, "Man of his Century: A Reconsideration of the Historical Significance of Karl Marx", *The Journal of Political Economy,* New York, vol. LI, No. 6, December 1943.

3. See S. F. Bloom, "The 'Withering Away' of the State", *Journal of the History of Ideas.* New York, vol. VII, No. 1, January 1946. See also Alfred G. Meyer, *Leninism* (Harvard University Press, Cambridge, Mass.: 1957), *passim.*

4. Most notable among these were Bernstein's emphasis on the democratic way to socialism, his general interest in the doctrine of evolution, and his concern with positivism and the natural sciences, rather than with the understanding of history in the Hegelian and early Marxist sense. In all these respects, Engels forms a trio together with Bernstein and the latter's veteran critic, Kautsky.

5. Engels, *Herrn Eugen Dührings Umwaelzung der Wissenschaft,* (Anti-Dühring) (Moscow: 1935), 291–92.

6. K. Marx, *Kritik des Gothaer Programms* (Critique of the Gotha Programme), as translated in Marx and Engels, *Selected Works,* vol. II, Foreign Languages Publishing House, Moscow, 1951, p. 29.

7. *See Aus dem literarischen Nachlass von Karl Marx, Friedrich Engels und Ferdinand Lassalle* (From the Literary Heritage of Karl Marx, Friedrich Engels and Ferdinand Lassalle), Stuttgart, 1902, vol III, p. 438.

8. *Das Kapital,* vol. III, 2, p. 355.

9. Cf. Raya Dunayevskaya, *Marxism and Freedom* (Bookman Associates, New York: 1958).

Sorel

For his contemporaries, Georges Sorel (1847–1922) was primarily the author of the *Réflexions sur la Violence* (1908). Later commentators have seen him according to their own stand as a disciple of Proudhon, as a theoretician of Syndicalism, as the representative of an irrationalist tendency in French thought in the years before the first World War or even as one of the spiritual progenitors of Italian Fascism. His writings of the 1890's have been considered a significant contribution to the discussion of Marxism that was just then gathering momentum. Sorel, together with Benedetto Croce and Antonio Labriola, has been credited with giving to Italian and French socialists the first adequate interpretation of historical materialism. His left wing radical critics censure him all the more severely for the reactionary attitude evident in the *Réflexions*, which eventually linked his followers politically and spiritually with the nationalist *Action Française*. He has not even escaped the charge of encouraging anti-Semitism—and this in regard to a time which was a turning-point in his intellectual life, when he came into relatively close contact with the philosopher Henri Bergson, who was of Jewish descent and background. If we add that after 1918 Sorel openly proclaimed his sympathy for Lenin, and that after his death his pupil Edouard Berth still found it necessary to defend him from the allegation of having been the intellectual founder of Fascism, it is easy to form a picture of a man who, at first sight, appears to be a bundle of contradictions.

This impression is understandable but inadequate as a judgement of him. Sorel was more than the "notorious muddler" that Lenin would have had him to be.[1] However contradictory, fragmentary and ultimately second-rate his work may seem today, its author cannot be denied a certain originality.

Sorel did not have a systematic mind. He was dependent philosophically on the fashionable currents of the 1890's. As a critic of Marxism, as a Syndicalist theoretician and as an opponent of the Enlightenment he never achieved more than a series of more or less original *aperçus*. But what he lacked in systematic power he made up for to a considerable extent by critical openness and independent thought. An inclination to paradox which drove him from one unresolved problem to another, was the counterpart of a never-failing readiness to withstand the spirit of the age. It is typical of the man that in 1889—in the very centenary year of the great Revolution that had emerged from the Enlightenment—he should have published his apprentice work, *Le Procès de Socrate,* in which Socrates, as the "ancestor of all intellectuals", was solemnly put on trial and his execution was justified.[2]

If Sorel's first appearance in print already declared him the enemy of Liberalism which he remained all his life, justice demands scrutiny of the moral grounds on which he took his stand. For what Sorel held against Socrates was not the undermining of the State (to Proudhon's successor the State, if not exactly to be despised, was certainly irrelevant), but something that went much deeper : the subversion of traditional popular morality. Even at the summit of his revolutionary career, when he was trying to unite Marxism and Syndicalism, Sorel never deferred to the Enlightenment by making individual reason the starting-point for a critique of society. He was always concerned that a collective, universally binding morality should replace the existing one. At one time it was socialist morality (as he understood it) that was to take the place of the declining liberal ethos; later on he saw nationalism, that is, the unconditional acceptance of France and its many centuries of tradition, as replacing the disintegrative democratic ideology which enjoyed a short-lived ascendancy after the Dreyfus

Affair (1894–1902). The struggle against the individualism and rationalism of the Enlightenment was the spiritual centre of Sorel's life. For this very reason Sorel was never a Marxist in the strict sense, not even between 1893 and 1905 when the Italian and French public saw in him the interpreter of revolutionary socialism.

The man who was to continue Proudhon's work in so individual a fashion was born on November 2, 1847 to a highly respectable family of Norman descent in the seaport of Cherbourg and died on August 28, 1922 in the Paris suburb of Boulogne-sur-Seine. As an eighteen year old he was enrolled at the Ecole Polytechnique, the Paris School of Engineering founded in 1794, and after his training he practised as a civil engineer for twenty-five years in various areas of France and Algeria. When he left the profession in 1892 in order to devote himself to private study at the age of forty-five he had reached the grade of Chief Engineer and was awarded the rosette of the Légion d'honneur—a distinction that a higher civil servant could hardly escape then in France. A small legacy from his mother (which, like most Frenchmen of independent means of his time, he invested in Imperial Russian bonds) enabled him to spend the remaining thirty years of his life in private research and writing.

In 1897 his simple and uneducated companion died. Increasing loneliness as he grew older may have contributed to the pessimistic tendency of Sorel's thought, but his fundamental opposition to the optimism of the Enlightenment certainly had deep roots in the Catholic faith of his parents, as did his concern for a universalist morality. This faith, as his biographers tell us, was touched with a Jansenist gloom. Sorel had broken with the Church at an early date, but his avoidance of formal marriage ties with his mistress, Marie, a simple *femme du peuple*, who had previously been in service, was due rather to a feeling for the bourgeois concerns of his mother and his other relatives, to whom she would have been most unwelcome as a member of the family. Sorel's high estimation of the family as the nucleus of the social order (a legacy from Proudhon who, as the son of a working class household did not need to compromise when it came to his own marriage) ought to have disposed him to marry Marie for even as an atheist he remained conservative in his moral outlook. His concubinage, which went along with a lifelong condemnation of the debauchery of Paris, was an inconsistency in this extremely contradictory man, but one must remember that Georges Sorel was a bourgeois by upbringing and that this was very hard to shake at a time when the middle class was at its zenith, having attained with the consolidation of the Third Republic what seemed its ultimate goal.

The democratic Republic had become not only in appearance but in essence the political expression of the French bourgeoisie. It was not necessary to be a Marxist to appreciate this. For the French public, from the Catholic Royalists on the Right all the way to the Anarcho-Syndicalists on the Left, the middle class nature of the Republic was self-evident. This had not always been the case. In 1848, when street fighting between the proletariat and the National Guard was raging in Paris, and again during the Paris Commune of 1871, for most of the French provincial bourgeoisie, the word "Republic" had sinister revolutionary overtones. It was the wave of republican agitation led by Léon Gambetta and Georges Clemenceau among the peasants and the lower middle class which finally made the Marseillaise and the tricolor symbols of the national feeling hurt by the military defeat of Napoleon III's Empire in 1870. The Jacobin tradition (from its origin warlike and national) was placed in the service of an extremely patriotic idea : war against Imperial Germany and for the recovery of Alsace Lorraine. The Right, of course, shared these nationalist sentiments, but its domestic political ambitions—restoration of the Monarchy and of the sovereignty of the Church—barred its way to power. In order to govern the Right would have to accept the Republic. This problem crippled it for decades and kept it from power. On the other hand the party of the tricolor Republicans, which had been ruling permanently since 1880, could always rely on the workers if it was a question of defending the Republic against the common enemy. The clericomonarchical Right could not gain this support. It had done the bloody work during the military overthrow of the Commune in 1871. To the Parisian working class in particular, the Army and its monarchist allies were responsible for the mass shooting of the Communards. Hence by 1889 one hundred years after the Revolution, the Republic had become legitimate in France because the ruling Republican party claimed to represent democracy, and its strength lay in the fact that the peasants and the lower middle class formed the overwhelming majority. Whoever enjoyed their confidence could successfully confront both the Royalist reaction and the Socialist revolution. For this reason Monarchists and Anarchists alike had to abandon any hope of a democratic basis for their political aims.

This was the situation when Sorel resigned from the civil service at forty-five to retire to a Paris suburb. It was the same situation which made it possible for Hippolyte Taine or Ernest Renan to endure the Republic, without on that account exhibiting the slightest regard for the Jacobin tradition.[3] For Jacobinism had its roots in Rousseau and these *grand bourgeois* liberals were deeply antipathetic to his ideas. An attempt has been made to connect Sorel's early published writings, in particular *Le Procès de Socrate,* with the liberal-conservative works of Tocqueville, Taine and Renan.[4] But these three, for all their bitter criticism of the French Revolution, were closer to the Enlightenment than Sorel, who from the beginning of his career as a writer sounded a traditionalist note which was part of his religious heritage. The struggle against the Republic and its supporting ideology could be conducted from the Right or from the Left. Sorel gave his opposition to liberalism and democracy both reactionary and revolutionary emphases. He never wavered in his attachment to the main cause : bourgeois democracy was the enemy to be fought. The middle class, the class to which he himself belonged and whose conservative notions of morality he never discarded, was doomed.[5]

In accordance with a radical tradition deeply rooted in France since 1848, someone who thought along these lines could be counted as belonging to the party of "red Republicans". But Sorel always rejected this party, as Proudhon had done fifty years before him. The "red Republicanism" of Blanqui (1805–1881) had arisen from the communist sects and secret societies established in the 1840's and wrecked in the Commune of 1871. Sorel—close here to Marx—saw them as a mere precursor of the actual workers' movement reborn around 1880. Sorel was attracted to Marxism precisely because it transcended basic concepts stemming from Jacobinism, which identified revolution with the seizure of political power. The idea of obtaining power by means of a Parisian *coup d'état*—a notion central to Blanquism—had in any case become an absurdity with the stabilization of the Republic. Since the formation in 1880 of a Marxist party under the leadership of Jules Guesde, even surviving veterans of the Commune had come to accept this. Bourgeois society—so ran the new formulation based on "scientific socialism"—was subject to a law of development which would finally allow the working class full possession of political and social power. Sorel adopted this Marxian analysis but interpreted it in his own way. Marxists talked of class war : Sorel added to this the vision of the *general strike* originally worked out by Fernand Pelloutier (1867–1901).[6]

The revolutionary Syndicalism of Pelloutier and his friends, after a preparatory period between 1884 and 1892, had established itself in the nineties as a real force. Trade unions and *Bourses du Travail* (the latter being regional bodies which united the functions of unions with those of education) had to an increasing extent, at their annual assemblies since 1892, declared themselves in favour of the idea of a general strike as propagated by Pelloutier. In this way the democratic and reformist Socialism of Jean Jaurès (1859–1914) and the "orthodox" Marxism of Jules Guesde (1845–1922) were both faced with a rival which could not be dismissed in the same way as could the outdated tactics of Blanqui or the mere anarchism of Michael Bakunin (1814–1876). For Syndicalism—so called because the *syndicats* (trade unions) were conceived as instruments and nuclei of the new order—itself stood on Marxist ground, inasmuch as it adopted the Marxian analysis of capitalism : in this way tacitly completing the break with Proudhon, who maintained the principle of private property until his death. Pelloutier —like Sorel brought up as a Catholic and from the educated middle class, but in contrast to him a youthful enthusiast who sacrificed health and life to the emancipation of the proletariat —united in his thought the Proudhonist withdrawal from parliamentary politics with the Marxian recognition that private property could not be preserved. He thus arrived at the basic idea of Syndicalism : the nucleus of the new order would have to be discovered in the working class movement itself. The *Fédération des Bourses du Travail,* founded in 1892 and whose Secretary he had become, in 1895 took the initiative in setting up the *Confédération Générale du Travail,* which eventually adopted the general strike as part of its programme : as an instrument of revolutionary struggle which would remove the ground from under the feet of bourgeois society.

This was the vision which around 1898 Sorel opposed to the official Marxism of the workers' party led by Guesde and Lafargue. The rift intensified after 1905, when a united Socialist Party (S.F.I.O.) emerged from the fusion of the Guesdists and Blanquists with the movement led by Jaurès. All factions of the S.F.I.O. accepted Marxism formally but they interpreted it variously : Jaurès in the traditional republican-democratic sense for which the tricolor was no less meaningful than the red flag; Guesde and his followers with a heavier emphasis on the antithesis of proletariat and bourgeoisie; Syndicalism as already described. To Sorel only Syndicalism deserved to be taken seriously. But Syndicalism was to a considerable extent nourished by illusions based on the fact that large-scale industry was still in its infancy. The Paris to which Sorel moved in 1892 was anything but a centre of modern industry. The elite of the Paris working class which Pelloutier, still associated with Guesde, began to influence from 1893 on, were largely employed in small firms. "Paris knew nothing of Marxism. . . . It is true to say that there was no large-scale industry in the Paris of 1892. There were a large number of small businesses and a very intelligent working class, much given to reading, the elite of which were able to associate with a rebellious bourgeois such as Pelloutier."[7]

Despite this, Marxism was accepted by a section of the radical intelligentsia who more or less consistently professed its attachment to Socialism. There had been, since 1880, a workers' party led by Jules Guesde with a programme that coincided with the Marxism of the Socialist International (founded in Paris in 1889) as represented by Engels and Karl Kautsky. The level of its literature, however, did not accord with the standards demanded by those Parisian intellectuals who were seeking the way to Socialism. This was the point at which Sorel became important : as the interpreter of historical materialism. The first volume of *Capital* had been available in French translation since 1875 and had won Marx a reputation as a first class economist. Yet this was hardly sufficient to make Marxism the theoretical basis of French Socialism, which looked back with pride on a century of revolutionary tradition. Besides, Proudhon and Bakunin, calling Marx a "German Jew", had contributed an image of him that was a bogey. Even a man such as Jaurès, who despised anti-Semitism, had reservations about accepting a system of analysis which had not evolved on French soil and, in so far as he appeared around 1890 as an interpreter of classical German philosophy, it was obvious that Jaurès was closer to Kant and Fichte than to Hegel (wholly uncomprehended in France at that time), and that he found Lassalle more sympathetic than Marx.[8] Sorel, who wished to make historical materialism the basis of a new form of analysis, had first to demolish the sterotype of Marx as no more than a significant critic of bourgeois economics. Whereas the official representatives of social-democratic Marxism in France, with Jules Guesde and Marx's son-in-law Paul Lafargue in the vanguard, were content to provide a French paraphrase of the popularisation of Marx's thought propagated by Engels and Karl Kautsky, Sorel (for a time in concert with Antonio Labriola, Professor of Philosophy in Rome, and his pupil Benedetto Croce) addressed himself to the task of providing the educated public with some notion of what exactly was of consequence in historical materialism.[9]

Sorel's first public appearance as an interpreter of Marx in 1893 coincided with the death of Benoît Malon, whose *Revue*

Socialiste, under the aegis of its autodidactic editor-in-chief, had made its way only very slowly and incompletely from its inherited Proudhonism to a kind of primitive quasi-Marxism. In July of 1893 the first number of a new monthly appeared : the *Ere Nouvelle,* founded by the Rumanian student Georges Diamandy, expressly aimed at acquainting French readers with authentic Marxist writing. The review's business manager was the Hungarian Leo Frankel, who in 1871 had been the solitary "Marxist" among the leading figures of the short-lived revolutionary Paris Commune. Two foreigners—of the sort later to be known as "rootless cosmopolitans"—thus began the task of cultivating the new Marxian theory in the birthland of Socialism. The *Ere Nouvelle,* which survived for seventeen months, published contributions from Engels, Kautsky, Bebel and Bernstein in association with Kautsky's *Neue Zeit,* but also printed original articles by leading French Socialists including Jaurès and Sorel. The latter's main contributions were two long essays, "L'ancienne et la nouvelle métaphysique" and "La fin du paganisme", both published later as books under the titles *D'Aristote à Marx* and *La Ruine du monde antique.* Sorel introduced himself as a philosopher of history and the short article "Science et socialisme" which he published in May 1893 in the official academic *Revue Philosophique* was also essentially concerned with the Marxian conception of history. As a contributor to the *Revue Philosophique* he was in a position which allowed him, courteously but precisely, to correct the then conventional academic notions of the work of Hegel and Marx. His own understanding, however, was grounded not so much in a study of German philosophy (for which his knowledge of the language did not suffice) but in his acquaintance with Labriola and in his lifelong interest in Vico. Sorel came to Marx by way of Vico. What the author of the *Scienza Nuova* meant to him can be seen in his "Etude sur Vico" in *Le Devenir Social* of October-December 1896, the journal founded after the death of the *Ere Nouvelle* by Sorel, Lafargue, Gabriel Deville and others, which was to be the leading theoretical organ of French Marxism from 1895 to 1898. Together with the *Critica Sociale* founded by Turati in Milan in 1891 (with which Labriola and the then still very youthful Croce were associated) *Le Devenir Social* expressed the Marxist thought of the two leading Romance language countries. Towards the end of 1897 Sorel broke with Deville and Lafargue and in the following year he made his debut as a theoretician of Syndicalism.[10]

To understand Sorel it is important to realize that the "revisionist" debate introduced by Eduard Bernstein in 1898 affected him quite differently from his associates. Whereas Labriola, together with Kautsky and Plekhanov (in the name of the exiled Russian Marxists in Geneva) held to "orthodoxy", Jaurès adopted Bernstein's critique of Marx and Croce turned in boredom from Socialism,[11] Sorel deviated in the direction of Syndicalism. The first literary document of this transformation was an article entitled "Avenir socialiste des syndicats" in the Spring 1898 issue of *Humanité nouvelle,* reprinted later in his *Matériaux d'une théorie du proletariat* (Paris, 1919). It is worthwhile comparing this collection of his essays with the *Réflexions sur la violence,* if only because the later versions refer specifically to the Russian Revolution. The essay "Pour Lénine" written in September 1919 for the fourth edition of the *Réflexions* accords with a postcript to the *Matériaux d'une théorie* written in 1918, in which he wrote : "The bloody object-lesson to come in Russia will make all workers understand that there is a contradition between democracy and the mission of the proletariat."

In the October Revolution Sorel saw the confirmation of his conviction, expressed already in 1898, that the seizure of power by the proletariat would not occur through parliamentary and democratic means. This was not really at variance with Jacobin-Blanquist expectations and anyone acquainted with the intellectual prehistory of Bolshevism is aware that from 1903 Lenin quite emphatically acknowledged his indebtedness to the Jacobin tradition and equated any criticism of it with defection from revolutionary Marxism. But Sorel in 1918–1919 wholly misread the Russian situation in a way possible only for a distant observer who was handicapped additionally by his ignorance of

Russian language and tradition. He took the window-dressing of "rule by soviets" literally, believed that the Russian workers had power in their hands and, for the rest, found excuses for Lenin's dictatorial conduct which he—in common with all Socialists descended from Proudhon—had consistently denied the Jacobins. He was even able to discover a plausible explanation for Bolshevik terrorism, one that possessed the advantage of fanning anew a sentiment embedded deeply in the consciousness of the Catholic provincial bourgeoisie : the atrocities of the Cheka were probably the work of the Jews![12]

All the same, it would be unjust to Sorel to measure his work by his understanding of the Russian Revolution. Anything happening outside France hardly came within his range of vision. Italy was an exception to this and in Italy he had friends and pupils (among them Mussolini, who turned away from him at one point only to return to him in the end). Sorel was aware of the importance of German philosophy, and in his last years he was still open enough to the stimulus of the American pragmatism of William James.[13] But otherwise his eyes were blinkered. Throughout his long life he never left France (except to work in Algeria which then belonged to France). He never visited Italy, a second homeland spiritually. His inclination towards nationalism after 1908, which around 1914 made him an ally of the *Action française,* had its psychological roots in an indifference to everything that was not grounded directly in French experience.

Sorel was not a "revisionist". With certain "revisionist" views he was in accord, in particular with the criticism of the political strategy outlined in the *Communist Manifesto,* which he was not alone in finding too Jacobin. "If one of the characteristics of utopian socialism is not to have taken the actual power of the working class into account, the *Manifesto* . . . still belongs to the age of utopia". The comment is by Jaurès,[14] but it could have been Sorel speaking. Never an admirer of Jaurès, they were in agreement on this point. Sorel in general saw Jaurès as the embodiment of the hated Republican tradition which was indeed bourgeois, in so far as it was rooted in the humanism and pacifism of the Enlightenment. Sorel had always attacked

Jaurès and heaped abuse on him and, through his influence on Charles Péguy, to whom Jaurès on the eve of the first World War was a symbol not only of pacifism but also of treason, he shared a certain degree of moral guilt for the insane action of the nationalist fanatic who assassinated Jaurès on July 31, 1914.[15] When Jaurès at the height of his career announced at the Toulouse Socialist Congress in 1908 that "the coming of Socialism will mean the accession of the entire working class to the highest elevation of human culture, and the accession of present-day human culture in an infinitely superior form for an immense majority of citizens", he was saying virtually the opposite of what for Sorel—both in his Syndicalist and in his nationalist phases—amounted to the particular truth of his age : the decrepitude of bourgeois culture and the necessity of opposing something radically new and undreamed of to it.

The year 1907–8 was Sorel's *annus mirabilis*. Apart from his major work, the *Réflexions,* he also published *Les Illusions du progrès,* the title of which was a programme in itself and in which he opposed the bourgeois Enlightenment to the Socialist actuality to come. These works have to be read in conjunction with his earlier work, *La décomposition du marxisme* (1906), and the essay collection *Saggi di critica del marxismo* (Milan, 1903), in which he had already demonstrated that Marxist theory was consistent with his own highly individual voluntarist ethics. His transition to nationalism found theoretical expression in his *La Révolution Dreyfusienne* (1909). Sorel could not forgive the bourgeois Radicals of the Clemenceau variety and the Socialists around Jaurès for having turned the fight for Captain Dreyfus' rehabilitation into a political campaign against the Army and the Church, which in the end put the Radical party in office. His literary activity in these years before the outbreak of the first World War points in two directions : backward to the legacy of Pelloutier, which had to be preserved from reformist adulterations; forward to the coming tactical alliance with Maurras and the *Action française* (1910–14), which was also to subserve the struggle against bourgeois democracy. All these considerations converge in the *Réflexions* of 1906–8.

Marx, he thought, was right in making the antagonism between classes the central point of his theory, and in subordinating the analysis of what was empirically knowable to revolutionary practice, to which science must minister.[16] What the bourgeois critics thought on this point was wholly irrelevant, for they necessarily represented only the standpoint of one of the two contending parties. The much deplored one-sidedness of Marxism was the very secret of its greatness. This judgement, already expressed in the *Saggi di critica del Marxismo* in 1903, recurs in the writings of 1906-8—but with a new undertone, already apparent in the title *La décomposition du marxisme*. It is consciously ambiguous, for the "decomposition"—in Sorel's view anyway—affected only the pseudo-Marxism of Social Democracy. Its leaders rejected, together with the Blanquist legacy of the *Communist Manifesto* (which was of no consequence to Sorel, and which he willingly discarded), the notion of class struggle. The German Social Democrats especially were still attached fundamentally to the Lasallean tradition of State Socialism, even though officially they acknowledged Marx.[17] Hence the emancipation of the working class was in fact frustrated, for it was conceivable only if the State were to disappear together with class society. Here Sorel returns to the idea, derived from the Syndicalism of Pelloutier and his friends, that Socialist intellectuals of middle-class origin represent a danger for the workers' movement: not only because they are inclined to introduce bourgeois forms of thought (among which Sorel also counted Blanquism) into the working class, but above all because as politicizing representatives of the intelligentsia they can not, or do not want to renounce the State. Politics is their vocation, and no amount of weekend speechifying about the future withering-way of the State can alter the fact that the Socialist intellectuals want above all to take possession of State power.

In order to understand adequately the transformation that has taken place in Socialist thought, one must examine the composition of the modern State. It is a body of intellectuals invested with privileges and possessing so-called

political means of defence against the attacks made upon it
by other groups of intellectuals eager to possess the profits
of public office. Parties form themselves in order to take
over these posts and are analogous to the State.[18]

The State itself is no more than an association of intellectuals! From this viewpoint it is possible to see why Sorel for a
time appealed no less strongly to the later founder of Italian
Communism, Antonio Gramsci, than to Benito Mussolini
(around 1912 still a very radical Socialist from the Romagna).
Starting from Sorel, it was just as possible to arrive at Communism as at Fascism.[19]

Even though Mussolini's later adherents misused Sorel's
writings in the twenties and thirties (to the extreme annoyance
of Gramsci, who saw this as a conscious deformation of Sorel's
fundamentally revolutionary attitude[20]), the assertion that in
some points he was Mussolini's mentor is not without
foundation. Sorel's last statements on this subject amount to a
declaration that he had in no way inspired Mussolini's fusion
of the nationalist with the socialist idea.[21] But it is hardly possible to deny that the Sorel of 1910 to 1914 was guilty of some
such synthesis : for this precisely was the connecting link in the
alliance of the Sorelians with some adherents of the right-wing
Action française who inclined towards Socialism. But here we are
concerned with the Sorel of 1906–08, who had not as yet
surrendered the hope that the Syndicalist movement would bring
about a renewal of Socialism and set the proletarian revolution
going. Even in his late work of 1920 (published in Rome in
1928), Sorel acknowledged his debt to Proudhon and grounded
his temporary deviation from Marx (which, significantly,
did not prevent him from supporting Lenin) on the statement
that Marxism had not explained how the bourgeois concept of
property was to be replaced by a new form of proletarian
ethics. To a certain extent Sorel remained true to himself :
Proudhon had been his starting-point, and at the end of his
life he returned to him. Admittedly, little is said about Proudhon and more about Pelloutier in the writings of 1906–08, but
at that time Syndicalism had not yet collapsed. How far

Pelloutier (who died in 1901 from tuberculosis when only thirty-four) would have agreed with Sorel when from about the end of 1906 into early 1908 he tried to compress Marx, Bergson and Syndicalism into a consistent political doctrine and philosophy of life, is irrelevant. Pelloutier's successors among the leaders of the *Confédération Générale du Travail* seem to have taken hardly any notice of Sorel's concerns. In the so-called *Charte d'Amiens* of October 13, 1906, the *Confédération* had adopted Syndicalism (that is, total independence of any political —even the Socialist—party) into its programme. The anarchosyndicalist labour leaders, above all Victor Griffuelhes, Paul Delesalle and the former veteran of classical Anarchism, Emile Pouget, had pushed through a resolution to this effect, which was accepted unanimously. This explains Sorel's short-lived enthusiasm for the *Confédération,* the after-effect of which can still be discerned in his *La décomposition du marxisme.* There, *inter alia,* we read :

> Catastrophe—which was the big stumbling-block for those Socialists who wanted to adjust Marxism to the practice of the politicians of democracy—in fact corresponds perfectly to the general strike which, for the revolutionary syndicalists, represents the arrival of the world of the future. The latter cannot be accused of having been deceived by Hegelian dialectics; and, since they reject the orientation of even the most advanced politicians, they are not imitators of Blanquism.[22]

Sorel wanted to make it quite plain that this would mean the fulfilment of Marxism in its proper sense[23], which was naturally contested by Marxists of the orthodox school of Kautsky and Guesde. Nevertheless, it is clear that the workers' leaders of the time—and precisely to the extent that they adhered to the revolutionary Syndicalism of Pelloutier and his spiritual heirs— did not lay very great store on Sorel's literary activity. Edouard Dolléans, the historian of the French trade union movement (an unimpeachable witness, since he himself was a follower of Syndicalism), has given a quite unambiguous judgement on this point.

An attempt has been made to trace the tendencies of revolutionary Syndicalism to the influence of Bergsonism . . . not directly, but indirectly, through an intermediary: Georges Sorel. In fact Sorel did contribute to the *Mouvement socialiste* a series of articles on "creative evolution", which were published by Alcan in 1907.[24] Even though Georges Sorel encountered some militants, they did not read him. A. Merrheim did not know him; Victor Griffuelhes always protested when anyone mentioned the influence of Sorel to him: "He knew nothing about Sorel really," says Maxime Leroy, "and knew of him only from conversations, vaguely: 'I read Alexandre Dumas,' he liked to say, thus stressing . . . his annoyance at the preaching of violence by parlour theoreticians." Working-class Syndicalism, on the other hand, did influence some writers, notably Georges Sorel, who tried to deduce systematizations from working-class practice after the event.[25]

In short, Sorel's influence on the elite of the French workers' movement of his time is a legend put about by the *littérateurs* whom he so despised. It is to Sorel's credit that he always described himself as no more than the interpreter of the movement —with what right remains doubtful. In any case the synthesis of Marxism with Bergson's philosophy was his own highly personal contribution. The philosopher's main work, *L'Evolution créatrice* (1907) made a considerable impact on Sorel, as is apparent from his own series of articles on the theme to which he gave the same title. Even after his later adherence to the nationalism and anti-Semitism of the extreme Right (which began in 1909 with his pamphlet *La Révolution Dreyfusienne* and reached a dramatic height around 1912 with his discovery that Jewish rationalism was inimical to the heroic and Christian tradition of France), Sorel made an exception of Bergson, the life-force philosopher. To him, Bergson was a comrade-in-arms in the now extremely urgent retreat from radical intellectualism. Bergson's Jewish descent was his private misfortune for which he was not responsible, and played no part in the victorious rejoicing which spread over Paris around 1908 among the Radical and Socialist Dreyfusards, whose triumph Sorel thought must be ruinous for France, because their anti-clericalism meant that the popular belief in Joan of Arc (the secret source of French patriotism) was irretrievably lost. Whoever destroyed the Catholic myth undermined the national existence of France! On this point Sorel agreed with Maurras, even though he did not share the latter's hope in a restoration of the Monarchy. But how was it that in 1906 Bergson appeared in a pamphlet dedicated to the general strike? The philosopher's own political outlook was hopelessly liberal and democratic, like that of his contemporary and fellow Jew, the sociologist Emile Durkheim, whom Sorel could not abide. Nevertheless, Sorel managed to find in Bergson a philosophical support for his own belief in revolutionary spontaneity:

> We ought not to expect that the revolutionary movement could ever take a direction appropriately determined in advance; that it could be, like the conquest of a country, regulated in accordance with an intelligent plan; or that it could be studied scientifically other than in its present manifestation. It is wholly unforeseeable.[26]

Bergson had broken with the determinism then dominant in France. This was the legacy of Auguste Comte, the after effects of which could be traced in Taine's historical writings. However, Bergson did not give a political emphasis to the fundamental unpredictability of the future, and his evolutionism was quite opposed to all revolutionary action in the Sorelian sense. But Sorel had his own method in these matters. He drew his arguments from all available sources, unburdened by the intention of the thinkers he cited who, in his opinion, often did not know how to apply their own intuitions. In the *Décomposition* he compared the revolutionary working class movement with the Church. The latter, despite all papal corruption, had been saved time and again by the monks. Socialism, similarly, would be saved by those who were determined to declare permanent war on bourgeois society.

> This role played by the monks is not devoid of analogies to that of the revolutionary syndicates which are the salvation

of Socialism; deviations towards trade unionism, which are a deadly menace for Socialism, recall those relaxations of monastic rules which end up in cancelling the separation between their followers and the world that was the intention of the orders' founders.[27]

We must now come to the work to which Georges Sorel owes his fame, if not his importance. The bourgeois public began to take note of him at the precise moment when he was about to lose his faith in the regenerative power of the proletariat and turn to nationalism. The *Réflexions* had an effect beyond their author's intention : not on the workers' movement (and certainly not on Lenin, as is sometimes asserted without any grounds), but on that section of the student youth which was then freeing itself from positivism and finding new teachers in Bergson, Sorel and Maurras. An incidental result of this was the establishment of the Cercle Proudhon, in which Royalists and Syndicalists met together for the first time. "La Monarchie et la classe ouvrière", the slogan of George Valois (a nationalist of working-class origin), was intended to unite Maurras with Sorel. This did not really happen, for Maurras remained a prisoner of the traditional paternalism of the Catholic-conservative social theorists of France. Valois (whose real name was Alfred Georges Gressent) had turned to Royalism in 1905. In the meetings of the Cercle Berth represented his teacher Sorel and, together with Valois, edited the *Cahiers du Cercle Proudhon,* in which "plutocratic" democracy and disintegrating liberal rationalism were put on trial systematically. Berth's later attempts to excuse this synthesis as a tactical manoeuvre have about the same credibility as Mussolini's subsequent effort to represent Fascism as a necessary detour for the realization of the distant goal of Syndicalism. In fact, by 1925 Valois assembled his own Fascist splinter group which abandoned the out-of-date clerical monarchism of the *Action française* and completed the entry into the new age.

If one now raises the question of the extent to which Sorel's work retains lasting significance beyond these possibly accidental

constellations, it is well to read with some care the preface
to the first edition of 1906 and the subsequent Introduction of
July 1907, couched in the form of a letter to his then pupil Daniel
Halévy. His thought, with its pessimism about civilization, was
in certain respects a continuation of the *fin de siècle* attitude of
the 1890's, then prevalent throughout western Europe among a
section of the educated bourgeoisie. This was a middle class
which had lost its faith in the Enlightenment, no longer took
political Liberalism really seriously, saw Socialism as a more or
less dangerous enemy and satisfied its metaphysical cravings
by variations on a theme to which Nietzsche had introduced
it : the coming redemption of man by the Superman. Sorel's
thought, in certain significant respects, fitted in with this attitude : not as an imperialist and prophet of coming world
wars as Spengler was to be in Germany a little later on, but by
recourse to the idea of a creative cycle, proposed by Vico, in
which culture in each case makes an attempt—even if initially
primitive—at regeneration. To use Hegel's term, a new principle has made its entry on the world stage or, as
Sorel puts it, a final and decisive struggle is under way in which
the existing state of things yields : in this case the now old and
tired bourgeois civilization, which was about to be rejuvenated by
the workers' movement—but only if this movement knew how
to preserve its *revolutionary myth* from corruption.

   This thesis is the centre-point of the Introduction and of the
work as a whole. The concepts of "violence" and "myth" are
balanced reciprocally, for what sets the masses in motion and
enables them to overthrow the *status quo* is the myth. Without
it there would be no real revolution.

> So long as none of the myths is taken up by the masses,
> it is possible to talk indefinitely of insurrections, without ever
> producing any revolutionary movement; this circumstance
> makes the general strike so very important, and also makes
> it so very inimical to the Socialists, who fear to be con-
> fronted with a revolution.

A few sentences later, the reader is told :

> The revolutionary myths of the present . . . enable the actions, emotions, and ideas of the popular masses, who are preparing for a showdown, to be understood; they are not descriptions of things, but expressions of desires. Utopia, on the contrary, is the product of intellectual labour. . . . It is a construction that can be taken apart. . . . Whereas our contemporary myths lead men to prepare for a struggle to destroy the *status quo,* the effect of utopia has always been to direct men's minds to reforms. . . .

Marx had opposed theory to utopia. Sorel—who would be a Marxist at any price, but in reality returns to Proudhon—sets myth against utopia. In this context myth does not mean poetic fantasy in contradistinction to scientific truth, but a prophetic anticipation of that which is to come. The masses, collectively and unconsciously, produce such myths when a new age is knocking at the door. And the myth of the working class is the idea of the general strike.

But why do the Socialist parties who adhere ostensibly to Marxism not recognize this? One reason, according to Sorel, is that Marx himself did not realize it. He was ahead of his age and had formulated his critique of capitalism at a time when the working class movement had not yet developed its appropriate forms of struggle. Another reason is that his adherents, being mostly intellectuals, reject instinctively both myth and the use of violence.

> We know better than he what strikes are, because we have been able to observe economic conflicts of considerable extent and length. The myth of the general strike has achieved popularity and has fixed itself in people's heads; we also have ideas about violence that he could not easily have formed; therefore we can supplement his teaching, instead of annotating his texts as his unfortunate students had to do for so long.

At first sight the combination of these two theses seems extraordinary. It is a simple matter of fact that the general strike was not at all so novel an idea as Sorel suggested, for it had been proposed in the 1860's among the Belgian Socialists who belonged to the First International—men like de Paepe, whose minds were haunted by something very much like the later Syndicalism.[28] Apart from this it seems astonishing that the idea of violence should be represented as foreign to Marx. But one must always bear in mind that Sorel was really no Marxist, but a Proudhonist. In 1861 Proudhon had published an eight-hundred page work under the ambitious title *La Guerre et la Paix, recherches sur le principe et la constitution du droit des gens,* in which he intoned a veritable hymn on the role of war as purification, liberation and service to the cause of righteousness. War was not only the father of all things, but over and above that a manifestation of the still more universal principle of force, which for its part formed in historical time the basis of all legislation. Only with the coming of democracy was this principle replaced by another: that of majority resolutions, and hence of peace. Proudhon did not neglect to add that consequently war had become an anachronism, but the majority of his readers never got beyond the first part of his tedious work in which he developed an historical-philosophical apology for war. His political associates reproached him and he wrote peevishly to an acquaintance on June 3, 1861; "All my friends are filled with consternation; they understand nothing; or if they understand, it is only to disapprove and complain. Does this mean that I have gone mad, or is the world growing dull-witted?"[29]

Sorel's whole originality in 1906–08 consisted in replacing the term "force" by "violence". Proudhon had advocated the "right of force", and simultaneously indicated that as a means of dividing the fit from the unfit, war had once (even if in the age of barbarism) been a means of compensatory justice. Sorel does not hold a different opinion, he merely transfers the debate onto another plane. In place of national war, for which in fact he has no use, he puts civil war. This is not only inevitable if the working class is to assume power, but salutary, for it deploys energies which a now decadent bourgeoisie no longer possesses and is hardly able to conceive. In the past there was still a ruling class resolute for battle, but—at least in the France of the Third Republic—that was now gone. The humanitarian pacificism of a worn-out bourgeoisie corresponded to the parliamentary

Socialism of Jaurès and the "rich intellectuals who came to Socialism by way of Dreyfusism . . . and . . . provided capital for the Party newspapers" :

> The decadence of capitalist economy supports the ideology of an intimidated middle class filled with humanitarian ideas, which attempts to free its thought from the conditions of its existence. The race of bold leaders who had established the greatness of modern industry disappears, in order to make room for an excessively effete aristocracy desirous of a life of peace.

Apart from Nietzsche, it was Carlyle whom Sorel took as his model here—Carlyle whose glorification of the great captains of industry could be counted among the bold intellectual feats of Victorian England and among other things perhaps explains why the same Carlyle defended Negro slavery in his notorious article, later a pamphlet of 1849, *The Nigger Question*.[30]

The class struggle, as Sorel understands it, will bring this wretched sentimental humanitarianism to an end. "At this point the role of violence seems uniquely great in history : for it can work indirectly on the middle class in order to recall them to their class feeling." Syndicalism would indeed be meaningless without a worthy opponent. This opponent is the State, and in particular the Army. "The Army is the support of the State which is most obvious, palpable, and most firmly interwoven with its origins"; and since the Syndicalists do not want to reform but to destroy the State, they must necessarily come into conflict with the Army, especially since they also reject patriotism. On the other hand, Sorel wants it made clear that the general strike and the subsequent overthrow of the bourgeois order do not imply a new version of the infamous revolutionary atrocities of 1793, which arose out of a quite different situation. "Accordingly we have the right to hope that a revolution carried through by genuine Syndicalists would not be defiled by the atrocities which defiled the bourgeois revolutions." We can take it that the theoretician of "violence" was in earnest here, for the French workers' movement would not have borne with another interpretation. Its leaders had adopted the general strike into their

programme precisely because it appeared to be a means of social
upheaval that was both effective and bloodless. Yet the section
on the destruction of the State and the role of the Army which
directly precedes the sentence quoted leaves one—to put it
mildly—with a certain impression of incongruity.

As regards the readiness of the bourgeoisie and the governments of Western Europe to use force against working-class upris-
ings, Sorel had only to look over the frontier for reassurance. In
Italy, where his ideas fell on fruitful soil in the case of both the
Syndicalists and their Fascist pupils, the publication of the
Réflexions in book form in 1908 coincided with a foretaste of
events to come. The strike movement of the agricultural workers
in Parma and Ferrar led to an armed countermove by the landowners of those areas; these proprietors still laboured under
somewhat old-fashioned ideas, and their behaviour showed what
would happen once it came to a really large-scale confrontation.[31]
Italian Liberalism, from the start a somewhat powerless affair,
had already before 1914 found itself in a state of dissolution
which could not be modulated by the parliamentary manoeuvres
of the ruling elite led by Giovanni Giolitti. Logically-minded
ideologues of this upper-class Liberalism of the calibre of Benedetto Croce or Gaetano Mosca were even then united in their
conviction that—in Italy at least—Liberalism and democracy
were irreconcilable. In this they could point to Sorel, who in his
own way expressed the same belief.[32] The later developments
released in Western Europe by the first World War were to show
that Sorel's specific criticism of bourgeois democracy was, strictly
speaking, meaningful only for France and Italy. The Socialist
movements in these two countries were deeply divided. The same
was true of Spain with the difference that there Liberalism was
even weaker and bourgeois democracy did not have to discredit
itself for the simple reason that it never came to office (apart
from the short period between 1931 and 1936, when the outbreak
of the Civil War brought the Republican experiment to a bloody
end). 1914 was a turning-point for France in this respect also
inasmuch as it buried the illusion that revolutionary Syndicalism
had the backing of the working masses. In reality it was supported
by an elite which was completely isolated in 1914 by the wave

of patriotism which overwhelmed the entire working class, and later looked to the Russian Revolution by way of consolation for this disappointment. It has already been remarked that Sorel believed Lenin's seizure of power was the realization of his own ideas—a misapprehension that he shared with others. The victory of Italian Fascism in 1922 was more closely related to the teachings proclaimed in the *Réflexions*, for the future Duce even before 1914 was among Sorel's readers and admirers. To be sure Mussolini believed at this time that Sorel was a theoretician of revolution—a conviction he shared with his then political associate Pietro Nenni, later the leader of the Socialist Party. Italy—unlike France and like Spain—was ripe for revolution, at least in the negative sense which Sorel associated with this concept. To say that the myth of violence developed in the *Réflexions* was eventually of primary service to the counter-revolution is only to state the obvious.[33]

Like his spiritual relative Vilfredo Pareto (1848–1923), with whom he was friendly for many years, Sorel belongs to a group of thinkers at the turn of the century who may be described as representatives of a specifically bourgeois cultural pessimism. They saw the clearly marked dissolution of Liberalism as the end of an epoch that had begun with the Enlightenment and reached its final high point towards 1870. Sorel, unlike Pareto, did not mourn but rather tried to hasten the decline of Liberalism. It is remarkable that Pareto's profound aversion to Socialism, against which he directed a detailed critique (*Les Systèmes Socialistes*, 1902–1903), caused no rift in his friendship with Sorel. The Marchese Pareto (he came from the Italian nobility, even though he was born in Paris of a French mother) obviously recognized the theoretician of Syndicalism as one who thought along similar lines, and did not resent his literary recommendation of the general strike. That parliamentary democracy—at least in the form in which it functioned, or rather did not function in Italy at the time—was condemned to extinction, Pareto had already recognized before Sorel turned to politics. And when, in contrast to Sorel (whom he survived by one year), he was showered with public honours by Mussolini in the last months of his life and appointed Senator of the Kingdom of Italy, the recognition went not to the author of bulky sociological treatises that were wholly incomprehensible to the Duce, but to the merciless critic of democracy and the harbinger of elitist forms of government.

Nevertheless, Sorel's pessimism exhibits features very different from those of Pareto. Sorel (unlike the withdrawn, immensely rich and fastidious Italian aristocrat living in Switzerland) wanted to be the theoretician of the workers' movement, and for a number of years identified himself with it. Pareto's sybaritic way of life accorded with a highly personal attitude to existence which was fundamentally opposed to Sorel's puritan moralism. Sorel's constant indictment of the moral decadence of the bourgeoisie, his concern for healthy public morals and his insistence on the necessity of equipping Socialism with an appropriate "producers' morality" was anything but bourgeois. Condemnation of parliamentary corruption was common to both men, but Pareto had retired full of disgust at Italian politics because in his opinion (shared also by others) the ruling class had not fulfilled its national task. The personal enrichment common in this political milieu was particularly scandalous in a then still poor and undeveloped country and Pareto held Parliament responsible for not going ahead full steam with economic development, which he wanted to see happen through free enterprise and without the slightest concession to the collectivism of the Left. What was in his mind was an "educational dictatorship" which would enable the elite to do what was right and necessary without recourse to democratic and humanitarian rhetoric. Sorel did not take this problem too seriously and in the France of the Third Republic, despite all Panama scandals, he did not need to. He believed in the possibility of a national regeneration through the newly nascent working class. The "myth of the general strike" and the associated elevation of the workers to the status of heroes was his answer to the question posed by the decline of Liberalism.

It is in Sorel's favour that he did not countenance the dual morality typical of Italian Fascism—religious instruction for the masses and cynical atheism on the part of the educated upper stratum. His notion of "myth" is often misunderstood in this respect. Sorel did not recommend the conscious dissemination of (revolutionary or reactionary) illusions, as is sometimes argued. When he called the general strike a myth, or when he asserted that it was Marx's merit to have been more than a mere scientist, this did not entail a dismissal of the question of truth. The trite and cynical notion common in Italy since Machiavelli, that history could be cheated, remained as alien to Sorel as to almost all French thinkers, with the significant exception of Charles Maurras. Sorel's puritan morality, a heritage from his Jansenist forbears, did not permit this kind of double-entry book-keeping. This must be stressed since Sorel sometimes expressed himself in an ambiguous manner. For him myth is the product of a collective will-to-believe, which does not allow itself to be manipulated and in that form possesses something akin to a presentiment of future events. In this sense he also sees religion as a myth—although in his nationalist phase around 1912 he came close enough to the Maurrasist notion of placing the Church at the disposal of politics to repel his former disciple Charles Péguy, who took Christianity seriously.[34]

Clearly there is an inner contradiction here. Sorel was not a systematic thinker and consistency in the connection of his ideas, which often arose from chance stimuli, was not his strong point. Self-contradiction was part of his nature and the notion of myth as he conceived it was ambiguous enough to permit occasional inconsistencies in its application. If myth offered access to true, i.e. supra-empirical reality, then the thinker who had perceived the mythical character of a certain structure of thought would be tempted to do the newly approaching era an occasional service by ignoring banal facts. Sorel did not always resist this temptation. On the other hand, one cannot deny that he was very much in earnest in his concern (shared by Renan) about the decline of the bourgeois world. For this world was his own, just as the world of French Catholicism was his. Sorel was thoroughly middle class and he abhorred the bourgeoisie of his time precisely because the better characteristics it had once displayed—above all the moral seriousness and the puritan sexual ethics to which Sorel adhered—appeared to have been mislaid. Sorel saw himself as living in an epoch of decadence similar to that of late classical antiquity, and his interest in the idea of *ricorso* developed by Vico—renewal by the retrieval of archaic and heroic modes of behaviour and belief—was a way out of the predicament into which his historical consciousness had plunged him. If a return to these buried values could not be achieved by holding firm to bourgeois-peasant tradition; if—to express it in sociological terms—the incursion of capitalism could not be rescinded, then salvation had to be sought in the working class and in the revolutionary general strike. It was logical enough that, at the moment when he despaired of the revolutionary role of the Confédération Générale du Travail, he should have taken up another movement for renewal—nationalism.

How far this corresponded to the developments associated with the names of Nietzsche and Spengler in Germany—a country Sorel neither knew nor understood—hardly needs to be stressed. However, France had been volcanic soil since 1789 and even if French Socialism had no prospects of achieving a successful revolution, it had at least a revolutionary mentality, which for a time captivated even conservative and pessimistic thinkers of the calibre of Sorel. The *Refléxions* are a unique testimony to such an encounter, possible only in a Catholic culture, for only there could Socialism itself attain the character of a counter-Church. The one-time Catholic Georges Sorel had always reproached the liberal Enlightenment for having introduced a process of dissolution, at the end of which sheer nothingness must come if no new faith were to replace the old. This is the ultimate sense of his attempt to allot the myth of violence a fitting role in the arrival of a new age. In this sense Sorel must be called a conservative thinker, for it is part of the essence of conservatism to see the movement of history as an interaction of constructive and destructive forces, in which the role of creative rebirth falls to the *ricorso*—even when effected by barbarian incursions. The inner tension of a system of thought that moves between the two poles of an archaism ultimately rooted in the Middle Ages and a myth of the total overthrow of the *status quo* without ever finding a real resting point, is more than a psychological phenomenon. We are faced here with a spiritual correlative of a social upheaval which is not yet at an end. The political health of present-day Europe permits no judgment as to whether the crisis proper already lies behind us in the form of the two great wars of 1914–18 and 1939–45, or whether yet more convulsions of a similar nature await us.

Sorel contributed to the journals *Ere Nouvelle* (1893–94), *Devenir Social* (1895–97) and *Mouvement socialiste* (1899–1910). His main works are *Le procès de Socrate*, 1889; *La ruine du monde antique*, 1898; *L'avenir socialiste des syndicats*, 1898; *Saggi di critica del marxismo*, 1903; *Introduction à l'économie moderne*, 1903; *Le système historique de Renan*, 1905; *Décomposition du marxisme*, 1906; *Insegnamenti sociale della economia contemporanea*, 1906; *Réflexions sur la violence*, 1906–8; *Les illusions du progrès*, 1907–8; *La Révolution Dreyfusienne*, 1909; *De l'utilité du pragmatisme*, 1921.

NOTES

1. *Materialism and Empirio-criticism* (1908–09), quoted from the English translation in *Collected Works, vol.* 14, 292. The judgment was not aimed at Sorel's political writings, which at that time were still more or less on the Syndicalist level, but at his epistemological study, *Les préoccupations métaphysiques des physiciens modernes* (1907). In regard to Sorel's relation to Bergson's then very influential critique of rationalism, see Pierre Andreu, *Notre Maître, M. Sorel* (Paris: 1953), 239–68, and the same author's "Bergson et Sorel", in *Etudes bergsoniennes* (Paris: 1952), vol. III.

2. The study in the criticism of religion published in the same year, *Contribution a l'étude profane de la Bible*, treats the Old Testament as a "popular" book—more exactly, as the self-representation of a peasantry still rooted in its tribal customs.

3. See H. Stuart Hughes, *Consciousness and Society: The Reorientation of European Social Thought 1890–1930* (New York: 1958).

4. Georges Goriely, *Le pluralisme dramatique de Georges Sorel* (Paris: 1962).

5. I. L. Horowitz, *Radicalism and the Revolt against Reason* (London: 1961).

6. Edouard Dolléans, *Histoire du Mouvement Ouvrier*, vol. II, 1871–1936 (Paris: 1946), 23–56.

7. Daniel Halévy, quoted from Dolléans, 41.

8. See Jean Jaurès, *Les origines du socialisme allemand;* new edition, with a Foreword by Lucien Goldmann (Paris: 1960).

9. Neil McInnes, "Les débuts du marxisme théorique en France et en Italie", in *Cahiers de l'Institut de Science Economique Appliquée* (Paris: 1960, series S, no. 3), no. 102. With reference to Croce's relation to Labriola see Hughes, *op. cit.,* 82 ff. Croce's later turning away from Marxism, which seemed to him to be a materialistic misunderstanding of Hegel, coincided in time with Eduard Bernstein's critique of Marx (1898–99), but depended on other intellectual premises, since Croce was a liberal on the one hand and a Hegelian on the other. This intrinsically interesting theme cannot be pursued further here.

10. The *Devenir Social* possessed in the person of Labriola a contributor who could certainly be counted among the best contemporary interpreters of Marx. As a representative of the orthodox tendency he turned sharply against Bernstein in 1898 and broke almost simultaneously both with Sorel and with his former pupil Croce. See in this regard the new edition of his then polemic, *Discorrendo di socialismo e di filosofia* (Laterza, Bari: 1947). The French translation of his main work, *Essais sur la conception matérialiste de l'histoire,* appeared in 1897—still with a Foreword by Sorel. This book had, *inter alia,* the curious effect of converting the nineteen-year-old Leo Trotsky, then (1898) in prison in Odessa, once and for all to Marxism.

11. See Croce's work of 1899, *Materialismo storico ed economia marxistica,* with the postscript "Come nacque e come mori il marxismo teorico in Italia (1895–1900)". As has been remarked with some justice, Croce was inclined to confuse his intellectual autobiography with the cultural development of Italy. What "died" around 1900 was not Italian Marxism, which at that time was rather in the process of emerging, but Croce's dilettante concern with this subject. Nevertheless, around 1915 it was the confrontation with Croce which caused the young Antonio Gramsci to devote himself in earnest to the understanding of philosophy. In Croce, Italian Liberalism possessed a cultural dictator who incited his Marxist critics to efforts that, even if circuitously, were eventually of benefit to philosophy.

12. For Sorel's attitude to the Jewish question and his growing inclination to make concessions to the anti-Semitism of the French Right, see *Jewish Social Studies* (New York: 1953, vol. XV, Nos. 3–4) for the article by Edmund Silberner, "Anti-Jewish Trends in French Revolutionary Syndicalism". See also Gaëtan Pirou, *Georges Sorel* (Paris: 1927), 50. Horowitz, *op. cit.,* 39–41, dodges the, for him, embarrassing issue by means of confused phrasing.

13. *De l'utilité du pragmatisme* (Paris: 1921). The tendency of Sorel's late work is directed against the Henri Bergson whom he had prized so high in earlier years, and to whom James is now suddenly opposed. Sorel

would seem to have neglected the community of interest of these two thinkers, who both grounded their work in psychology.

14. *Cahiers de la Quinzaine,* November 17, 1901. Quoted in Georges Lefranc, *Jaurès et le socialisme des intellectuals* (Paris: 1968), 47.

15. Péguy, of course, would not have been capable of that, even though he did not shrink from wild outbursts against Jaurès. The assassin belonged to the circle of the *Action française,* whereas Péguy—the former Dreyfusard turned nationalist—must definitely be described as a Christian Democrat. Everything separated this scholar of peasant stock from Charles Maurras, the atheist for whom the Church was no more than a means in his struggle against democracy. In addition, since 1912, Péguy had severed his link with Sorel.

16. "La necessità e il fatalismo nel marxismo", *Saggi,* 92.

17. *La décomposition du marxisme,* 34.

18. *La décomposition,* 53.

19. In regard to Gramsci's relation to Sorel, which was in fact two-edged, see especially *Il materialismo storico e la filosofia di Benedetto Croce (Opere,* vol. 2, Turin: 1952), *passim.* As late as November 1928, six years after his seizure of power and when Gramsci was already in prison, Mussolini allowed the publication of a late work of Sorel's in the *Nuova Antologia* (Rome); the Fascist editors removed only one sentence in which Sorel acknowledged his debt to Lenin. The essay, published under the title of *"Dernières méditations"* (but not in fact Sorel's last written work) was presented to the readers of the *Nuova Antologia* as his political testament.

20. See Antonio Gramsci, *Passato e Presente* (Turin: 1953), 186–7.

21. *Cahiers de l'Institut de Science Economique Appliquée* (Paris: January 1962, series S, No. 5), 83. For the relation of Mussolini to his actual or alleged mentor, see also Ernst Nolte, *Der Faschismus in seiner Epoche* (Munich: 1963), 203. Cf. also the remarks of the same author on Sorel's pupil Edouard Berth and the latter's role in the *Cercle Proudhon* in which around 1910 Syndicalists and radical adherents of the Royalist *Action française* came together; Nolte, 160. It is hardly open to doubt that here at least one may look for *one* of the intellectual birthplaces of Fascism, if this concept is understood in this context in a specifically Franco-Italian sense and has little to do with racialist theory.

22. *Op. cit.,* 64.

23. *Ibid.*

24. Georges Sorel, *L'Evolution créatrice:* this study appeared between October 15, 1907 and April 15, 1908 as a series of articles in the Syndicalist journal *Mouvement socialiste,* to which Sorel was a regular contributor. His work *Les Illusions du progrès* also appeared in its pages for the first time, as a series of articles from September to December 1906. For Pelloutier, see his brother Maurice's biography of the man: *F. Pelloutier, sa vie, son oeuvre* (Paris: 1911). See also Jean Maitron's

far-reaching and very detailed historical study: *Histoire du mouvement anarchiste en France* (1880–1914), second edition (Paris: 1955), *passim*.

25. *Histoire du Mouvement Ouvrier* (1966), vol. II, 126–127.

26. This statement in the *Décomposition* has a footnote reference in which Sorel remarks:

> One of the greatest illusions of the utopians was to believe that the pattern of the future could be deduced from a good knowledge of the present. As against such an illusion, see what Bergson says in *L'Evolution créatrice* . . .

27. *Op. cit.,* 68.

28. The Brussels Congress of the First International in September 1868 had before it a resolution worked out by de Paepe and his Belgian followers, which, in the event of a war between the European states, called on the workers to strike and to reject without exception all parties engaged in conducting the war. In a private letter to Engels of September 16, 1868, Marx described this as "Belgian idiocy": obviously because in the situation obtaining then it was incumbent on him to emphasize that a German-French war (as stated in the resolution introduced by the German Social Democratic delegates) would be advantageous only to Czarist Russia. In any case, the idea of striking against war was already familiar to the Belgian trade unionists at that time.

29. See the Introduction to the new edition of Proudhon's *Qu'est-ce que la propriété?* (Paris: 1966), 15.

30. Thomas Carlyle, *Critical and Miscellaneous Essays* (London: 1901), 348–383.

31. See Dennis Mack Smith: *Italy. A Modern History* (Ann Arbor, University of Michigan Press: 1959), 256: "It was a foretaste of the future when, in 1908, the landowners of Emilia collected a defence fund and formed a motorized volunteer force equipped with arms. This force assisted the troops in street-fighting at Parma and marched through a barrage of missiles and boiling water to surround and occupy the working-class quarters of the city. Similar scenes were to occur more frequently in the not so distant future." As the same author remarks, this was the moment when some of the Syndicalist leaders began to flirt with the nationalism of the right-wing extremists, in the hope of overthrowing the bourgeois State with their help. "Some of the Syndicalist leaders, Arturo Labriola among them, now divined that their best hope of revolution was by joining the nationalists." *(Ibid.)* Arturo Labriola, who was closely allied with Mussolini, should not be confused with Antonio Labriola who had helped to found Italian Socialism a decade before.

32. Dennis Mack Smith, *op cit.,* I, 259, 341. Croce, who in 1920–21 was a member of Giolitti's Liberal government, saw no danger in Fascism, and thus made his own contribution to the suicide of Italian Liberalism.

33. On this, see Dennis Mack Smith, *op. cit.,* 322 ff. Mussolini, born 1883 in the Romagna, relatively uncultured and by disposition attached

to anarcho-syndicalism, was never a Marxist in the period before the war
—contrary to a widespread legend. This was so even though around 1912
he used the class-struggle phraseology of the radical journalism of the
time, as was usual in his milieu. Hence he turned with all the greater
enthusiasm after 1914 to a synthesis of nationalism with the teaching of
Sorel as prepared by Arturo Labriola and other former Syndicalists.
The belief that Italy could be regenerated only through war was common
to both ways of thought, and had already been expressed in 1911 by
some leading Syndicalists to justify the colonial war then being waged in
Libya. See Smith, 267.

34. On Sorel's relation to Christianity in general and to Catholicism
in particular, see his essay "De l'église et de l'état", in *Cahiers de la
Quinzaine,* vol. III, no. 3, October 1901.

Translated by John Cumming.

Adorno

Resurgent energies released by the sudden expansion of a culture are traditionally given credit for those mysterious explosions of creativity whose inner mechanism remains obscure. The reverse case, that of a social order whose dissolution promotes news forms of consciousness, has less to commend it so far as public opinion is concerned. The favourite epithet for the spirit of such an age is "self-conscious" or "cerebral", the conventional reproach a sustained lament over the passing of greatness. Even quite major achievements tend to be viewed with suspicion—one need only recall the unfriendly reception accorded to the new psychology in its own homeland (not to mention the argument that its founder had generalized unduly from the nervous complaints of Viennese ladies). When new art forms are concerned, criticism frequently abandons its proper concerns for metaphysics. Stylistic novelties will be deplored, not on aesthetic grounds, but as signalizing a falling away from the standards of a lost "organic" age. Such censure fastens impartially upon *fin-de-siècle* weariness and radical innovations borne from a desire to have done with worn-out modes of expression. Traditionalism consigns all departures from a supposedly fixed and immutable norm to a cultural limbo labelled "decadence". If the critic happens to be domiciled east of what used to be known as the Iron Curtain, he is likely to protest that these fashionable novelties are in truth the last despairing manifestations of a dying bourgeois culture.

Judgments of this kind, whether advanced by Christian or Communist *bien-pensants*, employ a Hegelian concept (the "spirit of the age") to obscure Hegel's principal discovery : contradiction is not external to reality, but built into its structure. Obsolescent forms typically co-exist with the first stirrings—frequently crude enough—of new modes of consciousness. Because a culture has disintegrated it does not follow that its ultimate accomplishments are "decadent" in the pejorative sense assigned to the term by traditionalists or blood-and-soil enthusiasts. What can legitimately be inferred is something else : the likelihood that reflective intelligence has become dissociated from a sensibility linked to petrified customs and dying creeds. Unquestionably such a state of affairs does not favour modes of expression normally dependent upon acceptance of ancient folkways. But to acknowledge this is merely to say that some achievements are historically unique and irrecoverable. It is no indictment of a mature civilization to concede that its best minds are unlikely to be engaged in the composition of epic poems.

Historical judgments in any case do not exhaust the significance of what by its nature transcends the social texture of life in any given epoch. Because both Hegel and Marx were aware of this, it has been possible for critics steeped in the Hegelian tradition to evade the intellectual straitjacket imposed upon loyal party members by the prevailing orthodoxy in Eastern Europe. Such guerilla action, however, remains perilous and at best is confined to an avant-garde. Westward the outlook brightens for the nonconformist, albeit for reasons unconnected with the prestige of Hegelian Marxism. Freedom to expound this (or any other) doctrine is purchased at the cost of a genial tolerance extended to all comers—a spurious equalization of chances which in practice favours the owners of the mass media and the purveyors of commercial slush (frequently the same people). In the competitive struggle to market his ideas, the philosopher is no better off than the middle-brow novelist or the producer of pop art—indeed rather worse off. If he benefits from the freedom casually granted to critics of the new consensus, he is also made aware that his strictures will not impinge directly upon those in control. For the most part his audience will be confined to a minority among the educated.

Considerations of this sort are relevant to the work of a Central European critic comparatively unknown in Britain, though not in the United States, where for some years he figured among the influential German-born emigrants cast adrift by the National-Socialist upheaval. If the name of Theodor Adorno evokes an immediate response from Americans familiar with contemporary sociological literature, the simplest explanation is Adorno's co-authorship of the weighty (in every sense) collection of studies issued in 1950 under the title *The Authoritarian Personality*. Although sponsored by the American Jewish Committee, this investigation into the psychology of religious and racial animosities was not limited to the topic of anti-Semitism. In the approved manner of other melting-pot studies it had much to say about ethnic minorities and acculturation in general, the typical stresses of immigrant life in a "pluralist" culture not always being clearly discriminated from the more specific issue of racial paranoia. The material was processed and put together by investigators affiliated to the Institute of Social Research—itself transferred to the United States by the group of scholars who had originally staffed it in Frankfurt am Main until compelled to emigrate by the advent of the Third Reich.

It was perhaps fortuitous that Adorno (who from 1934 to 1937 spent much of his time at Oxford working on a critique of Husserl's philosophy) should have been associated with this particular enterprise. But having taken the plunge and agreed to contribute a lengthy theoretical chapter, he brought to bear the complex theoretical apparatus—derived in about equal parts from Marx, Freud and Max Weber—which the *Institut für Sozialforschung* had gradually assembled in the 1920's, and which by 1933 had made Frankfurt one of the intellectual centres of the Weimar Republic. If the finished product seemed barely digestible to some readers, part of the fault perhaps lay with the soggy academic prose in which the author's perceptions had to be wrapped in order to achieve the gravity proper to a work published under the auspices of the Social Science Research Council and the Research Board of the University of

California. In any case Adorno's involvement with this particular branch of learning had no further consequences, and the
entire episode was terminated (to everyone's relief, one may
surmise) with his own and the Institute's return to Frankfurt in
the late 1940's.

He was returning to the city where he had been born in 1903,
the son of a wealthy businessman and a mother of Italian non-
Jewish origin, a gifted musician from whom he inherited his
passion for music (and whose name he took as a writer). Casual
reminiscences suggest an uncommonly happy childhood, followed by schooling in Frankfurt, where he also attended the
university and obtained his doctorate with a dissertation on
Husserl (the basis of the book-length study published many years
later). The offspring of a well-to-do father willing to support his
son's brilliant career as philosopher, composer, and musicologist,
he was in an unusually fortunate position, well integrated into
the social and cultural life of his native city, and thus spared
some of the tribulations common among intellectuals who grew
up in the turbulent years of the Weimar Republic. Something
of the ease and grace that goes with such happy circumstances
has clung to him—also perhaps a certain inability to make contact with the common lot of men. When in 1925 he moved to
Vienna to study music, it was natural—given his talent and his
family connexions—that he should establish personal ties with
Schönberg, Alban Berg, von Webern, Křenek, Steuermann,
Kolisch and other representatives of the modern school. Back in
Frankfurt his habilitation as *Privatdozent* in 1931 was sponsored
by Paul Tillich. By then the *Institut für Sozialforschung* had
come into being, but contact at first was informal. It does not
seem that Adorno during these pre-Hitler years took much
notice of the Institute's political and ideological affiliations.
His personal friendship with Max Horkheimer, then and for
many years its director, acquired a political character only under
the impact of events which shattered what until then had been
a conventionally brilliant academic career.

Yet the American interlude in the career of the Institute, and
of Adorno himself, has a significance transcending the biographical circumstance that this group of predominantly German-

Jewish intellectuals chose to spend the Hitler years in the United States rather than elsewhere. By 1933 the *Institut für Sozialforschung* had come to represent a remarkable distillation of several distinct, though interconnected, forms of contemporary thought : Marxism on the one hand, sociology in the tradition of Weber and Simmel on the other, with psychoanalysis lately added to the list and rapidly becoming an instrument of interdisciplinary thought in the vaguely mapped territory connecting social, educational, and critical studies.

The Marxism was of a non-denominational kind; Lukács was briefly associated with the Institute but so were heretics like Karl Korsch who had broken not only with the Communist party, but with Leninism as a doctrine. To balance the party-line rigidity of the eminent Sinologist Karl Wittfogel (in later years the most embattled of anti-Stalinists in the America of Truman and Eisenhower) there were others who had never renounced their attachment to the Social-Democratic tradition. No reader of the *Zeitschrift für Sozialforschung* could for a moment be in doubt as to the Marxian inspiration of the critical essays on contemporary philosophy and sociology contributed by the Institute's director. But—and this constituted the peculiar fascination of the journal in the 1930's—the Marxism was not that of Moscow. Indeed Marx was rarely mentioned, Lenin never. The cryptic terms employed by Horkheimer and Adorno to designate their system of beliefs served as an outward sign of an orientation which systematically discriminated between Marxism and what was going on in the Soviet Union.

Hence the decision after 1933 to move the Institute to Switzerland, and later to New York, rather than to the East, came as no surprise to the initiated, who at that time still included some Soviet sympathizers. Coming at a moment when the Weimar Republic lay in ruins and when orthodox Communists (Lukács among them) had transferred themselves to the Soviet Union, the decision to "go West" took on a symbolic note whose meaning became clearer as the years passed and the Institute's identification with the cause of Western democracy gradually assumed a more principled character. It is no coincidence that those former members of the group who made their fundamental choice in those years have remained on the Western side of the great divide. If even so pronounced a critic of contemporary Western society as Herbert Marcuse has settled down in California (where the politically less engaged and intellectually more tolerant Leo Löwenthal had preceded him), it is no cause for wonder that Horkheimer and Adorno returned to Frankfurt in 1948–49; soon to occupy prominent positions in the university and in particular at the revived and reorganized Institute for Social Studies—now shorn of its ancient political connexions and transformed into a flourishing centre of the new academic sociology.

Yet something of the old attachment has survived and been transmitted to a new generation. To read the work of Professor Jürgen Habermas, perhaps the most original and distinguished of the present generation of West German philosophers, is to make contact with a mind at once profoundly Germanic, wholly contemporary and unmistakably steeped in the Hegelian-Marxist tradition.

Nor is he alone. The massive *Festschrift* presented to Adorno on the occasion of his sixtieth birthday in 1963 can stand as a monument to something besides his own individual work, and possibly of greater lasting import : the fusion of classical German philosophy with empirical research in the social sciences, in psychology, and in the most up-to-date forms of literary and art criticism. West Germany today, unlike its Eastern neighbour beyond the Wall, provides a meeting-place of Marxism and modernism. Some such encounter had already begun in the later years of the Weimar Republic and, but for the catastrophic eruption of counter-revolution and war, might have set the tone for the intellectual elite in the country as a whole. If its actual resonance is now confined to the *heimatlose Linke*—the homeless Left of the Federal Republic—the blame rests with others : not least with the East German Communists who (Brecht and Bloch notwithstanding) have remained firmly stuck in the primitive populism of their Russian masters, complete with Victorian morals, "socialist-realist" *Kitsch,* and an undialectical copy-theory of perception lengthily and boringly expounded not only in the official party literature but even in so heterodox a work as Lukács' multi-volume treatise on aesthetics.

To inquire how this group of intellectuals came to evolve its peculiar synthesis of traditional and contemporary thinking is to touch upon a highly sensitive nerve, for the question leads straight to that forbidden topic, the German-Jewish symbiosis (forbidden to some Jews as well as to most Germans, one might add). The subject is not rendered less delicate by the pro-Western orientation of an intelligentsia which had notoriously made Paris its spiritual home at a time when patriotic Germans were taught to resist the inroads of the subversive Gallic spirit. The ancestors of this particular tradition include Marx and Heine—two Francophiles from the Rhineland who on this account alone appeared suspect to German nationalists. The circumstance has often been noted that German Jewry represented the only consistently pro-Western element in the Reich founded by Bismarck and irretrievably wrecked by Hitler. From 1918 to 1933, during that chaotically brilliant interlude between two upheavals, liberalism and Marxism alike were heavily dependent upon a group which stood a little apart from the main body of the national community—and consequently represented one of Germany's few links with the outside world. The subject cannot be pursued here. It must be enough to say that the modernism of Ernst Bloch, Walter Benjamin or Theodor Adorno was as important a factor in rendering them unpopular as their more or less orthodox Marxism. Benjamin, in some ways the most original representative of that remarkable generation, combined religious mysticism and Marxism in proportions difficult to unravel even for assiduous students of his essays and letters (now published in West Germany by Suhrkamp). The significance of this extraordinary writer is far from exhausted when one has described him as the friend of Brecht, the translator of Proust, and the author of that historical and critical masterpiece, *Ursprung des deutschen Trauerspiels*. He is one of those disturbing figures in whom an impending catastrophe casts a premonitory shadow. His suicide in 1940, when detained with other fugitives while trying to cross from France into Spain, was among the many unrecorded tragedies of that disastrous year.

It has to be said that "tragedy" is not a term one readily

associates with Benjamin's friend and pupil Theodor Adorno.
The two men had become acquainted when Adorno was still a
student, while Benjamin—his senior by more than ten years—
already held a position of some importance as a reviewer for the
Frankfurter Zeitung and other journals. Adorno's early work
centred on musical composition, but his and Benjamin's writings
in the later 1920's overlapped in the area of literary criticism.
Retrospectively Benjamin appears as the inventor of a critical
manner, even a distinctive style, which owed something to his
philosophical training as a neo-Kantian, more to his early
familiarity with the tradition established by the Romantic
school of literary historians, and most of all to his personal
idiosyncrasies.

Of this style it has been said with truth that no one but a
German can possibly fathom its complexities, and that few
Germans even are likely to have either the patience or the erudition necessary to cope with its intricacies. There is indeed something faintly perverse about a passion for language (Benjamin
rivalled Proust and Valéry in his concern for the medium, and
Adorno has inherited the trait) resulting in a mode of expression
so mannered, hermetic and remote from ordinary discourse.
German admittedly is not an ideal instrument for a writer who
aspires to the clarity of the great French essayists—unless, that
is, he takes the easy way out (as Heine did) and settles for
superficial elegance and a sustained endeavour to be bright and
amusing.

Ever since Karl Kraus, in a celebrated essay titled "Heine
und die Folgen" (*Die Fackel,* April 1910) had pronounced sentence upon this particular style (by then a mere parody of its
original) the more serious practitioners of the craft had felt under
an obligation to differentiate themselves from the purveyors of
feuilleton. The solution they hit upon was to write as though they
were addressing themselves to their friends plus a small circle
of the elect : an operation which went easily with the aestheticism
of the period (cf. Lukács' *Theorie des Romans,* first published
in 1916). What Benjamin added to this esoteric manner was the
complexity of the born metaphysician. At its best the finished
product was Kantian in its intellectual rigour and almost

Goethean in its profusion of metaphor. But—and here one re-enters the domain of public affairs—the cultivation of this style was at variance with the democratic beliefs held by the left-wing intellectuals of the Weimar Republic, whether liberals or Marxists. Neither Benjamin nor Adorno escaped from the dilemma, though the former (urged on by Brecht) did his best for a while to sound matter-of-fact when applying the sociological canon to his favourite topic, the great French poets of the previous century. The problem appears to be insoluble. In Adorno's case it has, since his return to West Germany, led to the typically Central European compromise whereby a scholar is permitted to address newspaper or radio audiences in what is assumed to be their normal idiom, on condition that he composes his serious writings in the crabbed and hermetic fashion proper to the academic world. The truth obliges one to add that Adorno's natural bent is best served by a diction remote from ordinary usage, a circumstance which lends a certain charm to his occasional descents into the popular arena.

It is a tribute to the seriousness of the West German public that so difficult a writer has over the years become an established figure beyond the academic compound and (by way of paper-back reprints) begun to reach a wider audience. But then there are two Adornos (not counting the former head of the Radio Research Programme at Princeton in 1938–41, and the one-time director of the Research Project on Social Discrimination at the University of California, Los Angeles, in 1944–49). There is the author of weighty studies on Husserl and Hegel, and along-side him the essayist who won his spurs as a music critic in the 1920's and who has retained something of the facility of the born reviewer. Adorno's range is extraordinary, and while his output cannot compare for sheer size with that of Lukács, he has consistently maintained standards of logical stringency and literary elegance beyond the modest aspirations of East European theoreticians. By now his published work extends over four decades—and setting aside the years spent in the United States and Britain—may be regarded as a rounded whole. Beginning as a composer and interpreter of modern music in Vienna and

Frankfurt in the early 1920's, then moving to literary criticism and aesthetic theory later in the decade, he published his first major work, a study of Kierkegaard, in the calamitous year 1933, having himself just turned thirty. Aesthetics has remained at the core of his thinking, but the philosopher and the sociologist were given free rein in the years following his enforced departure from Germany in 1934, while his return fifteen years later inaugurated a new phase, culminating in 1966 in a major philosophical study, *Negative Dialektik*. This, as it were, completes the circle, for Adorno's aim here is nothing less than the restoration of classical German philosophy in general, and the Hegelian tradition in particular, to what he regards as their rightful place in the philosophical canon.

A systematic account of the entire *oeuvre*, if it were practicable, would presumably disclose numerous links between the creative, the critical, and the more strictly philosophical concerns underlying the development of a writer who has filled such a multiplicity of roles—always with distinction, at times in an unexpected guise (e.g., as the unnamed source of Thomas Mann's reflections on Beethoven in chapter VIII of *Doktor Faustus*). Even the bare enumeration of the writings published or reprinted in West Germany since the war has a suitably encyclopaedic ring. Recent essay collections (some of them in paperback format) include one under the title *Moments musicaux* which assembles critical studies going back to 1928. A number of rather more technical *Lehrschriften zur musikalischen Praxis* appear in a volume titled *Der getreue Korrepetitor* (Berlin: S. Fischer Verlag, 1963). *Drei Studien zu Hegel* (another paperback issued by Suhrkamp in 1963) reprints the earlier *Aspekte der Hegelschen Philosophie* plus two additional lectures (one of them delivered at the Sorbonne). *Eingriffe. Neun kritische Modelle* (Suhrkamp, 1963) presents the author in the guise of a semi-popular *praeceptor Germaniae* on topics ranging from the contemporary function of philosophy to the educational value of television.

Lastly there is the 1963 *Festschrift* already referred to (*Zeugnisse. Theodor W. Adorno zum sechzigsten Geburtstag*, Frankfurt am Main : Europäische Verlagsanstalt): a 500-page volume assembling friends of the author ranging from Professor Scholem of Jerusalem University to M. Pierre Boulez. There is hardly an aspect of the contemporary scene in the humanities not touched upon in this distinguished collection, but then its catholicity is no greater than that of Adorno's work itself. Nor are the contributors to this volume in any way to be described as outsiders, although they include some prominent respresentatives of the New Left. One discerns a note of authority in their pronouncements, however critical they may be of the prevailing consensus in the Federal Republic. If this is an Opposition, it is a well-established one, unlike its precursors in Weimar days. Adorno himself is now a public figure. The Professor of Philosophy and Sociology, and director (since Horkheimer's retirement) of the *Institut für Sozialforschung* at the Johann Wolfgang Goethe University, has become a power in the land (or at any rate the *Land Hesse*) and something of an oracle whose views are sought by the newspapers on topics ranging from the reform of higher education to the merits of a Wagner festival at Bayreuth. His former pupils occupy university chairs and editorial positions. They are even beginning to form something of a school.

At this stage one is unavoidably confronted with the problem of trying to extract a coherent viewpoint from a body of work so rich and variegated, yet at the same time so heavily weighted on the side of criticism. This applies even to Adorno's special domain, that of musical composition, since here, too, he has after all made his mark as a critic rather than as a practitioner. The layman can only register the astonishing expertise reflected in writing that ranges effortlessly over the past two centuries. Here is a writer apparently as much at home with the finer shades of a Beethoven or Mahler symphony as with the intricacies of twelve-tone composition or the recent history of jazz.

A few impressions impose themselves even upon the outsider: the central position occupied in Adorno's thinking by the musical tradition of Vienna, where he received his training; his relative lack of interest in work antedating that of Beethoven; the resolute championship of Schönberg, Berg and Webern. His own standing as a theorist (his sociological studies on the role of music in contemporary society are something else again) is evidently a function of his ability to analyse the technical problems of composition. It is this which gives to his studies of Mahler, Stravinsky, or Schönberg the solidity lacking in criticism which treats art merely as a social phenomenon. But this being said, one is left with the problem or having to account for a sensibility attuned to the stylistic peculiarities of atonal music, joined to an intellectual disposition which invariably seeks to establish the precise significance of new work in the context of musical history. This last of course has been the Hegelian contribution. What makes Adorno's work remarkable is that with him the fusion of aesthetic and historical concerns is spontaneous, unforced, and as it were organic. In other domains he had been preceded by the neo-Marxists of the 1930's, notably by Benjamin, to some degree by the early Lukács (before his adoption of the intellectual standards of Soviet populism and pseudo-realism). In relation to music he had the field to himself, and the proof that formal appreciation can be fused with sociology was his own accomplishment. So far as can be judged, the resulting doctrine has been accepted by the practitioners themselves; the real test, after all, of any theoretical construction.

When one turns to Adorno's writings on literature and philosophy, it is precisely the absence of such a criterion which makes the reviewer's task difficult. Music is commonly said to be a more subjective form of expression even than lyric poetry, yet composition after all presents technical problems which can be discussed with reference to generally accepted standards of past achievement. The case is different in literature, where the medium of communication is simply language—and everyone is supposed to be able to master its use. This of course is an illusion; on the other hand it is possible to feel that Adorno is unduly concerned with formal problems.

A reviewer of his *Noten zur Literatur* (*Times Literary Supplement,* February 16, 1962) made the point that their author "approaches literature and even sociology . . . from a bias of internal structure and communicative energy whose model is, ultimately, that of music. This bias allows him to regard language

as merely one of several available codes of imparted meaning."
Behind this concern for the formal structure of linguistic expression there evidently lurks the notion that musical and literary
composition have a common denominator in an underlying sensibility informing the distinctive style of any given period. This
is the aesthetic of Proust, who in turn derived such notions from
the symbolists. Adorno, like Benjamin before him, has felt the
fascination of Proust's work, not least perhaps because it offered
a field for interpretation drawing simultaneously upon Marxian
and Freudian modes of thought. Rather more unexpectedly he
has championed Valéry—*inter alia* on the grounds that his
affected coldness and indifference permits a deeper insight into
the alienation imposed upon men in present-day society than
does the facile "engagement" of writers who delude themselves
about the real nature of contemporary life. (Cf. *Noten zur
Literatur I*, pp. 183–84).

The reproach of aestheticism is indeed not one that Adorno
could afford to ignore. One would imagine it to have been a
sore point with him, for if anything has hampered the acceptance of his work it is the disjunction between his emphatic
commitment to democracy and his inability to cast off a stylistic
armature impenetrable to all but an elite of readers. It is surely
more than a personal quirk that so determined and clear-sighted
a humanist should have chosen to express himself in a style
refined and formalized to the point of complete artificiality.
There appears to be some discordance between the medium
and the message : the former developed in response to the
aesthetics of symbolism, the latter inherited from Marx and
Freud : radical thinkers brought up on the great nineteenth-
century realists.

Adorno has written on Goethe and Balzac, but in a manner
more appropriate to the discussion of Baudelaire or Valéry.
Curiously, there is no such discordance in his finely phrased
essay on Eichendorff (*Noten zur Literatur I*), where for once
the critic's idiosyncratic tone does not come between the subject
and the reader : perhaps because Eichendorff (like Schumann,
who set his lyrics to music) stirred some deeply buried yearning
for natural simplicity in his learned interpreter. At his best

Adorno's legendary erudition is joined to a felicity of phrasing
in which the psychologist may discern an echo of untroubled
days in a sunlit countryside before 1914 (charmingly evoked in
Parva Aesthetica). At his worst, e.g. in his study of Kierkegaard,
the ostensible topic disappears behind a wearisome display of
dialectical fireworks. The intermediate zone is represented by an
epigrammatic manner plainly derived from French models :
extreme condensation allied to a relentless search for the *mot
juste*. It is the reverse of a popular style—but then the business of
criticism has never, in Germany, been a popular affair.

A modernist then—but also a Hegelian for whom the tradition
of classical German philosophy issues and culminates in Marx.
Before hastening to describe this as a conventional left-wing
position, one had better face the awkwardness inherent in
Adorno's understanding of this particular heritage. He might,
after all, have adopted Marx without committing himself to
Hegel (which is more or less what Benjamin had done). Alternatively he could have championed the Hegel of the *Phenomenology* and the *Aesthetics* without troubling about Marx.
It is a tribute to his consistency that he resisted these easy
solutions, just as it is a mark of his fundamental seriousness that,
having opted for Hegel's solution of the Kantian problem, he
applied his dialectical method to the critique of Husserl (proof
of which may be found in *Zur Metakritik der Erkenntnistheorie* :
published in 1956, but re-worked from an earlier draft in
1934–37, when the emigrant in Oxford had leisure to reflect
upon the topicality of Hegelian theorizing).

Beyond these technicalities lay a wider issue : the 1930's were
a test for rationalists recently converted to a view of history as a
self-activating totality whose mechanism could be discovered by
the exercise of reason. They were doubly a test for Central European intellectuals exposed to the torrent of unreason let loose by
the Third Reich. The catastrophe suffered by the entire German
Left, Communist and non-communist alike, extended from their
lives to their beliefs, for in addition to having their careers shattered, men of Adorno's generation experienced the collapse of the
confident humanism that had sustained them in earlier days. In
these circumstances the defence of the rationalist position at its

most uncompromising—in the line leading from Kant via Hegel to Marx—had the significance of a moral as well as an intellectual affirmation. Face to face with the *Walpurgisnacht* in Germany —a gathering of demonic spirits from which irrationalists like Heidegger sought to extract what they could for the promotion of their own private contribution to the general madness—these opponents had to stand fast and Adorno at any rate did.

It is less easy to pin-point the precise connexion between the defence of rationalism and the commitment to a Hegelianized form of Marxism. There was after all an alternative : the radical empiricism of the Vienna Circle, most of whose surviving members in those years likewise had to seek refuge abroad when the German cloaca spilled over into Hitler's native Austria. One could even (those were the years before Professor Popper's conversion to liberalism) be an empiricist in philosophy and a socialist in politics. To those familiar with the sociology of Karl Mannheim this was a possible option. It was, however, an option precluded by the basic orientation of the Frankfurt group whose understanding of Marxism, while significantly different from the Soviet variety, retained the traditional link with Hegel. During the early 1930's the *Zeitschrift für Sozialforschung* carried so many critical notices of empiricist and positivist literature as to give the impression that its editors saw themselves conducting a war on two fronts : against the prevailing irrationalism of the Third Reich, and against the empiricism traditionally dominant in the Anglo-American world. With the decision to move to the United States, this orientation underwent a change, possibly because closer acquaintance with the America of Roosevelt and Dewey suggested a different view of the situation. Yet the theoretical position staked out in Adorno's critique of Husserl in the mid-1930's was reaffirmed when twenty years later he finally published *Zur Metakritik* and (a year later) his *Aspekte der Hegelschen Philosophie*. The dialectician has to combat on two fronts : against the traditional ontology whose revival had finally issued in Heidegger's irrationalism, and against the empiricist narrowness which confuses philosophy with scientism, thereby renouncing the critical function of the intellect.

Speculative metaphysics conceals its emptiness behind pompous tautologies (Being = Nothing), while empiricism contents itself with the registration of surface phenomena which it mistakes for the whole of reality. Dialectics does neither. It employs the Hegelian method beyond and against Hegel's own system, thus laying bare the contradiction inherent in the attempt to inflate an individual consciousness (that of the philosopher) to the dimensions of the universe. But it does not for this reason renounce the task of understanding the world. There is a logic which pervades reality and a method proper to its portrayal. The subject-matter of this analysis is not a substance underlying its own appearances, but the concrete totality known as history.

The exposition of this theme takes up the bulk of Adorno's last and most ambitious work, the 400-page tract bearing the title *Negative Dialektik*. Here the programmatic aim of the earlier writings has come to fruition: classical German philosophy is subjected to a critique which turns the concepts of idealist logic against the various systematizations undertaken by German thinkers since Kant. What remains when this process of auto-destruction has been completed is—the dialectical method itself. This is shown to have survived Hegel's grandiose but utopian attempt to encompass the material world within the logical straitjacket of his own system: in aberration ultimately traceable to the deeply rooted habit of allotting the primacy within the subject-object relation to the thinking subject. In contrast to this idealist perversion, Adorno opts for the "materialist" dialectic of Marx: there is neither an ontological primacy of spirit over matter nor a logical primacy of the reflecting individual mind. This last consideration also serves to "place" the existentialist heresy. At the same time Adorno will have nothing to do with dialectical materialism in the conventional meaning of the term. What Communist doctrine describes as the union of theory and practice has in his view become a particular kind of practice to which theory is subordinated. This practice perpetuates a repressive social order. "Philosophy, which at one time appeared outdated, survives because the proper moment for its realization has been missed." Radical criticism accordingly sets itself the task of freeing philosophy from the trammels imposed upon it by all the orthodoxies of our age, and of past ages too.

> Already with Plato the dialectic is intended as a means of yielding something positive by way of negative thinking; later this was pregnantly described as the Negation of the Negation. This book intends to free the dialectic from such affirmative purpose, without yielding anything in the realm of concreteness. The development of its paradoxical title is among its aims.

The argument that this revival of a purely theoretical mode of thought represents a retreat from Marx to the pre-Marxists is rebutted (page 144) on the grounds that it is not the critic's fault if theory and practice have fallen apart. The Communist enterprise having terminated in the effective subordination of critical thinking to a despotic authority, philosophy is obliged to recover the autonomy it had momentarily sacrificed to the "union of theory and practice". There can indeed be no return to metaphysics, but the critique of reality must nonetheless appeal to meta-political standards of judgment. Its ultimate criterion is mankind itself—the life of men and the immorality of a society which denies them the elementary rights and freedoms they need.

Whatever may be thought of this solution, the boldness of the enterprise commands respect. Candour, it must be added, compels the observation that even in this, his *opus magnum*, Adorno does not present a systematic exposition of his theme, but something less formal : a lengthy and brilliant polemical tract which is also a *profession de foi*. The argument does not, properly speaking, unfold. It is hurled at the reader in an unbroken sequence of staccato affirmations whose precise and lucid phrasing does not altogether make up for the absence of a discernible logical skeleton. In short, what we have here is an essay, not a treatise. It is, moreover, couched in the author's highly personal idiom—itself an adequate guarantee against pseudo-popularity, but also, alas, against practical effectiveness. But then we have it on Adorno's authority that the time for such considerations is past : the practitioners have failed us.

The revolution has not really changed the world. The task once more is to understand it.

If this is Adorno's final judgment on the contemporary situation in Europe (and he is not, as a theorist, concerned with other regions of the world), the conclusion imposes itself that he has indeed reverted to something like the "critical critique" of the Young Hegelians. Doubtless he would reply that no other position is today compatible with intellectual integrity, as may be seen from the parallel development of a form of neo-Marxist revisionism in Eastern Europe. In the end one is left with the impression that Lukács and Adorno have opted for contrasting and complementary solutions of the same problem, the *sacrifizio dell' intelletto* of the one corresponding to the willed obscurity and disdainful pride of the other. Survivors of an age when for a brief moment the "union of theory and practice" appeared possible, these writers in their different ways seem to furnish proof that the critical spirit is once more reduced to the familiar role of contemplation.

Post scriptum : this appraisal of Adorno's work preceded by two years his sudden death in August 1969. The present tense has nonetheless been preserved, since any other procedure would have changed the entire tone of the article originally published in the *Times Literary Supplement* on September 28, 1967.

A New Twist in the Dialectic

In December 1966 a sympathetic observer of the Parisian intellectual scene, writing in the London *Times Literary Supplement,* drew attention to the recent rise to prominence of a group of theorists associated with Louis Althusser, a professional philosopher and the holder of a teaching post at the prestigious Ecole Normale Supérieure in the rue d'Ulm, but also a major controversial figure within the French Communist Party. Shortly thereafter further news of him reached the general public from two different directions. First there was a well-publicized clash between Althusser and the Party's official philosopher, Roger Garaudy, at a meeting of the Central Committee, of which both men were members (Garaudy, being then also in the Politburo, carried more political weight, but has since been expelled from the Party altogether). Next, the trial of Régis Debray in Bolivia brought out the improbable connection linking this rebellious offspring of the Parisian *haute bourgeoisie* with two figures as remote from each other as Louis Althusser (Debray's old teacher) and the late Ernesto Guevara. Lastly, the French upheaval of May-June 1968 introduced a further complication, inasmuch as Althusser reacted to it with a deafening silence. It has since been explained that he was ill; also that he was privately critical of the illusions entertained by the students.

On Czechoslovakia he has been likewise silent, whereas

Garaudy publicly urged Brezhnev and Co. to quit the scene of their labours (*"Allez-vous en!"*)—rather to the embarrassment of his colleagues in the Politburo who were well aware that a sizeable minority of the Party's *militants* was shocked by this kind of language. Since then there has been further trouble. Jeanette Vermeersch (Thorez's widow) resigned from the Central Committee in protest against the Party's official stand on the invasion of Czechoslovakia, while Garaudy (later expelled) escaped with a fairly mild rebuke from his Politburo colleagues for having made too many unauthorized statements calling upon French Communists to repudiate Stalinism (of which he used to be an uncritical apologist until 1956, when the scales suddenly dropped from his eyes). Meanwhile silence enveloped Louis Althusser and his immediate circle at the Ecole Normale. One can hardly suppose that they were happy with the Kremlin's behaviour. On the other hand, unlike Garaudy (and Louis Aragon) they refused to agonize about it in public.

The relevance of all this for outsiders is difficult to grasp, and the present writer counts himself among those who have been baffled by these cross-currents. Perhaps some light is cast by a study of Fidel Castro's curious utterances about the invasion of Prague. On the one hand (he said) it was a flagrant interference with national sovereignty. On the other hand, it was necessary to "save socialism" from the revisionists. And anyway the principle of national sovereignty was bourgeois humbug. It had no absolute value, only a relative one, and could not be allowed to take precedence over the interests of the world revolution. This used to be Lenin's attitude after 1918. It may also reflect Althusser's view, since his Leninism is unqualified, and thus account for his curious silence.

Doctrinally, Althusser is a "dogmatist," but of the learned and sophisticated variety. His refusal to compromise works both ways. If one is a rigid defender of what one conceives to be the Communist interpretation of Marxism, one will tend to cast a cold eye on humanism, and this it what Althusser and his pupils have become famous for. At the same time these rigorists display an intellectual *hauteur* which cannot be to the taste of *Pravda*. Freud and Lévi-Strauss are among their oracles, along with Marx and Max Weber. The primitive Leninism of the 1930's and the petrified Stalinism of the 1950's have alike been left behind. The school specializes in theoretical analysis and expects its adherents to be well up on game theory and the latest wrinkle in Parsonian sociology. Evily disposed people have been known to hint that Althusser is really after the replacement of Stalinism by structuralism. (I shall come to this topic later.) It has also been suggested that the remedy is worse than the disease, since after all Stalinism merely kills the body whereas structuralism destroys the mind. Without going quite so far, the present author is obliged to confess that he has not found the writings of the school as rewarding as he had been led to expect. Perhaps the promised illumination is still to come. Meantime here is a corpus of work that merits attention.

To start from the wrong end, let us ignore Régis Debray's pamphlet on guerrilla warfare, familiarity with which may now be taken for granted. It bears the traces of its intellectual origins, but for a more up-to-date production of the school one has to look at André Glucksmann's analysis of the May-June upheaval in France. This followed an earlier work on military strategy published in 1967 under the challenging title *Le Discours de la Guerre*. There is no evidence that its youthful author had any first-hand acquaintance with the problems involved in military planning, but then he was writing not about war but about the theory of war. To be exact, he was presenting an exegesis of political and military theorizing from Clausewitz to Mao Tse-tung.

The book has a certain morbid fascination for a layman like the present reviewer, but one would have to consult a practitioner—Debray perhaps, or Malraux—to get an expert opinion. Prospective readers of *Le Discours de la Guerre* are warned that a thorough knowledge of Hegel's *Science of Logic* is an essential precondition for the understanding of Glucksmann. He is very good at expounding simple soldierly dicta, e.g., "The mutual definition of the terms within a contradiction excludes the possibility of any non-contradictory universality." He also has some sound advice on how to get from one point to another, for example: "The logical manipulation of a contradiction progressively reduces the role of external factors. From differences to contradictions, from their multiplicity to the principal contradiction, from the doublet of aspects (principal/secondary) to the asymmetry of their development (unevenness), there must always be a move from the exterior, which may pose the terms of the problem, to the interior which resolves it." Now why hadn't one thought of that before? *C'est clair comme le jour, mais il fallait y penser,* as they say in Paris.

Glucksmann on the French non-revolution in May-June 1968 is original too, though a trifle perverse. Being rather more sophisticated than the armchair revolutionists of the thirties, he relates the *general* crisis of *modern* society to the national crisis of *French* society. This is a trick the Althusser school, of which Glucksmann is a member, has picked up from Antonio Gramsci, though on philosophical grounds they tend to be critical of him as being too much influenced by Hegel. It is quite a sound approach, provided one sticks to the rules of the game. If one is going to be serious about the method, one must not pretend, for example, that the near-collapse of the over-centralized French bureaucracy in 1968 was part of a global "contestation" pitting the exploiters against their victims from (literally) China to Peru. Unfortunately Glucksmann will have it that the factory occupations in May were symptomatic of a world-wide tension within modern society. What they were really symptomatic of was a perennial problem of *French* society. But then empirical history does not matter much to the Althusserian school. Neither does the nation and its past.

M. Garaudy, in his latest semi-autobiographical tract has a chapter on political morality which has stirred up a considerable rumpus inside the Party. *Peut-on être communiste aujourd'hui?* is in its way a rather moving document. Among other things it explains how the author managed since he became a Communist at the age of twenty in 1933 to retain his faith, in the teeth of everything: not only the 1939 Hitler-Stalin pact, which it took some courage to defend (especially since he was a soldier at the time, and got beaten up for his obstinacy), but the 1956 revelations about Stalin. This appears to have been the worst crisis of his life, and he got through only by drawing upon an unquenchable source of truly religious faith in Communism as an ideal, as distinct from the sordid reality of Stalinist Russia. (It is not irrelevant that the young Garaudy had his moral conscience awakened by Kierkegaard and Karl Barth before he turned to Marx, and that his closest friends have always shared his belief in the compatibility of Christian ethics with Communism.) In the more theoretical parts of his book he is rather good on the intellectual arrogance of the Althusserian school, its remoteness from the concerns of ordinary human beings, and its commitment to a kind of neo-positivism with deep roots in the French intellectual tradition.

This learned and eloquent pamphlet probably puts into words what is closest to the hearts of French Communists today—especially Communists of working-class origin like Garaudy himself. The Althusserians mostly come from a different stratum, and Garaudy scores a point when he observes of their master (p. 271): *"Ainsi l'on en arrive aisément à considérer que l'idéologie est bien assez bonne pour le maniement des masses en réservant la Théorie pour les technocrates de la philosophie"* ("Thus one arrives easily enough at the notion that ideology is good enough for manoeuvring the masses about, while reserving Theory for the technocrats of philosophy.")

Since Garaudy is himself a professor of philosophy (albeit at a provincial university, not in Paris) this kind of remark cannot be dismissed as an expression of the layman's traditional suspicion of the clerisy. What divides the two men is Garaudy's commitment to a socialist form of humanism, i.e., faith in the ability of *all* men to understand what the world is about and specifically what history is about. Althusser has become famous for asserting that Marxism is *not* a form of humanism, and that the writings of the young Marx—notably the celebrated *Paris Manuscripts* of 1844—represent a form of philosophical idealism which he subsequently repudiated. The real commitment of Marx from about 1845 onward (according to Althusser) was to the proletarian revolution, not to mankind. But who is to bring the revolution about? Why, the Communist Party of course (this is no longer Marx, but Lenin, as interpreted by Althusser). Hence appeals to "socialist humanism" must be dismissed, and so, of course, must complaints about interference with such bourgeois-democratic principles as national sovereignty or liberty . . . Hence his silence on Czechoslovakia, while Garaudy publicly (see the *Nouvel Observateur* of October 21, 1968) condemned the Soviet intervention as "contrary to the principles governing the basic problem of the [various] roads to socialism."

In the end, though, Garaudy's lively and vigorous polemic falls short of its aim. A moralist, to be genuinely effective, must sacrifice all else to the truth. Now Garaudy does his best to be honest, but his best is not quite good enough. In his book he says all the proper things about Stalin, but averts his eyes from the awful truth about Stalinism as a system of rule. He also subscribes to the official mythology about the French Communists' share in the wartime Resistance movement, including what he calls *"l'appel patriotique du 10 Juillet"*, which the Party leadership is supposed to have issued after the 1940 armistice. There was no such "appeal" at that date (the "document" in question is a post-war forgery) and the authentic CP declaration circulated in September of that year, while it contained a few rude remarks about Vichy, was anything but a call for resistance to Hitler, who at the time was still Stalin's ally.

It is sad to find a moralist sacrificing his conscience for the sake of his friendship with the late Maurice Thorez, but not altogether surprising. And anyway he had taken on an impossible task. If I may plagiarize from a rather cutting *Manchester Guardian* editorial on the latest Papal encyclical and its repercussions in England : "Anyone who tries to speak in the same breath as prophet, philosopher, pastor and politician is liable to find at the finish that he has panted to no purpose . . . Prophets absolutize, philosophers analyse, politicians generalize, pastors particularize." Politicians also tell lies, and while one may admire Garaudy's steadfast loyalty to Thorez, he really ought not to have covered up for the former Party leader quite to the extent he did in his book.

Where he is effective is in blasting his philosophical opponents out of their methodological funk-hole. Although not an original thinker, Garaudy is a trained philosopher and quite capable of spotting a contradiction when he sees one. When he says (p. 272)

"*Althusser combat l'interprétation 'historiciste' du marxisme, et il la combat contre Marx lui-même*", he is saying the obvious, but there are occasions when it does no harm to do that. He gets even closer to the target when he writes (pp. 273-74): "*En réalité Althusser ne se contente pas d'opérer un retour au rationalisme dogmatique; son propos, qu'il a explicité dans un article sur le retour à Freud (Nouvelle Critique de janvier 1965) est d'être à Marx ce que Lacan est à Freud.*" This hits the nail on the head rather neatly, although I had perhaps better explain that Lacan—"*le génie du moment*"—has sprung into sudden fame with an enormous tome relating Freud to Lévi-Strauss and his school. It also needs to be explained that Althusser and his pupils, in a laudable effort to get away from Hegel and Hegelianism, are much concerned with the uniqueness of the historical event: specifically events such as the October Revolution. Such breaks in historical continuity are not predictable (see Althusser's essay "*Contradiction et Surdétermination,*" in his *Pour Marx*, pp. 87ff), and they do not obey any "law". This is heresy from the Soviet standpoint, according to which the October Revolution was "lawful," in the sense of being inscribed in the logic of history.

Althusser realizes quite clearly that this is (a) nonsense; (b) non-Marxist; (c) not what Lenin himself thought. But the October Revolution *did* take place, and of course it must not be treated as the Napoleonic gamble it really was. Althusser's solution of the problem is to assert that the event was "overdetermined", in the sense that a number of seemingly unrelated circumstances (the war, the collapse of Tsarism, the availability of Lenin and the Bolshevik party) all converged toward the same result.

Now the concept of "over-determination", which plays a key role in Althusser's thinking, has in fact been taken over from psychoanalysis, while other notions systematically employed by his school have been borrowed from Foucault and Lévi-Strauss. Well, and why not? Garaudy raises no objection in principle. What he complains of is a tendency to substitute a different approach for that of Marx without actually saying so. He is right in diagnosing such a tendency, although of course he may be wrong in substance : a different issue altogether. After all, it is arguable that present-day Marxists would be better off without the Hegelian dialectic, not to mention its castration by Engels and his descendants. Only, if this is what Althusser believes, he ought to say so more plainly and without pulling his punches about Lenin.

I shall get around to the Master in due course. First let us have a look at one of his acolytes : M. Nicos Poulantzas, a Greek-born sociologist attached to the Centre National de la Recherche Scientifique, and the author of a learned essay entitled *Pouvoir politique et classes sociales de l'état capitaliste*. For a young man of thirty-two this is quite a remarkable effort : grimly professional, rigorously logical, and littered with footnotes in the best scholarly manner. Poulantzas has digested his Communist classics (Marx, Engels, Lenin, Gramsci, and Althusser; no one else counts, certainly not Lukács who is dismissed as a Hegelian in disguise), but he also cites Weber, Schumpeter, Parsons, Lasswell, MacIver, Theodor Geiger, and Ralf Dahrendorf, at the drop of a hat. Indeed he seems to have read practically everything produced in this century, although not a great deal written before that date. Again, like Glucksmann, he does not bother with empirical history—the little he says about it testifies to a marked disdain for anything so tiresome as a mere fact. What he is after is an analysis of his chosen topic : the capitalist state.

Now here is an initial difficulty. One can leaf through the entire works of Marx and Engels without coming across any systematic treatment of this particular topic. Marx had a good deal to say about the capitalist mode of production. He also had much to say about bourgeois society. And he occasionally remarked upon the fact that the state (by which he meant the bureaucracy) was normally—but not invariably—in the service of the socially dominant class. But nowhere does he speak of a "capitalist state" (or for that matter of a feudal one). At most he suggests that the modern state serves the interests of capital. But what of the state as such? For Marx it is simply the embodiment of force, a centralized apparatus to be taken over (or destroyed) by the revolution. The state is what society is not :

the concentrated essence of political power and for the rest a neutral administrative machinery. There is no "capitalist state" : not in Marx anyway.

Here then is a poser. Was Marx a Marxist? Did he know what he was doing? The answer one gets from Althusser and his disciples is : "Only up to a point". Marx, one is told, originated a new manner of theorizing, but he was not altogether clear about all the implications of his own work. The reason is that he lacked some of the conceptual tools that were needed to clarify the method he was employing in his investigations. Moreover, in so far as he made use of Hegel's terminology he went seriously astray. Fortunately it has now become possible to dispense with these blinkers and transform Marxism into a genuine science. How? By getting rid of all that German metaphysical ballast and replacing it by the kind of sophisticated system-analysis that Althusser, Lacan, Poulantzas, Foucault, and others are agreed in describing as structuralism. The *real* Marx—the one whose genuinely novel theoretical discoveries have to be laboriously deciphered with the aid of Althusser's conceptual tool-kit— was a structuralist before his time. He just didn't know it.

How could he? After all, structuralism had not yet been invented. That is to say, it had not yet been established (by Lévi-Strauss and his school) that what matters in the investigation of a social system is the inter-relationship among its parts. There is a certain totality of relationships in every society such that all the particular sectors are held in balance by the regulative principle of the system : in the case of capitalism, the accumulation of capital. As a sociologist Marx knew this, but as a philosopher he was hampered by his Hegelian inheritance. So, instead of concentrating on the internal logic of the system he was analysing (capitalism), he tried to place it in a historical perspective, midway between European feudalism and the socialist future. Moreover, he suggested that a genuine analysis of capitalism became possible only at a certain historical moment when the "internal contradictions" of the system had begun to reflect themselves in critical theorizing (of a socialist nature).

This link between "crisis" and "criticism" was part of the Hegelian inheritance. It led to the notion that theoretical

concepts are themselves historical, in that they "reflect" a particular state of affairs, instead of being timeless and applicable to
all eternity. Althusser (who much prefers Spinoza to Hegel) is dis-
satisfied with all this and he can point to the alarming consequences of treating theoretical concepts as though they were
fluid and needed revision every now and then. What he is really
saying (see *Lire le Capital,* Vols. I and II) is that Marx would
have done better to dispense with Hegelian terminology and to
present his theory of capitalism as the scientific analysis of a certain structural totality: scientific because true and therefore
timeless.

Very well, let us provisionally accept all this. Let us disregard
the awkward circumstance that Althusser's rationalism is in the
straight line of descent from Auguste Comte, and that Marx
had read Comte and did not think much of him. For the sake
of argument let us also concede that Marx was trying to perform
the kind of structural-functional analysis of *bourgeois* society
which Weber and Parsons subsequently applied to *industrial*
society (not quite the same thing). We are then still left with the
problem of accounting for the man's failure to spot the existence of a "capitalist state". There he was, writing all those
volumes of *Capital,* and all those political pamphlets about the
seizure of power, and yet it never once dawned on him that
there was a "capitalist state". Why did it not occur to him to put
two and two together? So long as he was busy analysing the
relationship of bourgeois society to the state, why did he not
make the point that the state was "capitalist"?

The obvious answer is: because he did not think there was
such an entity as the "capitalist state". He thought in terms
of a capitalist *mode of production* compatible with *any* kind of
state: autocratic, democratic, or whatever. But the reader won't
find this stated by Poulantzas (or by Althusser either). Instead he
is offered a series of hints to the effect that the notion of a
"capitalist state" can be extrapolated from Marx's writings, if
only one tries hard enough. Moreover, there is the argument
that Marxism has been developed further—by Lenin and
Gramsci, for example. Only Gramsci says nothing about the
"capitalist state" either! Instead he talks of an *Italian* state,

which, to be sure, serves the basic aims of the ruling class, but that is another matter.

What of contemporary Marxist theory on this question? Poulantzas cites Henri Lefebvre, Maximilien Rubel, and Herbert Marcuse (p. 132), shakes his head over them, and dismisses them as "historicists"—the worst thing a structuralist can say of his opponents. They all share, it seems, a common error: that of taking seriously the Hegelian distinction between "civil society" and "the state". Thence derives *"ce corrélat de la problématique historiciste qu'est la perspective anthropologique de 'l'individu concret' et de 'l'homme générique' conçus comme sujets de l'économie"*. Poulantzas (having learned from Althusser that the Marx of the 1844 *Paris Manuscripts* was still a speculative philosopher) will have nothing to do with this "historicist perspective". It does not occur to him that the distinction between state and society (which was in fact introduced for the first time by a group of eighteenth-century theorists including Montesquieu and the Scottish historians) may have been the intellectual reflex of an actual event: the emergence (for the first time in recorded history) of an autonomous market-centred society *not* subordinate to the state.

All he can see is that Marx inherited this terminology and he wants no part of it. *"Sans s'étendre sur la critique de cette conception, contentons-nous de remarquer qu'elle conduit à des conséquences très graves, qui aboutissent à l'impossibilité d'un examen scientifique de l'Etat capitaliste."* The "grave consequences" are these: if the state as such became visible for the first time at a particular historical moment, then a theory of the state is something different from an analysis of the particular political order characteristic of present-day society. Philosophy, in other words, would then conserve its autonomy—instead of collapsing into sociology—so long as people remember that there was once something called history, and that history has to do with men, not just with classes and their relations. Philosophy and history are in fact inter-related—which is just why the Althusser school wants to eliminate both.

Nous voilà enfin au coeur de la mêlée. It is not just a matter of "historicism" in the Hegelian sense. Poulantzas has something quite sensible to say (p. 222) about the needless trouble which some Hegelians get into trying to disentangle "ideology" from "science". His brief remarks on this topic are effective against Lukács (and against Lenin, whom he does not criticize), but this is mere shadow-boxing. What we want to know is where history —actual profane empirical history—comes in. The answer is that it doesn't come in at all. At any rate, the present reviewer can't find it. And for this it seems to me Louis Althusser must take some of the responsibility.

Now it has to be conceded that in getting rid of the Stalinist heritage, including the dreadful clap-trap about "bourgeois science" and "proletarian science", Althusser and his pupils have performed a valuable service. At least the air has once more become breathable. But the accumulated stench from the Stalin cloaca was not the only bother. French Communism had become addicted to a debased form of metaphysics which certified the coming victory of the revolution by appealing to dialectical "laws of motion" supposedly valid for nature and history alike. The demolition of this faith was long overdue, and once more Althusser deserves credit for it. Lastly, there was the heritage of Engels' philosophical writings including his interpretation (or misinterpretation) of historical materialism in his letter to J. Bloch of September 21, 1890—a text usually cited by his apologists as proof that he knew all about the limitations of economic determinism. In fact, what Engels puts forward in this regrettable document is an eclectic doctrine which takes at its face value the surface configuration of society. His uncritical acceptance of the theoretical model underlying the notion of the *homo oeconomicus* represents a return to the pre-Marxian standpoint.

However, this is not the end of the matter. The autonomy of science in the writings of Althusser signifies a commitment to a particular kind of theorizing: that associated with the structuralist school. A return to positivism is inevitable if one casts philosophy overboard, but structuralism has a special attraction for French Marxists because it is in tune with the Comtean tradition. It can also appeal to the prestige of contemporary anthropology, psychology, and linguistics. However, as we have seen, it can be argued with a little ingenuity that Marx was himself a structuralist before his time; he certainly looked for patterns and relations. Althusser's pupils are fond of citing from the Sixth Thesis on Feuerbach: "The human essence is no abstraction inherent in each single individual . . . it is the ensemble of social relations." This sort of thing was and is a necessary corrective to German metaphysical speculation (not to mention the flatulent idealism of Schiller and his imitators down to Hochhuth). Marx was critical of Kant for the same reason that he preferred Shakespeare to Schiller.

On the other hand, he had no use for Comte, and it is easy to guess what he would have thought of Michel Foucault's discovery that "Man" was invented quite recently (around 1800— See *Les Mots et Les Choses,* p. 319) and is due to make his disappearance shortly (*ibid.,* pp. 396-398). What will take man's place, it seems, as a human ant-heap in which the individual no longer exists as such. If one believes this, one must also believe that there is nothing to be done about it, in which case one can hardly claim to be in the Marxist tradition. Foucault, in fact, cites Nietzsche in support of his reflections on the imminent Death of Man (*"L'homme est une invention dont l'archéologie de notre pensée montre aisément la date récente."*)

Now there is no need to burden Althusser with Foucault's gloomy prophesies. One may also grant that every set of problems needs to be reformulated from time to time, and that it will do the Marxists no harm if they have to bring their conceptual apparatus up to date. Lastly, it is arguable that Marx himself lacked the perspective necessary to perceive just what he was doing that had not been done before. This is a perennial problem in philosophy and science: the great innovators who advance into *terra incognita* have to make up their tools as they go along, and these tools necessarily partake of the nature of the "old world" that is being left behind. In Marx's case, it is now conventional to deplore his residual Hegelianism, but the Althusserian Marx suffers from a more specific fault: he was so far in advance of his time that he found it impossible even in *Capital* to apply the sort of methodology that would have been appropriate to the kind of work he was doing. Instead, he fell back upon inherited thought patterns (*Lire le Capital,* I, pp.

33–35. Hence the prevalence of a terminology embodying a particular vision—that of the dialectical process, kept going by its "internal contraditions".

For Marx, the latter exist in germ already from the start, and the subsequent history of an epoch (antiquity, the middle ages, or whatever) is simply the explication and externalization of a hidden logic of self-contradiction. In *Pour Marx* (pp. 92 ff) Althusser shows very clearly that the understanding of an event such as the Russian Revolution demands a different conceptual model. He is less convincing when he turns his attention to those passages in *Capital* where Marx employs Hegelian terms by way of suggesting that relatively simple forms of economic life (commodity, money, etc.) already contained *in nuce* the more highly developed stages of the capitalist production process. In this case the method simply cannot be divorced from the theoretical conclusions worked out with its aid. Althusser's solution of this awkward problem is to suggest that Marx did his scientific work (whose validity he takes for granted) in spite of being saddled with concepts that were quite unsuitable for his purpose. What he discovered (with the help admittedly of an "ideological" commitment to Hegel's logic of contradiction) was a particular structure to which this logic was not applicable (*Lire le Capital*, II, pp. 399-401).

It is to be observed that Althusser and his pupils have nothing to say about the subject matter of Marx's economic investigations. They are solely concerned with his methodology. In so far as it is tainted with Hegelianism, they regard it as irrelevant and contingent. An empiricist like Raymond Aron can describe Marx as pre-modern because still indebted to Hegel. The originality of Althusser's performance consists in demonstrating that Marx actually employed a method of his own for which he had not found a suitable mode of expression, and that he unconsciously made up for this lack by employing the antiquated Hegelian terminology. The only trouble is that we are never told what his new method was. *Lire le Capital* concludes with a rhetorical question : *"quelle est donc la nouveauté de la méthode d'exposition suivie par Marx pour qu'il soit contraint de l'exposer en un language ancien qui la trahit?"* (ibid, II, p. 401). No clear answer is to be found anywhere, but the drift of Althusser's thought is plain enough : having got rid of the dialectic, in the "materialist" form conserved by Marx, he is free to search for the structure of social reality without bothering about the notion that this historical process exemplifies a logic of contradiction (or the passage of essence into existence, or that of unconscious reality into consciousness, or any other philosophical superstition).

Now the point here is that for Althusser theoretical thinking, if it is to take itself seriously, cannot operate with the sort of logical model Engels had in mind when in the Preface to Vol. III of *Capital* he wrote : "It is self-evident that where things and their interrelations are conceived not as fixed but as changing, their mental images, the ideas, are likewise subject to change and transformation . . . they are not encapsulated in rigid definitions. . . ." If the changing substance of the historical process enters into the very structure of the conceptual model, then how can there be such a thing as science?

The question is legitimate. The answer is that Engels, not for the first time, had made a muddle of a logical problem for whose solution he was not equipped. Althusser is so appalled by this discovery (see *Lire le Capital,* II, pp. 64–67) that he hardly knows what to say, whereas Garaudy (*op. cit.,* pp. 275–78) bends all his efforts to the task of demonstrating that Engels was merely explicating the plain meaning of what Marx had said earlier. In actual fact Marx could never have done his theoretical work if he had not believed in the possibility of defining his object scientifically. Althusser's polemic against "empiricism" and "pragmatism" is directed against Engels, and to that extent represents a justified reaction on the part of a theorist when confronted with a conceptual model which makes theoretical thinking impossible, and moreover takes pride in demonstrating that there can be no such thing as an adequate scientific definition because "the only real definition is the development of the object itself, but this development is no longer a definition". (*Lire le Capital,* II, p. 65, citing *Anti-Dühring.*)

This kind of stuff connects Engels with Nietzsche, and one can hardly blame Althusser for wanting no part of it. He is less persuasive when he tries to expel the dialectic from those passages in Marx's own work where theoretical thinking is meant to give an adequate report of the actual historical process—something Engels could not do on his pragmatist assumptions, because for him the concepts merely "reflect" a changing set of circumstances, and thus lack any theoretical dignity. When Althusser affirms that authentic *theorizing* is incompatible with this kind of historicism, he is saying the obvious. And when he lauds Spinoza for having effected an unprecedented revolution in thought (*Lire le Capital*, II, p 50), he performs an important and necessary task. But to call Spinoza *"le seul ancêtre direct de Marx"* (*Ibid.*) is to open one's flank to criticism (see Garaudy, p. 273). The mathematical model employed by Descartes and Spinoza does serve as a reminder that there is such a thing as theoretical discovery, and of course Marx thought he had *discovered* something—why else go to all that trouble?

As a corrective to the kind of debased Hegelianism which no longer recognizes any difference between ideas and mere ideologies, this is all very well. But Althusser seems to underrate the difficulty of applying the rationalist model to historical reality. If there is such a thing as a logic of history—and for the past two centuries philosophy has been in search of a method suitable to this topic—it is unlikely to disclose itself to thinkers for whom Hegelianism merely represents a grandiose aberration.

The attraction structuralism has come to possess for Althusser and his school should now have become somewhat less mysterious. At bottom both he and Lévi-Strauss are in search of something that lies beyond the flux of history. The unifying link is the theory of language, inasmuch as its study holds out the hope of laying bare the most general features of man's conceptual structure and therewith a means of deciphering our cultural heritage without falling into relativism. To the obvious question, *whose* conceptual structure—the Brazilian aboriginal's or the modern scientist's—philosophy may reply, in the words of a contemporary British logician (P. F. Strawson), "There is a massive central core of human thinking which has no history". If this area can be cleared up, we shall have access to "the commonplaces of the least refined thinking" as well as "the indispensable core of the conceptual equipment of the most sophisticated human beings."

Plainly it is this goal which for some of our contemporaries has taken the place of the traditional concern with the decipherment of historical processes. That France, for so long the stronghold of rationalism and positivism, should have become a centre of structuralist writing—for in the last resort this is what the whole movement is about—need not surprise anyone familiar with the intellectual climate of Paris. I merely observe, in passing as it were, that the historical movement which has led us to this point is quite capable of leading away from it. For when all is said and done, the current predominance of rationalist, structuralist, and anti-historicist (not to say anti-historical) modes of thought is just as much an aspect of the contemporary world as the rise of nuclear science, the new calculating machines, the growth of authoritarian and bureaucratic tendencies in politics, and the phenomenon of a cult literature whose theme is no longer the death of God, but the coming disappearance of Man.

From historicism to
Marxist humanism

If an historian of ideas were asked to identify the central problem of his task at the present time, what feature would he stress? The relation of history to sociology? The need for a universalist outlook transcending the limitations of race, nation and locality? The built-in reservations of the scientific approach? At any rate it is unlikely that he would feel able to neglect the reproach of "historicism" flung at his predecessors ever since it began to dawn upon thinking people in the second half of the nineteenth century that behind the new historical consciousness there lurked a related view of values hitherto treated as absolute and unchanging. Once nature had been shown to possess a history, it was not long before the subversive notion occurred to anthropologists, sociologists, critics of religion, and students of political thought that human nature too might have an historical dimension, and that men might not consequently be bound for all time by the moral precepts worked out by the theologians and philosophers reflecting upon the circumstances of their own age and place. Hence the "anarchy of values" contemplated with horrified fascination by writers as remote from each other as Kierkegaard, Nietzsche and Dostoevsky, and the fin de siècle malaise clearly perceptible behind the cheerful cynicism of Shaw and other life-forcers—some of them not long after converted to Fascism on the grounds that one ideology was as good or bad as another. The historian, even though himself in many cases quite innocent of such a philosophy (or any other), could not in the circumstances escape the suspicion that he was up to no good.

Historicism in this sense of the term clearly possesses a signification quite different from that subsequently given to it by Professor Karl Popper, whose well-known refutation of what he took to be the characteristic modern heresy centred upon the logical impossibility of predicting the future. Popper's comprehensive ignorance of the philosophical tradition he was criticizing enabled him to fasten upon Hegel the wholly unfounded charge of having inaugurated the disastrous habit of making political theory dependent upon historical prediction. The baseless accusation rebounded upon the European heirs of positivism when their American colleagues began to apply mechanistic and deterministic notions about "social engineering" all too plainly derived from the unhistorical approach prevalent in the physical sciences. Like the "social statics" of Comte and Spencer, these conceptual models ignored whatever could not be measured or quantified—in other words, whatever was specifically human, and thus of interest to historians. The predictable result has been well illustrated recently by the fraud-cum-farce known as the "anti-poverty programme" : not to mention the war in Vietnam, which was to have been won by dropping so many tons of bombs a square mile, thereby paradoxically stiffening the will to resistance in the face of such senseless destruction.

Whatever Hegel's faults, he never made the mistake of supposing that the human element could be removed from the equation. Nor, for that matter, did his philosophy lend support to the notion that history was subject to inexorable causal laws. What turned "historicism" into a problem for later thinkers operating within the mental climate he had helped to create was, rather, an uncomfortable awareness that no one could any longer foresee where the historical process was going to. History thus became a threat to the intellectual and moral certainties shared by rationalists and romantics alike : the metaphysical dimension preserved in Hegel's idea of *Geistesgeschichte* had to be abandoned. By the later nineteenth century this evacuation of *Geist* from *Geschichte* had been completed by the positivist school; but the first step was notoriously taken by Ranke, with his hopeless search for history "as it really was" before the mind got to work on "the facts". By the time Dilthey around 1900 had worked out his typology of world views, this phase was over and the issue had been settled. Historiography had become a matter for professionals who studiously avoided what were known as "value judgments" (though needless to say they automatically imported their patriotic and religious values into their writings).

Alongside this growing mountain of specialization there persisted the ancient search for a universal history of the spirit, but by now emptied of the moral certainties which inhabited the Hegelian system. Dilthey's solution of the problem amounted to an admission that reflection could yield only partial and contradictory insights into a higher, or deeper, reality whose true nature remained hidden. Once this had been accepted, the irrationalists, with their cult of intuition and empathy, were free to let their fancy roam, unhampered by the antiquated notion that values must be anchored in theoretical comprehension of mankind's nature and history's logic. One *Weltanschauung* being as good as another, the choice between them reduced itself to arbitrariness even for a professed rationalist like Weber, who in the end accepted what he called the "plurality of values" in a suitably resigned spirit :

> It is necessary to choose which of these gods one wishes to serve, but regardless of the choice, he will always find himself in conflict with one of the other gods of the world.

Nietzsche had already chosen the Superman, and Spengler, the poor man's Nietzsche, thereafter effected the transition from aesthetics to politics : if everyone was free to choose the "god" he wished to serve one might as well choose the god of war. The circle was closed.

Of the books under review, the two-volume collection of Horkheimer's essays, *Kritische Theorie,* is the one most profoundly marked by this particular problem. This is hardly surprising when one considers that the author was born in 1895, made his philosophical debut in 1925 with a doctoral dissertation on Kant's aesthetics, became director of the Frankfurt Institut für Sozialforschung in 1930, and after 1933 transferred the Institute successively to Geneva, Paris, New York and Los Angeles, before returning to Frankfurt in 1950 to become once more head of the reconstructed Institute and, more briefly, Rector of the Goethe-Universität. His publications during this period included sociological investigations composed or edited in collaboration with American colleagues of very different background, as well as a philosophical study, *Dialektik der Aufklärung* (1947), written jointly with his long-standing friend and colleague Theodor Adorno. This work already struck a note of disillusionment induced by the rise and fall of the Third Reich with its attendant horrors—not foreseeable in 1932 when Horkheimer published the first of his collected essays in the *Zeitschrift für Sozialforschung*. The concluding piece in *Kritische Theorie*, dated 1941, deals critically with the new phenomenon of "culture for the masses", and in other ways anticipates the author's subsequent conversion to a decidedly pessimistic view of present-day society.

The 1947 work still maintained an uneasy balance between the militant rationalism of the earlier essays and a growing realization that the heritage of the Enlightenment was ambiguous—whence the title *Dialektik der Aufklärung*. By 1967 a collection of studies published under the title *Zur Kritik der instrumentellen Vernunft* rang the changes on a theme already familiar from Professor Herbert Marcuse's writings: modern industrial society has found its intellectual complement in an "instrumental" employment of reason which lacks the critical dimension because it has been emptied of philosophy in the traditional sense of the term. The introduction to *Kritische Theorie* makes the additional point that Marxism—the esoteric faith of the Institute and its collaborators during the 1930's—has become inadequate, the industrial proletariat having been integrated within the social order in East and West alike. This preface is dated "April 1968", yet the subsequent upheaval in France is unlikely to have shaken Horkheimer's conviction that the era of proletarian revolution is closed. For the rest, verbal applause of "the onward march of totalitarian bureaucracy" is dismissed as "pseudo-revolutionary", and liberal democracy, where it still exists, is characterized as the lesser evil, in terms unlikely to appeal to the student Left, in West Germany or elsewhere. Max

Horkheimer, in the 1930's very much a Marxist-Leninist, may today not unfairly be said to have become a Social Democrat: albeit one who invokes Rosa Luxemburg's rather than Kautsky's critique of Bolshevism.

After this brief but inevitable detour through the maze of contemporary ideological affiliations, can one specify a connexion between Horkheimer's philosophy and his politics? He naturally affirms that what has vanished since the 1930's is not his personal faith in the enduring importance of reason and freedom, but the fleeting chance of transcending bourgeois liberalism in the direction of authentic socialism. At the same time, however, his 1968 preface strikes an idiosyncratic note unusual to say the least, in a former spokesman of the Old Left.

> Metaphysical pessimism, an implicit element of every genuine materialist thought, has always been familiar to me. My first acquaintance with philosophy was mediated by Schopenhauer; adherence to the teaching of Hcgel and Marx, the will to comprehend and transform social reality, did not, for all the political antagonism, blot out my experience of his philosophy.

In fairness it has to be said that this affirmation is borne out by the 1933 essay, "Materialismus und Metaphysik"—perhaps the most impressive piece of writing ever to emerge from Horkheimer, and certainly the most moving. For the impassioned commitment to Marxism was backed up by sentiments remote from the nauseating cheerfulness normally characteristic of "progressive" literature. Materialism, the reader was told, cannot fail to qualify its hopes for a better future by a sombre recollection of what it has cost mankind to emerge from pre-history, and thus it necessarily carries a pessimistic trait: "Past injustice cannot be made good. The sufferings endured by earlier generations obtain no redress." Since the author of these words was in 1933 fully committed to what in the same essay he discreetly styled "dialectical materialism", it does seem that his earlier immersion in Kant and Schopenhauer had left lasting traces. This severe training also showed up to advantage in his subsequent critical treatment of positivist and vitalist writings. Clearly there was some advantage in having come to intellectual maturity at a time when rationalism and humanism were already under attack, but still able to mobilize philosophical champions not intimidated by the prestige of scientism.

For all that, Horkheimer's writings during the decade from 1932 to 1941, now reprinted unchanged from the *Zeitschrift für Sozialforschung,* make it plain why the intellectual position then assumed by their author turned out in the end to be untenable. Alfred Schmidt's friendly but not uncritical epilogue to *Kritische Theorie* is nicely balanced between the respectful attention due to a veteran of battles fought and lost long ago, and the need for reconsideration of what Horkheimer and Adorno in the 1930's termed "critical theory" and what is perhaps more commonly known as Hegelian Marxism. Schmidt, who represents the next generation—he was born in 1931—is himself the author of a penetrating exegetical study of one particular aspect of Marx's thought which for obvious reasons did not attract much attention in the stormy 1930's (his doctoral dissertation, *Der Begriff der Natur in der Lehre von Marx,* the publication of which was sponsored by Adorno and Walter Dirks, representing the reconstituted Institut für Sozialforschung).

That Marx was primarily a social philosopher, and that his "materialism" had little in common with the dogmatic metaphysical neo-Hegelianism of the later Engels: these commonplaces of present-day discussion in Continental Europe were not so much argued by Schmidt as taken for granted. This assessment in turn rested upon the critical and exegetical labours performed three decades earlier by Horkheimer, Marcuse, Adorno and their associates. And yet the "critical theory" of the 1930's for all its self-conscious awareness of the distance separating it from the received truths of Soviet scholasticism, had not altogether emancipated itself from some of the fallacies inherent in the notion of "dialectical materialism", as interpreted by the "School of Frankfurt" in those days. For the political sphere this is obvious, and Schmidt's 1968 epilogue makes no bones about it: the Institute's "revolutionary conception" (as he tactfully puts it) had to be abandoned "under the pressure of world-political events". But it also applies to Horkheimer's and Adorno's interpretation of the "critical theory", and ultimately to the theory itself, in so far as it fell short of its proclaimed purpose.

It is noteworthy that Schmidt cites more or less orthodox French Communist theoreticians such as Louis Althusser and Roger Garaudy, alongside non-party heretics, such as Sartre and Henri Lefebvre, among the representatives of a "new Marxism" about to take shape in the aftermath of an increasingly tedious debate between old-fashioned Marxist-Leninists on the one hand and new-fangled existentialists and eschatologists on the other. It is likewise significant that, for all his reservations in detail, he still subscribes to the programmatic aim formulated by Horkheimer and Adorno in the 1930's: that of establishing a connexion between critical theory and political practice. That this practice is itself theoretical—inasmuch as it is necessarily guided by analysis of the actual situation, not by romantic rebelliousness and unmeditated rejection of the status quo in the anarchist manner—goes without saying both for the authors of the "critical theory" and for their latter-day descendants.

What then is it that differentiates Horkheimer's position in the 1930's from the sophisticated neo-Marxism of the present Frankfurt school and its French or Italian counterparts? Primarily, it would seem, a new awareness that Marx's approach—not to mention its popularization by Engels and others—was not wholly adequate to the task he had set himself: that of transforming philosophical "interpretation" into "revolutionary practice". With the wisdom acquired by painful experience it has become possible to see more clearly why the realization of the "critical theory" did not yield the results expected by its authors. At a remove this also applies to the original enterprise of the Frankfurt school, an undertaking which ran parallel to the more orthodox (in the Leninist sense) theorizing associated with the name of Georg Lukács.

In both cases the attempt fell short of its goal in so far as it failed to establish a satisfactory link between theory and practice. But it also ran into a purely intellectual obstacle ultimately traceable to the dissolution of Hegel's school and the rise of "historicism" in the sense defined above: the relativization of concepts and values which classical liberalism and classical socialism once had in common. In the end, there was not much to choose between the assertion that these values were class-bound, and the notion that they represented a passing phase in the history of "Western man" "German Christianity", the *Volksgeist,* or some other vehicle of evolution. Once philosophy had collapsed into sociology, the question whether class or race was to be regarded as the privileged instrument of a wholesale trans-formation of values reduced itself to an arbitrary choice between hypostatized agents of destiny.

In the light of what has been said about Horkheimer's genuine attachment to humanism, these remarks may seem unfair. It is perfectly true that on occasion he displayed a clear awareness of the situation, and indeed did his best to preserve the heritage of German idealism against neo-positivist scientism and romantic organicism alike (see "Der neueste Angriff auf die Metaphysik"). That relativism in theory corresponded to Fascism in practice had been publicly affirmed by Mussolini, and Horkheimer in 1937 gave himself the satisfaction of citing the Duce as witness in his eloquent address to an invisible jury whose members were invited to consider the potentially disastrous result of yielding to the temptation to cast philosophy overboard. But this circum-stance illuminates the paradoxical nature of the whole enterprise, for the author undermined his own position by presenting the reader with a thoroughly historicist and relativist critique of neo-liberalism and positivism. The tolerance of the Enlightenment, he observed, had originally comported a critique of "feudalism", whereas modern philosophy represented

> the ideological capitulation of liberalism before the new autocracy, the confession of its impotence, the transition to an authoritarian viewpoint.

Whether accurate or not—and one notes with some amusement that Bertrand Russell was among the thinkers whose utterances provoked these reflections in 1937—Horkheimer's characteriza-tion of the doctrines he objected to was thoroughly reductionist :

> Neo-romantic metaphysics and radical positivism both have their roots in the sad situation of large portions of the

middle class who have lost their faith in the ability to improve matters by virtue of their practicality (*durch eigene Tüchtigkeit*) . . .

Possibly, but what on earth does this kind of sociologism have to do with a philosophical critique of inadequate or self-contradictory standpoints?

It would be tedious to pursue this theme through the two stout volumes of Horkheimer's collected essays. The central dilemma remains the same from start to finish, and it is never resolved. The moralist, whose normative values are plainly derived from Kant and his successors, is shackled to the historicist who unwittingly relativizes his own utterances in the act of "unmasking" his opponents. Challenged by a critic to produce his philosophical credentials, Horkheimer replies that political philosophy

> long ago transformed itself into the critique of political economy. Either it unmasks the historical situation or it falls prey to belletrist epigones.

In the 1930's Marx's *Paris Manuscripts* were already available, but the draft of what later became *Capital*, the *Grundrisse* of 1857–58, had not yet been published. Hence the "critical theory" was unable to make the point that the author of *Capital* was a humanist whose scientific studies concretized an eminently philosophical anthropology. Had Horkheimer established a valid connexion between his critical excursions (often extremely acute) and his normative judgments, the Frankfurt group would not in the end have fallen between the two stools of its humanist commitment and its unavowed gamble on the realization of socialism in the USSR. As it was, the post-war repudiation of Communism led straight to a reaffirmation of what Horkheimer in the 1930's had described as bourgeois liberalism. The 1947 *Dialektik der Aufklärung*, written in collaboration with Adorno, even toyed with romantic notions whose Nietzschean origin was plain for all to see—"Odysseus oder Mythos und Aufklärung".

What really matters, of course, is not the spiritual biography of Horkheimer, Adorno, Marcuse or any other member of the circle originally associated with the *Zeitschrift für Sozialfor-schung,* but the major problem which they somehow failed to resolve in the 1930's and 1940's. Their Hegelian training had immunized them against the positivist notion that "value judge-ments" have no place within the serious business of analysing the "real" world. They saw clearly enough that the fact-value dichotomy was part of the spiritual sickness which had pro-voked the neo-romantic attempt to revive traditional meta-physics—not to mention the political frenzy culminating in the Third Reich. Even if in those days they were understandably a trifle vague about the precise connexion between the anthro-pology of the young Marx and the ethico-political assumptions built into the structure of *Capital,* they had at any rate grasped the central importance of the theory-practice problem. That men perceive the true nature of the world in the act of changing it—this much at least could be inferred from the 1845 *Feuerbach Theses* alone. Hence the philosophical dimension of Marx's thought did not have to be sacrificed in the name of scientism. As Mr. Alasdair MacIntyre has recently put it, in the revised edition of his *Marxism and Christianity,*

> the nature of the world is such that in discovering the order of things I also discover my own nature and those ends which beings like myself must pursue if we are not to be frustrated in certain predictable ways. Knowledge of nature and society is thus the principal determinant of action.

This having been the unspoken credo of the Frankfurt school, one may legitimately ask why it was never clearly spelt out. Perhaps a residual commitment to the "dialectical materialism" of Engels and his successors, including Lukács and Lenin, made it appear hazardous to anchor "scientific socialism" in the Feuerbachian anthropology of the *Paris Manuscripts.* But, in so far as authentic theoretical issues come into play, it is fairly obvious now that the school had come up against an unresolved dilemma close to the heart of the Hegelian inheritance. Both Hegel and Marx had exempted their pronouncements on the human condition from the relativism potentially inherent in their approach, on the grounds that a philosophy conscious of its own historical role is thereby placed in a privileged position.

Such a claim is implicit in Hegel and explicit in Marx, who had already perceived the threatening dimension of "historicism", but was confident that he possessed an answer to it : the theorist who commits himself to the arduous task of "changing" a world which is a *verkehrte Welt,* a world standing on its head, is able to universalize the values of the oppressed class, because that class endures in an extreme form the alienation imposed by history upon the whole of mankind. Historicism is a problem only for those who are blind to the logic of the total process. For the same reason, the fact-value dichotomy is troublesome only for the private individual who confronts a "given" environment and then wonders whether he ought to do something about it : whereas if he identified himself with the effort to "stand the world on its feet", the tedious but necessary business of scientific analysis need not be artificially shut off from the world-transforming and self-transforming realm of praxis. They are aspects of one and the same struggle to turn barbarous, sub-human pre-history into authentic history.

Well and good. But what if the enterprise issues in the monstrosities of Stalinism, or in the overpowering boredom of the atomized "affluent society", with its pop culture and pop sociology in the place once occupied by religion or metaphysics? Worse still, what if it turns out that capitalism and socialism are merely alternative ways of producing the industrial and technocratic society of the later twentieth century? Then we seem to have the contemporary dilemma and Marxism as such has no answer to it. Hence Horkheimer's disillusioned return to liberalism, Adorno's revival of idealist metaphysics (plain for all to see in his *Negative Dialektik* of 1966), and Marcuse's attempt to combine the politics of anarchism with the philosophy of the early German Romantics—a curious hybrid, more remarkable for his personal sincerity than for its illumination of the problems of contemporary society.

What currently distinguishes the outlook of the democratic Left in West Germany from Marcuse's *gran rifiuto* may be inferred from the collection of essays published in 1968 (on the occasion of the philosopher's seventieth birthday) under the title *Antworten auf Herbert Marcuse*. Edited and introduced by Professor Jürgen Habermas, himself a distinguished sociologist as well as a thinker in the Hegelian-Marxian tradition, this little volume brings together a number of exegetical and critical studies which add up to a polite but devastating critique of Marcuse's ontological credo—ultimately derived from Heidegger, whose pupil he was before turning to Hegel and Marx. Few people seem to be aware that Marcuse's first major publication, *Hegels Ontologie und die Grundlegung einer Theorie der Geschichtlichkeit* (1932), was an attempt to interpret the Hegelian legacy in terms derived from Heidegger's "existential analysis" : a fairly technical subject confined to those able to master German philosophical speculation, not to mention the language. This is decidedly a pity, since any attempt to discuss Marcuse's recent utterances in abstraction from his philosophical roots in the Germany of the 1920's misses an important dimension of his thought. Whoever doubts this is invited to consult the editorial preface which performs the remarkable feat of doing justice to Marcuse's intellectual tour de force in the 1930's—his unprecedented fusion of phenomenology which Marxism—while leaving not a stone intact of the politico-theoretical tower of Babel he has been busy erecting during the past decade. Habermas is clearly very fond of Marcuse, whose old-world charm is indeed difficult to resist. Equally clearly he is not enamoured of his most recent writings, or of their effect on a section of the New Left which combines political shock tactics with veneration for Rosa Luxemburg. One can see why the more doctrinaire student spokesmen fear and resent Habermas, just as they resent those Czechoslovak workers and intellectuals who actually believe in democracy, and in some cases have given their lives for it. When one has spent years establishing a Manichaean distinction between "the socialist revolution" (good) and "social-democratic reformism" (bad), it is annoying to be confronted with a standpoint that cannot be subsumed under these simplistic categories. It is even more irritating to be told that in comparison with the students of Prague one does not cut a very heroic figure.

There remains the recourse to Third World romanticism—
with Cuba rather than China as the preferred model—plus the
critique of present-day industrial society, as set out, for example,
in *One-Dimensional Man*. What a genuine Marxist sociologist
thinks of Marcuse's "technological determinism" can be discovered from Claus Offe's contribution to *Antworten auf Herbert
Marcuse*, where "the tradition of classical Marxism" is confronted with Marcuse's analytical model : a model indistinguishable (save for the author's private desiderata) from the analysis
of modern society developed by the theorists of the extreme
Right : Hans Freyer, Helmut Schelsky, and Arnold Gehlen.
The common factor is the conviction that science and technology
must fatally result in the establishment of a technocratic order
which perpetuates the alienation of man, disintegrates the substance of political democracy and consigns socialism to the attic.

Marcuse naturally deplores all this, whereas the former Fascists—now converted to technocracy, just like von Braun and
other organizers of planetary rocketry—are quite at home in
this Spenglerian universe, though needless to say they would
feel even more comfortable were the official language of scientism
German rather than Anglo-American. At the analytical level
their closeness to Marcuse's despairing critique of contemporary
civilization is unmistakable. The complementariness of their
respective positions is twofold : while it corresponds to the conventional right-left antagonism, it also extends to the dimension of the ancient quarrel between philosophy and science, for
the conservative authoritarians are "technicians" of their respective disciplines, whereas Marcuse's condemnation of industrial
society operates with large, vague and undefined concepts ultimately derived from an ontological tradition which the positivists
of the German New Right have abandoned. As theorists of contemporary society, all concerned have their roots in Max Weber's
sociology which treats bureaucratic structures as inseparable from
the steady growth of rationalization. What differentiates Marcuse from the neo-positivists—who in Germany at any rate
include right-wing authoritarians, as well as liberal empiricists of
the Anglo-French variety—is his attachment to existentialist
phenomenology ! The *homo philosophicus* whose existential

dilemmas furnish the theme of Marcuse's critical essays is not the socially-conditioned historical agent of Marxism, but the pre-existing subject-object of the historical process: a being whose problematic was the principal theme of what Heidegger in *Sein und Zeit* termed "existential ontology". In spite of Marcuse's constant appeals to empirical evidence, his analysis of the current situation is subordinated to, and grounded in, an attempt to lay bare the nature of man-as-such, as a being-in-the-world whose spiritual problems refract themselves in the tensions and conflicts of ordinary empirical history.

In adopting this position, Marcuse confronts his critics with a dilemma of which they are well aware: any attempt to define their standpoint in relation to his familiar theses must steer between the opposing cliffs of neo-positivist scientism (the official ideology of present-day liberalism in the West) and pseudo-Marxist historicism of the sort institutionalized in Eastern Europe. It must also avoid the temptation represented by the anti-historical structuralism of Althusser and his followers in France, for whom the philosophy of history represents a distraction from the serious business of analysing political economy. These West German critics, by contrast, share Marcuse's concern with the historical dimension and his important insight into the uncomfortable truth that the prevailing modes of thought in East and West alike are distinguished by an almost pathological fear of any theorizing that does not simply reproduce the categories of the established order. Where they differ from him is in questioning the attempt to ground a theory of history in a philosophical anthropology itself derived from the existentialism of Kierkegaard and Heidegger, the perennial theme of which is man's mortality—a biological fact which somehow dispenses the ontologist from the dreary task of studying human history in the "ordinary", or non-metaphysical sense.

Not that Marcuse shares this indifference, but his description of what happens to men in history depends for its resonance upon the legitimation of a claim he has in common with the ontologists: truth resides in universals which denote entities not present in actual experience, but rather constitutive of all experience. Even if this is granted, does it follow that a theory of history can be grounded in the perception of large general truths about man-as-such? The most unchallengeable of these verities —e.g., the statement that we are all going to die at some time —are notoriously also the emptiest. What is descriptive of everything in general cannot account for anything in particular.

The middle way between empiricism and ontology is a dialectic of theory and practice which measures social actuality against historical possibility. This is the standpoint of Marcuse's socialist critics who share his practical concerns, but not his philosophy (to say nothing of his recent political utterances). Their position necessarily implies a rejection of the defeatist assertion that modern man has been degraded to the status of a "one-dimensional" pseudo-being effectively manipulated by forces beyond his control: a "power elite" in charge of a reified technology whose immanent logic undercuts the traditional Marxist analysis. That Marcuse's *gran rifiuto* is not just aimed at capitalism, but at industrial society as such, should have been evident since the publication of *One-Dimensional Man* in 1964. But it has taken the student revolt, and the current revival of anarchism in general, to make it plain that what we have here is no longer a socialist theory, but an ideology of pure rebellion against technological rationality in every shape or form.

The authoritative re-statement of the classical socialist position, in contrast to Marcuse's anarchic utopianism, is to be found in the work of Professor Jürgen Habermas, starting with his important essay collection published in 1963 under the title *Theorie und Praxis,* and concretized more recently in his critical analysis of post-Kantian philosophy, *Erkenntnis und Interesse.* Taken together with his earlier historical study of the genesis and structure of bourgeois society, *Strukturwandel der Öffentlichkeit,* these writings represent the most impressive body of philosophy and sociology to have come out of Central Europe during the 1960's. They also provide a reference point against which the continuing relevance of the Frankfurt School can be measured. Habermas —at the age of forty himself professor of philosophy and sociology in Frankfurt—is in some sense the heir of this particular tradition. At the same time it is plain that he has by now both assimilated and transcended the heritage of the Institut für

Sozialforschung and its surviving members. The outcome of this theoretical and practical endeavour is an intellectual synthesis which conserves the original purpose of the "critical theory", while freeing it from the dead-weight of the German metaphysical tradition—and all this, *mirabile dictu,* without lapsing into positivist scientism, whether linguistic or structuralist. In fact much of his work in philosophy has been devoted to a systematic demolition of the inflated claims made by, or on behalf of, the positivist school.

It is not altogether easy to assess the work of a scholar whose professional competence extends from the logic of science to the sociology of knowledge, by way of Marx, Hegel and the more recondite sources of the European metaphysical tradition. There is no lack of competent specialists in any of these disciplines. Equally there are still a few "generalists" about—Marcuse is the best known, but there are others—who take the entire domain of contemporary philosophy and sociology for their province: only to be caught out by the specialists whenever they venture beyond the narrow range of their real expertise. The baffling thing about Habermas is that, at an age when most of his colleagues have painfully established control over one corner of the field, he has made himself master of the whole, in depth and breadth alike. There is no corner-cutting, no facile evasion of difficulties or spurious enunciation of conclusions unsupported by research: whether he is refuting Popper, dissecting the pragmatism of Charles Peirce, delving into the medieval antecedents of Schelling's metaphysics, or bringing Marxist sociology up to date, there is always the same uncanny mastery of the sources, joined to an enviable talent for clarifying intricate logical puzzles. He seems to have been born with a faculty for digesting the toughest kind of material and then refashioning it into orderly wholes. Hegel, whom he resembles at least in his appetite for encyclopaedic knowledge possessed this capacity in the highest degree, but he was cursed with an abominable style and a perverse fondness for obscurity, whereas Habermas writes as clearly and concisely as any empiricist. If his work does nothing else, it should dispel the notion that German philosophers invariably gain an undeserved reputation for profundity because no one can make out what they are saying.

The 1963 essay collection *Theorie und Praxis,* itself the sequel to a brief historical study of the genesis of modern society, starts with a reconsideration of the natural law tradition since Aquinas, and ends with a number of critical excursions aimed at romantic neo-Marxists like Ernst Bloch on the one hand, conservatives like Karl Löwith on the other. In between, Habermas subjects the Hegelian-Marxian heritage to the kind of analytical treatment which admittedly comes more easily to German writers than to outsiders unfamiliar with the finer shades of this particular topic. Even so, it needed a quite abnormal capacity for joining dialectical logic to historical insight to bring out the crucial link between "critique" and "crisis" in the way Habermas does in what is perhaps the most illuminating treatment the subject has yet received from a philosopher.

No one who has digested the relevant chapter is likely to suppose that the only alternative to the positivist misinterpretation of Marxism—shared by revisionists like Kolakowski, whom Habermas demolishes in a few pages—is the existentialist anthropology of radical theologians enamoured of the *Paris Manuscripts.* It took uncommon penetration to rediscover the precise significance which the term "critique" possessed within the objective structure of classical and modern thought for all those philosophers and non-philosophers, from the Greeks onwards, who prepared the way for Hegel and Marx. It also took remarkable detachment to perceive that the "critical theory"—so described in the 1930's by the Frankfurt school when the "crisis" of the European civil war was at its peak—stood and fell with an assessment of the historical situation which is no longer tenable : although paradoxically the Marxian method of social analysis has not been invalidated by the collapse of its unspoken assumptions. The reader who has assimilated what Habermas has to say on this tricky subject can save himself the bother of wandering backwards and forwards between Marx's empiricist critics, his existentialist defenders—including Sartre—and the surviving adherents of Soviet orthodoxy. They are all taken care of : that is to say, left at the post.

Erkenntnis und Interesse is a different kettle of fish, if that is not an unduly colloquial way of characterizing a rigorously professional analysis of positivism, pragmatism, and their Kantian antecedents. It may be convenient to quote the opening passage of the preface:

> I have undertaken the historically oriented attempt to re-construct the pre-history of modern positivism (guided by) a systematic analysis of the connection between cognition and interest. Whoever investigates the progressive dissolu-tion of the theory of knowledge, leaving in its place a theory of science, makes his way across abandoned phases of reflection. To retrace one's course along this route, with a perspective turned towards the original starting point, may be of help in bringing back the forgotten experience of reflection. The denial of reflection is positivism.

The execution of this programme obliges author and reader to traverse the waterless desert of scientism from its original source in Comte, by way of Ernst Mach and C. S. Peirce, to Popper's logic of science—already the target of Habermas's critique in the 1963 Adorno *Festschrift*. The chapter on Peirce, which does full justice to the founder of pragmatism without inflating his importance in the current transatlantic fashion, constitutes by itself sufficient reason for the book to be translated into English without delay (and introduced into the syllabus of American universities).

The real originality of *Erkenntnis und Interesse* lies elsewhere. Alongside a critical account of the empiricist tradition, or rather intertwined with it, Habermas presents an analysis of the manner in which epistemology in general, and Kantian idealism in par-ticular, dissolved into the conflicting theoretical standpoints of positivist scientism and post-Hegelian historicism (Dilthey)—with Marx's "metacritique of Hegel" inserted along the way as the (not wholly convincing) solution to a problem already posed by Kant and Fichte: that of mediating between the perception of reality by the individual thinking mind, and the inevitable conditioning of that mind by the socio-historical context.

The principle of criticism as "the union of cognition and

interest" is traced back to its Kantian source, and at the same time projected forward to its embodiment in the scientific work of Freud and the polemical writings of Nietzsche, for whom a crude interest psychology provided the means of "unmasking" philosophy as the illusory self-gratification of the reflecting subject. The two-fold movement of modern thought thus appears as a dialectical inter-connection between rival attempts to transcend the horizon of classical rationalist philosophy. Once the peculiar logic of this process has been grasped, one can see why the critical dissection of Peirce's pragmatism—a brain-cracking affair which should satisfy the most rigorous of contemporary logicians—is immediately followed by a destructive analysis of Dilthey's hermeneutics, in turn succeeded by an illuminating discussion of language and its function within the self-interpretation of *Geisteswissenschaft*.

The fascination of *Erkenntnis und Interesse* lies in the way Habermas brings out the intrinsic logic of this progressive dissolution of the rationalist heritage through the dialectical interplay of standpoints (positivism, pragmatism, historicism) rooted in assumptions originally shared by scientists and historians alike. The conclusion—namely that a radical critique of cognition (*Erkenntnistheorie*) must take the form of sociology (*Gesellschaftstheorie*)—seems wholly convincing : the more so since Habermas qualifies his acceptance of the Marxian approach by a careful dissection of an unfinished anthropology part-modelled on the natural sciences. He perceives the positivist strain in Marx and treats it as the source of later misunderstandings. Marx, he thinks, might have done more to clarify the enduring relevance of philosophy vis-à-vis the sciences :

> Philosophy is conserved within science as critique. A theory of society which purports to be the historical self-consciousness of the (human) species cannot simply negate philosophy. Rather the heritage of philosophy transforms itself into the critique of ideology, which in turn determines the method of scientific analysis.

So much for the structuralists, with their yearning for a science of society emancipated from history and philosophy alike.

Now plainly this orientation is itself open to criticism on the grounds that it translates into Marxian terms the familiar theses of German idealism. But then it so happens that Marx came out of this particular tradition. Among the services Habermas renders to the contemporary student of philosophy, not the least is the recovery of a dimension lost or abandoned in the heyday of positivist scientism. What he proposes is not a "return" to an unrecoverable past, but a deeper understanding of what is implied by the idealist approach that antedated the collapse into empirical practicality. He does not ignore the element of truth in the pragmatist enterprise, but stresses the failure of its originators to clarify the theory-practice relationship:

> Peirce and Dilthey had encountered the practical foundation (*Interessenbasis*) of scientific understanding, but they did not reflect it as such. They did not form a notion of interest-orientated cognition, and did not really comprehend what such a notion intends.

Habermas's own position is the reverse of a pseudo-materialist reductionism. It amounts to equating the concept of "reason" with a "will to reason", or "interest in reason", explicitly described as "liberating" (*einem emanzipatorischen Erkenntnisinteresse*). The root of this conception is traced to Kant, and more particularly to Fichte, who subordinated theoretical to practical cognition, and on this foundation developed the notion of a liberating, self-activating "interest" inherent in practical reason as such. There is no insuperable gulf separating material interest from rationality: they converge in practical activity that subjects both the self and the world to the freely chosen rule of reason.

This tardy illumination of a neglected aspect of the idealist heritage is all the more welcome because German philosophical speculation since Schopenhauer and Nietzsche has systematically obscured the fact that Hegel, for all his political conservatism, embodied one aspect of the Enlightenment tradition. The standard equation of German metaphysics with irrationalism has its roots in an incomprehension of what Hegelianism really signified—and not only for the Left Hegelians. In this respect

Habermas is the perfect antidote to Jaspers, or to Heidegger and his pupils, but he also introduces a corrective to a viewpoint made respectable by writers like Löwith who are innocent of Heidegger's extravagances (to say nothing of his political attitudes after 1933), but share his longing for a return to a pre-Kantian ontology of the Aristotelian type. Such an attitude implies the belief that modernism—in the narrow sense of post-medievalism —represents the secularization of a religious heritage (Hellenic or Christian, according to taste).

In *Theorie und Praxis* Habermas devoted a few passing reflections to the transformation of *Geschichtstheologie* into *Geschichtsphilosophie,* albeit with the accent on the radical innovation introduced by the "global consciousness" of the eighteenth century Enlightenment. For a systematic analysis of European philosophy, and its Hellenic sources one must turn to a very different work: Professor Hans Blumenberg's *Die Legitimität der Neuzeit.* This is one of those great treatises—historical, critical and speculative all at once—which for some reason do not seem to flourish outside Germany. Erudition by itself cannot explain the phenomenon, although Blumenberg's learning is in fact quite staggering, while his range encompasses the entire history of philosophy since the pre-Socratics. Inherent in his attitude is an urge towards systematization which, to put it crudely, is itself metaphysical and thus the antithesis to positivism and historicism alike. Within limits this statement is also applicable to Adorno, Marcuse and Habermas—hence their refusal to accept the fact-value dichotomy as an ultimate datum for the reflecting mind. But it has been left for Blumenberg to write a major treatise on the metaphysical tradition which unites intellectual history with a critical dissection of the concept of "secularization": a concept that has served two generations of writers in their efforts to make sense of the modern predicament. The fact that most of these writers were either theologians, or philosophers sympathetic to the theological perspective, does not, of course, invalidate the usefulness of this approach, but it does suggest that the rest of us have perhaps been a trifle too ready to operate with a set of notions originally devised to explain what their authors could only see as a falling-away from the true

—that is to say, the theocentric—view of man and the universe.

What Blumenberg has done, to put it briefly, is to present the disintegration of the medieval world-view as a consequence of latent contradictions already present in the scholastic tradition : ultimately in the synthesis of early Christianity and neo-Platonism inherited by the European middle ages. However, this formulation supplies only the feeblest sort of pointer to the importance of a work whose author is no mere historian but an original thinker in his own right, equipped with the sort of synthesizing faculty which was the pride of German scholarship in its great age—and its peculiar curse when put to destructive uses by obscurantists like Heidegger and charlatans like Spengler. By way of a belated revenge for the disaster these writers have inflicted upon their own country and all Europe, the half-buried tradition of the Enlightenment has now been disinterred : not by a shallow positivist, but by a philosopher who has thought his way through to a critical analysis of the problems that kept scholasticism going for a millennium after the classical tradition had run into the sands. This is all that can be said, within present limits, about a work perhaps best described as the answer to Heidegger's *Sein und Zeit*.

It may be as well to add that, for all his fundamental rationalism, Blumenberg shares some of the stylistic peculiarities of the school whose intellectual monopoly he has for ever destroyed. *Die Legitimität der Neuzeit* is not a book for the beginner, or for anyone who does not already possess an adequate grasp of classical, medieval and modern philosophy. But for someone willing to make the effort, it illuminates large tracts of a landscape which theologians and obscurantist metaphysicians had systematically blacked out—nowhere more successfully than in Germany, where irrationalism had already triumphed in philosophy before its prophets turned their attention to politics. It is no more than a minor and belated satisfaction that the catastrophe they promoted should at last have terminated their disastrous reign in the very sphere of historico-theological speculation they had for so long and so unchallengeably made their own.

Technocrats vs. Humanists

> An industrial society can only prosper if the workers under-
> stand the meaning of their task and are fully associated
> with the elaboration of all the decisions concerning them
> . . . for my own part I think, notably but not exclusively,
> of the Swedish example.

Thus M. Chaban-Delmas, France's new Prime Minister,
addressing the National Assembly a few days after Georges
Pompidou had taken the oath as President of the Republic.
The philosophic calm which greeted his declaration of principles testified to the conviction of the conservative majority
that this kind of fine talk was unlikely to be translated into
legislative action, let alone social reality. No doubt the sceptics
had good reason to shrug it off. M. Chaban-Delmas, after all,
belongs to the *haute bourgeoisie* of Bordeaux, where for the past
two decades he has functioned as mayor and devoted his considerable talents to industrial development, but hardly to the
furtherance of workers' councils.

As for M. Pompidou, it is true that during the presidential
election campaign of May and June 1969 he so far forgot
himself as to promise the voters to transform their country into a
"sunny Sweden". But it is also true that since his election he has
been silent on this topic, while exhorting his countrymen to

rival their West German neighbours, notably in the domain of foreign trade (now helped along by a remarkably skilful currency operation). On his list of priorities the task of turning France into a "great industrial country" (as he put it during his first presidential press conference on July 10, 1969) ranks decidedly ahead of Swedish welfare-stateism, not to mention anarcho-syndicalism. The General may brood in silence at Colombey, and the left-wing Gaullists may pursue the aim of worker-manage-ment "participation", but the France of M. Pompidou is unlikely to pioneer in this direction.

All the more reason, say the cynics, why Chaban-Delmas and his colleagues have to borrow the vocabulary of Defferre and Mendès France; and of course the cynics are right. But those sociologists who smell a whiff of "technocracy" in the Parisian air are right too. The fact is that the French political elite currently feels the need to cover its ideological nakedness with a new suit of clothing. The original formula was invented by the Saint-Simonians a century and a half ago : production is more important than property, and where property rights get in the way of technical or social progress, they must be sacrificed. This is the "technocratic ideology" that free-enterprisers and Marxists have come to detest : the former because it threatens to interfere with the blessings of an uncontrolled free market in property values; the latter because it ignores the class conflict and tries to make people believe that political problems can be reduced to purely technical or administrative ones.

The interesting thing is that whereas in the United States this kind of talk commonly issues from self-styled "liberals" (who are perhaps better described as Fabians in disguise) their French counterparts are fond of describing themselves as "socialists". It is partly a difference in national style, Americans being shy of the word "socialism" while the French love to talk about it, on the understanding that talk is not to be followed by action. In part it relates to a genuine difference in the political set-up : no French government can carry on in the teeth of really deter-mined hostility on the part of the unions, and the French unions (including those run by the Catholics) genuinely do believe in socialism and/or syndicalism. So does most of the teaching profession, a sizeable part of the technical intelligentsia, and practically everyone who matters in the country's literary life. Even the editors of the arch-conservative *Figaro,* the daily breakfast oracle of the Catholic bourgeoisie, went on strike when the paper's proprietor tried to assert control.

In brief, French capitalism lacks moral legitimation. In public life nobody—literally nobody, from de Gaulle and Pompidou downward—even pretends to believe in the sanctity of property. What the ruling stratum *does* believe in is technical progress, and of course "order" : that is to say, vesting authority in those best able to run the show. In short, the technocratic ethos is employed to legitimize what Marxists call capitalism and what sophisticated neo-liberals like Aron prefer to call "industrial society". Once this has been grasped, a number of things about contemporary France become less puzzling. One is the ability of the Gaullists to stay in office, and the presence in their ranks of numerous technocrats, who are in fact socialists inasmuch as they favour a planned economy and the steady shrinkage of the private sector. Then there is the sensational publishing success of M. Servan-Schreiber's glossy magazine *L'Express,* which has copied the Luce format but preaches Saint-Simonism to its half million affluent buyers (mostly businessmen, managers, or civil servants).

Lastly, there is the current paralysis of the French Left. This is partly a consequence of being weighed down by the Communist incubus and the failure of the French CP to renounce its dog-like devotion to Moscow. But in part it stems from a genuine intellectual dilemma : if French socialism is ever to gain a stable majority, it must not only overcome the rift dividing the democratic Left from the Stalinist rump; it must also define its understanding of what the term "socialism" signifies in the present age. Apart from the Anarcho-Trotskyist-Castroist-Maoist fringe, which inhabits a dream world of its own manufacture, the Left in France is up against a problem not wholly dissimilar from that which confronts the ruling coalition. Let us assume a peaceful democratic takeover and the preservation of the traditional liberties, if the Communists can be induced to beat a strategic retreat from Lenin to Marx. What then is to happen next? Is the economy, whether nationalized or not, to be run in accordance with purely technical criteria, or are the workers to be given a genuine say, even at some cost of efficiency? On the first assumption, how is one to avoid the kind of sullen resentment now observable all over Eastern Europe? On the second, how can one make plausible the claim that socialism will actually deliver the goods? Is there not a danger that the voter (including a large fraction of the industrial working class) will settle for Pompidou's "sunny Sweden" as the next best thing to Utopia?

It would be agreeable were one able to say that the problem has at any rate found an intellectual solution, but no such claim can seriously be put forward at the present time. It is not even advanced by M. Rocard, whose *Parti Socialiste Unifié*—perhaps the most faction-ridden and least unified of all the rival formations on the Left—was formed in 1960 for the express purpose of renovating socialist theory and practice. It had 15,000 members then. It has 15,600 now, almost half of them newcomers suddenly activated by the great 1968 upheaval, and out of the total membership it has been reckoned (see *Le Monde* of August 8, 1969) that one-third are teachers and students, a large proportion of the remainder belonging to the technical "cadres" in industry and the white-collar stratum. So far as an occasional visitor to Paris can see, all that has happened is that the latent tension between intelligentsia technocracy and working-class syndicalism has been institutionalized in the form of an endless battle for control of the PSU: a battle M. Rocard, a former *Inspecteur des Finances,* hence a technocrat by definition, looks like losing.

If and when he does lose control to the rival *gauchistes,* led by wealthy Castroites from the silk-stocking district of Paris, with a motley army of students and young workers yapping at their heels, he may (or may not) team up with the recently renovated Socialist party from which his own colleagues resigned in despair during the Algerian war. For the Socialist party has acquired a relatively youthful and dynamic new leader in the person of Alain Savary, and a very competent second-in-command, Pierre Mauroy. It has also attracted a small army of genuine left-wing *enragés* led by M. Jean Poperen, a former Communist who helped to found the PSU before abandoning it to its fate. But here is the snag : MM. Savary and Mauroy may be to the left of the Old Guard, but they also look and sound alarmingly intellectual and technocratic, whereas M. Poperen's new book, *Stratégie pour la gauche,* expresses a violent distaste for all technocrats, from Mendès France downward. For him it is still the proletarian revolution or nothing. (M. Poperen is himself a history professor at the Sorbonne.)

Nor do the complications end here. Savary quarrelled with Guy Mollet over Algeria in 1956 and later helped to found the PSU, before abandoning it in 1963. But he had previously been a Minister in the Mollet government (as had Mendès France before he quit). Middle-class by origin, he personifies a tradition that easily reconciles Socialism with patriotism, in the ancient manner to which the Communists have remained strangers. In 1940 young Savary, then a lieutenant in the Navy, was among the first to rally to de Gaulle, but retained his Socialist convictions and never became a Gaullist in the political sense. By 1945, after a dazzling war record, he embarked upon a political career marked by frequent clashes with his colleagues, resignations on matters of principle, and stormy exits from coalition governments and Socialist party councils. "When you hear a crash, that's Savary walking out," became a standard joke. A Socialist in the traditional Jaurèsian sense, he could hardly be called an orthodox Marxist.

All of which makes it the more remarkable that he has now come to the forefront on a platform calling for Socialist-Communist co-operation and banning any approach to the so-called "Centre" : the group of Catholic democrats who ran the presidential candidacy of the luckless Alain Poher. By implication Savary's rise in the Socialist party hierarchy thus spells the end of "Defferrism", i.e., the attempt to form a Social-Democrat coalition embracing the left wing of the Catholics. But does one ever know? Suppose the Comunists stick to their bone-headed Stalinist orthodoxy. Then a future Socialist congress may unseat M. Savary and revert to "Defferrism", although this is not going to happen if M. Mitterand has any say in the matter. But Mitterand has (for the time being) refused to lead his 15,000 adherents of the *Convention des Institutions Républicaines* into the Socialist party. Instead, he is busy preaching his own version of the gospel in the four corners of France.

Mitterand got eleven million votes in the 1965 presidential election, and he was very angry when in May 1969 the Socialists hastily nominated Defferre, instead of joining the Communists in a united front behind Mitterand. He is all for working with the Communists, critical of Social Democrats, and not too fond of his former chief, Mendès France. But is M. Mitterand a Marxist? Not at all: he comes from a bourgeois Catholic milieu, is still a believing (although unorthodox) Christian, preaches what he calls "social justice" and candidly admits in his recently published autobiographical tract that he has always had difficulty with all that complicated Marxist language. Yet he considers himself to the left of the orthodox Marxist Guy Mollet, whom he still blames for having voted de Gaulle into power in 1958. French politics are the reverse of simple.

Which brings us to "Jacques Mandrin", a pseudonym for a group of intellectuals affiliated with the CERES (*Centre d'Etudes, de Recherches et d'Education Socialistes*). Founded by ex-pupils of the *Ecole Nationale d'Administration,* where since 1945 the elite of the State bureaucracy has obtained its training, the CERES is now the brains of the renovated Socialist party. It is also the centre of (a) neo-socialist theorizing (b) youthful rebellion against elderly bureaucrats and moth-eaten dogmas. Both go together quite easily—much to the annoyance of a former Communist like Jean Poperen who is not taken in by spurious "modernizers" masquerading as left-wing rebels. He knows them for what they are: technocrats who want to revise Marxism-Leninism out of existence.

He is right too so far as "Mandrin" is concerned. The pseudonym was obviously adopted in a spirit of self-irony, for what could be more mandarin than the CERES, unless it be the *Ecole Nationale* itself? "Mandrin" first appeared on the scene with an *oeuvre* characteristically titled *"l'Enarchie ou les Mandarins de la société bourgeoise"*: another of those plays on words that only the insider can really savour. Not just "Enarchie" versus the familiar "Anarchy", but a bit of self-mockery too, for

ENA stands for *Ecole Nationale d'Administration,* and the "Enarchs" are the lucky ones who annually pass an examination so fierce that only 85 out of 1,000 candidates survive to enter the hallowed precincts of ENA. Of these eighty-five only fifteen can hope to enter one of the four elite services: the Inspectorate of Finance, the Council of State (for lawyers), the Diplomatic Service, or the *Cours des Comptes* which audits public expenditure.

But the cream of the jest is this: these men are mostly socialists of one kind or another. The Enarchs, as the school's graduates are familiarly known, have been running France pretty steadily under both the Fourth and Fifth Republics, ever since de Gaulle and Debré organized the *Ecole Nationale* in 1945 as a training centre for higher civil servants. Saint-Simonians to a man, they have little use for the French bourgeoisie—that wretched class which allowed France to be defeated in 1940 and to fall behind Germany industrially. The General fully shared this viewpoint and gave them all the backing he could. When he abruptly resigned in 1946, they divided their loyalties between the official Socialist party, Mendès France, and the group of ex-Socialists currently known as "left-wing Gaullists". Believers in the planned economy and a fast rate of industrial growth, they are suspicious of Pompidou and Giscard d'Estaing ("too bourgeois"), bored with the Communists whom they don't take seriously, and mildly interested in socialism. "Mandrin" represents that section of the Mandarinate which is actually inside the Socialist party: with the aim of reforming it, of course, and making it look "modern".

As political tracts go, *Socialisme ou social-médiocratie?* is a distinctly superior specimen: well-informed, intelligent, and occasionally very funny. The authors know all about the workings of the Socialist party machine, from the grass roots to the Paris headquarters at the Cité Malesherbes (or as they prefer to call it, the Cité des Mauvaises Herbes). They are notably good on the Twenty Years War between Mollet and Defferre which has now come to an end: Mollet having assumed the garb of Elder Statesman, while Defferre made only the briefest appearance at the 1969 convention which retired the Old Guard and put the reformers in.

The quarrel between the two factions, which for decades absorbed everyone's time and energy, is described rather amusingly in Taoist terms : the principles at stake in this never-ending contest were the Ying and Yang of a cosmic dualism which could not be terminated by the triumph of one faction over the other, seeing that the duality of sky-earth, spirit-matter, night-day (or what you will) cannot be resolved in this fashion. Moreover, the contestants were evenly matched, Yang-Mollet having behind him the tradition of Jules Guesde (1845–1922) and the bleak factory towns of the North, while Ying-Defferre was sustained by the ghost of Jean Jaurès (1859–1914), his own Marseilles organization, and the merry wine-drinking South. With Ying and Yang cancelling each other out for twenty years, the S.F.I.O. carried on imperturbably, while its popular following drifted away. No change was ever made in the sacred texts of 1905 and 1920, whereas daily practice could be as flexible as anyone chose. Mollet was a great one for combining doctrinal rigidity with parliamentary opportunism, and he regularly defeated Defferre and his friends whenever they tried to tamper with the Tablets of the Law. Thus secure in his conscience, he could permit himself pretty well anything when it came to practical politics :

> C'est que nos doctrinaires, à défaut d'avoir renversé le pouvoir de la bourgeoisie, ont maintenu la doctrine : il faut dire que leur longue marche, depuis 1920, réduit celle de Mao Tsé-toung à la dimension d'une promenade dominicale. (p. 72).

There is a great deal more of this, interlarded with a very shrewd analysis of the French class structure, the Socialist party's composition, the functioning of its congresses, and the mentality of its militants, for whom it has become a repository of hallowed traditions. Much of this likewise applies to the Communist party, and this is one reason why the CP now has to contend with an ultra-leftish current fed by the generational conflict as much as by Maoist or Trotskyist heresies.

There are some important differences, though : for example, the S.F.I.O. has always had numerous Protestant adherents (including Mollet and Defferre) who feel comfortable in its comparatively relaxed and democratic atmosphere, whereas the CP, with its rigid discipline and its endless heresy-hunts, bears a curious resemblance to the Roman Church. Its current arch-heretic, Roger Garaudy, not accidentally came to Marxism in his youth by way of Kierkegaard and Karl Barth, whereas the rigorously orthodox Louis Althusser stems from a Roman Catholic background. However, these are details. If a general conclusion can be extracted from what "Mandrin" has to say about the S.F.I.O. it also applies to its rival :

> Mais on ne détruit que ce qu'on remplace, et aucun de ceux qui s'y essayèrent successivement, le P.C., les Trotskystes, le P.S.U., la Grande Fédération, n'a réussi à remplacer le Parti Socialiste. (p. 50).

Nor (one may add) will the *gauchistes* replace the CP. The Communist party is deeply entrenched among the manual workers, and nothing short of a technological revolution can loosen its hold over the French working-class electorate. Which is not to say that it has any hope of coming to power. Moreover, if by some chance it did, its fossilized *apparatchiki* would not know what to do. They are much happier in opposition : witness their recent record, culminating in their mismanagement of a unique opportunity in 1968. It is true that they participated in the government in 1944–47, but they did so on Stalin's orders and because in those days they still hoped that Soviet intervention would drastically shift the balance of power in their favour. Now that these hopes are gone, they have settled down to the role of a permanent opposition. In a sense they have come to share effective power at the local level with the Gaullist majority, but on the tacit understanding that they will content themselves with the role of defending a sectional labour interest within a society run by others.

What then is to be done? "Mandrin" wants to renovate the Socialist party and make it relevant by appealing to the whole salariat. "Mandrin" likewise has no time for electoral politics and explicitly rejects the antiquated Social-Democratic notion that a parliamentary majority can legislate socialism into existence. The tract is duly contemptuous of the CP and sharply critical of romantic ultra-leftish Third Worlders. *"Cette fuite, verbale dans la jungle et réelle dans les mots, est l'expression d'une peur profonde de la réalité: on oublie que notre société est une société industrielle."* (p. 145.)

In the age of lunar rockets this hardly needs much emphasis, but Parisian ultra-leftism is the vehicle of a literary intelligentsia backed by a student proletariat which dreads unemployment but is not enthralled by the prospect of dreary office jobs and relentless mechanization either. The problem is common to all advanced countries. How does one square the circle? By identifying socialism with the "humanization" of modern society (says "Mandrin"), that is : by affirming humanist values in an age besotted by technology. Very well, but how does one get mass support for such a programme? By linking it up with working-class demands for *autogestion,* i.e., industrial self-government. Moreover, a planned economy is both more efficient and more responsive to human values than an unplanned one, and the bourgeoisie cannot really plan, even if it tries. This is also the view of Rocard and the PSU, yet to "Mandrin" these are "the Jehovah's Witnesses of the Left". Besides, the PSU has "technocratic" tendencies (p. 148). Coming from the CERES, this isn't bad !

Poperen has no use for the PSU either. Its leaders, he darkly says, played a double game during the May-June upheaval in 1968. On the one hand they tried to outflank the Communists by encouraging the students and the younger workers who were holding out for a prolongation of the general strike. At the same time they were really aiming at a government headed by Mendès France, whom Poperen detests because he represents *"la social-technocratie"*. Such a government, in his opinion, although publicly advertised as a "regime of transition" toward socialism, would in reality have been a "government of national union", and the Communists would have been tricked into supporting reformist measures designed to streamline French capitalism.

The argument is unconvincing in that it disregards the CP's real motive for sabotaging a "regime of transition": fear of being frozen out while socialism was introduced democratically. But it is certainly the case that there exists a "social-technocratic" ideology which is no more realistic than the tired reformism of the old parliamentary Social-Democrats. What the new ideology affirms is that socialism can be introduced by stealth. What it overlooks is that there inevitably comes a moment when the issue of political power has to be faced.

So far so good, but Poperen gets entangled in a contradiction he shares with the Communists. On the one hand he stresses the technocratic aspects of Gaullism; on the other he asserts that the state is becoming *more* bourgeois rather than less: *"L'Etat de la bourgeoisie ne fut pas toujours dirigé par la haute bourgeoisie: il l'est aujourd hui."* (p. 114.) This does not make sense. The only time when what Poperen calls *"L'Etat de la bourgeoisie"* was genuinely run along bourgeois lines was between 1870 and 1940, when the parliamentary Republic left the market economy to its own devices. One cannot describe Gaullism as *"une phase d'accélération du processus de technocratisation de la vie sociale et politique"* (p. 113) and simultaneously denounce it as "bourgeois". The fact is that if the regime had been bourgeois it would have collapsed in May-June 1968. What kept it going was a combination of factors, but the central fact was the decisive role of the "political superstructure", i.e. Gaullist control of a state apparatus which, so far from being merely retrogressive, had itself become the central energizing force in promoting the modernization of French society. Moreover, in a contest between the government and the strikers, the latter were at a disadvantage unless their leaders could make plausible the existence of a *political* alternative. Short of that, they appeared as troublemakers who were ruining the economy by prolonging the strike after their purely economic grievances had been satisfied.

In a way Poperen recognizes this. He even observes that, in the hypothetical case of a choice between "Union of the Left" and "National Union", the Communists in May-June 1968 "had no chance of winning and they knew it. The General was bound to win" (p. 77). But he attributes this state of affairs solely to de Gaulle's control of the armed forces, and to his accidental status as a national hero. Accidental? "The Left paid in May 1968 . . . for the support it had given de Gaulle since the days of the Resistance" (p. 88). But what alternative was there? Whom could "the Left" have put forward during the Liberation? The aged and failing Léon Blum? The Stalinist *apparatchik* Maurice Thorez, who deserted from the Army in 1939 and sat out the war years in Moscow? De Gaulle stepped into a vacuum. Naturally he made the most of it. But his Provisional Government of 1944–45 included Thorez and it nationalized a large sector of French industry and banking. In fact, the "technocratization" of state and society, which Poperen bewails, was set in train by a coalition between Gaullists and Communists. Poperen—a Communist resistance fighter at the time —has not forgotten that the Communists were driven from office three years later, but in assailing *"la social-technocratie"*, he forgets to mention that the CP was instrumental in opening this new chapter in French history. In short, he wants it both ways. It is all the fault of the Left for having turned de Gaulle into a national monument :

> Il n'y a de "héros national" que si le combat de classe se dissout dans la lutte nationale. Et il est plus facile de fabriquer ces "héros" que de s'en défaire. La bourgeoisie exploite à fond le personnage historique dont la gauche lui a fait cadeau. (p. 88.)

But the "historic personage" imposed himself precisely because in 1940–44 (and later again during the Algerian struggle) France *was* confronted with a national problem to which the Left had not found an answer. Anyway the General is now gone and the bourgeoisie can no longer hide behind him. Pompidou ought to make an easy target, and in some ways he does. He not only was a banker : he looks and talks like one. But lo and behold, he has filled the civil-service ranks of his administration with the sort of people whom Poperen classifies as representatives of *"la social-technocratie"* : ex-Mendèsists converted to Gaullism. Life is hard indeed.

In his memoirs—published a few days after Pompidou's election to the presidency—Mitterand likewise contents himself with half-truths. His record as a Minister in various Fourth Republic governments was fairly good, but not quite so spotless as he tries to make out. There are some things one is not supposed to mention these days in polite Parisian left-wing society: for example, that the Algerian revolt began in November 1954, at a time when Mendès France was Prime Minister and Mitterand his Minister of the Interior, and that both men reacted in approved Jacobin fashion: by affirming that Algeria was forever part of France and proclaming their determination to crush the rebellion by force.

What is more, they then had the support of the entire Assembly, from the Gaullists to the Communists. Four years later, when the parliamentary Republic had collapsed and de Gaulle had been called in to head a National Government, Mendès France and Mitterand voted against his investiture. This took no great courage, but it gave them a legitimation for what they called "republicanism": meaning loyalty to the defunct parliamentary regime. By 1965 Mitterand was reconciled to presidentialism. That year he ran against de Gaulle and collected eleven million votes. In 1969 he posed as the living incarnation of democratic socialism: the only man in France who could unite "the Left" on a common platform. For electoral purposes perhaps, but what happens thereafter?

The collection of essays titled *Liberté et organisation dans le monde actuel* tries to grapple with this set of problems, and so does Raymond Aron in the new Preface (dated March 1969) to his *Désillusions du progrès,* originally written in 1964–65 for the *Encyclopeadia Britannica* and now somewhat hastily revised. If there is a living embodiment of what Poperen calls "*la social-technocratie*" (other than Mendès France himself) it is Raymond Aron, with an important qualification: at heart a liberal individualist, he treats both technology and technocracy as necessary evils. At the same time he is enough of a positivist in the Comtean sense to believe that "industrial society", rather than "bourgeois society", must be the central category of an up-to-date empirical sociology. It is this, rather than his standing quarrel with the Parisian literary leftists, that separates him from the Marxists. They are, he thinks, imprisoned in nineteenth-century concepts.

This criticism, however, applies neither to Rocard nor to "Mandrin", both of whom are fully aware that—to put it crudely—science and technology have become the central driving force of the industrial production process. In sociological terms this means that the technical intelligentsia has become crucial to any kind of socialist strategy. Does it form part of the "working class"? This is more than a terminological quarrel, for if salaried employees are treated as an exploited class, someone will have to bring the labour theory of value up to date, if we assume that Marxism is to have a future. One cannot forever equate "labour" with "manual labour", and at the same time make a bid for the support of the white-collar employees. At bottom this is what the whole quarrel over "revisionism" is about, and has been for the past forty years, when some German Marxists first discovered what in those days they called the *Produktionsintelligenz*. It is also what the Czechoslovak reform movement was about, even though its figurehead was an authentic working-class Communist.

Does this mean that socialism is now threatened in its very essence? The question is ridiculous. The socialist movement has always consisted of two distinct strata : workers and intellectuals. To talk as though this were a new phenomenon is simply to display one's ignorance of history. What is at stake is something else : the technological development variously described as "late industrial" or "post-industrial" tends to do away with the rigid distinction between manual and intellectual labour. Technicians and skilled workers cannot be subsumed under the old categories, and their number is growing. One may also say that the upper layer of the old working class is becoming indistinguishable from the technicians properly so described. Here and there it merges with the lower ranks of the managerial stratum. From this circumstance liberals like Aron deduce that there is no longer a class division in the Marxian sense, but this does not follow. One may equally well assert that the white collar stratum is being proletarianized, in the sense that its position no longer differs substantially from that of the old industrial working class. "Brain workers" drafted into the salariat as a consequence of the new technology may still possess a socially privileged status, but they are no more independent than their colleagues on the factory floor. All they have is their jobs, and the first whiff of unemployment is enough to shatter the illusion that ownership of a house and expensive furniture makes them "members of the middle class" in the traditional bourgeois sense.

What distinguished the nineteenth-century bourgeois was not possession of a car (there were no motor cars in those days), but economic independence: he owned means of production and could thumb his nose at the government. His successor is just a highly paid clerk who can have the rug pulled from under him at a moment's notice. "Status symbols" become valueless when one's job is gone. Thus the salariat can be reached by socialist slogans (job security, for example) whereas the old independent middle class could not.

Now there is a catch in all this. In the first place, it applies equally to capitalism and collectivism, which is why the various Communist parties in advanced industrial countries are having trouble keeping their membership in line (elsewhere they still work with the Leninist or Maoist apparatus, which is fine for backward societies, but makes no sense in an industrial environment). Secondly, the "brain workers", or some of them, may get it into their collective heads that *they* ought to be running the show. At this point there emerges the phenomenon of Mendèsism, also known as *"la social-technocratie."* What this signifies is an attempt to introduce a planned economy and call it "socialism" while the traditional aims of the labour movement are ignored: above all, effective democracy in the workshop, at the point of production.

At the other pole, Anarchism and Third World romanticism combine to reject industrial society as such. The upshot is not revolution, but the kind of spontaneous revolt with a built-in mechanism that guaranteed its failure at the critical moment when the conquest of political power came within sight but could not be attempted because "the Left" was unprepared intellectually. Neither the Social Democrats nor the Communists had ever dreamed of a general strike actually occurring under their eyes, and the PSU was too weak and faction-torn to give effective leadership to the mass movement. The upshot, grotesquely enough, was to give French capitalism a shot in the arm by obliging it to modernize itself.

Yet the problem of social stratification remains, and the enforced modernization of society in France (and not only in France) under the impact of American-Soviet competition can only reinforce the pressures which caused the 1968 explosion. For this new society—and this is where Aron and his fellow-thinkers seem to me to have gone wrong—lacks legitimation. Its official ideology (liberalism in the West, communism in the East) is quite unrelated to what is really going on. The technocratic, or "social-technocratic," ethos does not help matters. A moonbeam from the larger lunacy of "progress", it translates into utopian language the illusions of a stratum that imagines itself to be in control of the new technological apparatus, whereas in fact it does the bidding of its political masters. The latter may be captivated by the jargon of technocracy, to the point of investing not only money but faith in moon landings. But however splendid the actual scientific achievement, there is no visible, tangible feedback into the life of the social organism. Or if there is, it is more likely to encourage authoritarian tendencies than to promote authentic self-government.

"Révolution et technocratie" (an essay in the collection mentioned earlier) takes a pessimistic view of the matter. The author (Lapierre) believes that a genuine "technocratic class" is in process of formation, in East and West alike. He takes issue with Marxists like Charles Bettelheim and liberals such as Raymond Aron who, for different reasons, dispute this thesis. Technocracy, in his opinion, represents *"une classe en formation"*, just like the old bourgeoisie before it had achieved political control. The new stratum already has an ideology, a number of more or less learned spokesman (e.g., Louis Armand and Jean Fourastié), and a host of journalistic sympathizers, with M. Servan-Schreiber in the lead. *"Cette idéologie a ses sources dans le saint-simonisme, le positivisme, la sociologie de Thorstein Veblen, les idées de Rathenau et d'Howard Scott."* (p. 45.) He might have

added the Fabians and that indefatigable popularizer, John Kenneth Galbraith. The term "ideology" here naturally signifies what it did for Marx and his followers : not just any body of ideas, but the unconscious presentation of a new world-view issuing from the slow growth of a social stratum which spontaneously generates collective illusions about the world, at the same time that it makes genuine discoveries. In this sense, the new technical intelligentsia does seem to be casting about for a social legitimation.

It is also beginning to sprout a philosophy : *"C'est ce que manifeste la grande mode du 'structuralisme'. Henri Lefebvre n'a pas tort de voir dans cette doctrine, qui transforme en dogmes les principes d'une méthode incontestablement scientifique, le support et la légitimation théoriques de la technocratie. L'idolâtrie du langage—système des systèmes—en est un trait caractéristique. . . . Le* logos *est coupé de la* praxis." (p. 47.)

In his own fashion Aron makes a similar point in his recent diatribe against Althusser and his school. *D'une Sainte Famille à l'autre : Essais sur les marxismes imaginaires* tilts at a number of opponents, but it really centres upon Althusser's attempt to transform Marxism into a rigorously "scientific" doctrine cut off from its author's own philosophical postulates. For reasons which Aron develops at some length, this enterprise runs up against an insurmountable obstacle : the unpublished draft of *Capital*—the famous *Grundrisse* of 1857–58 which saw the light only in 1939–41—makes it perfectly obvious that Marx never renounced his humanist starting point. That is to say, he analysed bourgeois production-relations in terms of what they did to man as such, not just in terms of how they caused the economy to function. Rationality was not enough for him : he held that socialism would signify the emancipation of the producer from the machinery to which he had become enslaved. Nor is this simply a biographical circumstance which can be treated as irrelevant. The concept of "exploitation" hinges upon an understanding of the labour theory of value which links an anthropological critique of society to a scientific analysis of capitalism. If this link is severed, Marxism becomes a "value-free" theory, just like structuralism (of which the Althusser school, not surprisingly, is greatly enamoured). If there can be a scientific theory of language, why not a scientific theory of society? Indeed, why not? Althusser is the Talcott Parsons of Marxism.

It is often said that liberalism and Marxism currently face a similar problem : that of coming to terms with a state of affairs to which part of their conceptual apparatus is no longer applicable. But while this applies to sociology and politics, it has no bearing upon philosophy. The notion that modern technology—or lunar rocketry for that matter—obliges us all to rethink human problems is itself an aspect of the technocratic ideology. Scientism is an *ersatz* philosophy born from the decay of traditional metaphysics. The only practice to which it relates is of a kind that perpetuates a state of affairs which both liberalism and socialism originally set out to alter : a radical disjunction between an authoritarian social structure and a privatized individual. Unless *praxis* is joined to *critique*, no amount of scientific rationality is ever going to change this.

One may of course assert with Michel Foucault that the entire historical enterprise associated with the names of Marx and Mill was no more than a tempest in a teapot (*Les mots et les choses*, p. 274) by comparison with the invariants discovered by the structuralists; but such modish affirmations are notoriously short-lived. *"Laissons ces préciosités du Nietzschéisme parisien"*, to cite Aron (an old humanist, hence in the last resort no friend of the new scientism). The fight will go on, if necessary "against the current" if it should turn out that technocracy is indeed "the wave of the future". People who want at all cost to be in the van of what they are pleased to call "progress" will just have to put up with the presence of unreconstructed humanists who draw no satisfaction from the ever-growing number of cars on the road, or the ever-growing size of death-dealing weapons. In the end the technocrats themselves may discover to their surprise that they cannot function unless someone tells them what the whole expenditure of energy is supposed to be *for*. And that someone won't be another technocrat.

Marx or Weber:
Dialectical
Methodology

For the past two decades the German Federal Republic has figured in the consciousness of the English-speaking world primarily as the residuary legatee of Bismarck's vanished Reich: a truncated body abruptly and permanently severed from its grandiose but catastrophic past. The severance, so far as an outsider could judge, extended to the country's intellectual life no less than to its somewhat parochial politics: so reassuringly humdrum by comparison with the ceaseless turmoil of the Weimar Republic.

Of late, however, there have been signs that this quiescent phase is coming to an end. Not only has the long reign of conservative somnolence in Bonn been terminated by the unexpected formation of a liberal-labour coalition. There have also been echoes of the American and French student revolts, and—at a considerably higher level—public debates between Marxists and theologians. Now, to confirm the worst fears of American pragmatists and British empiricists, there is a new *Methodenstreit*, or methodological dispute, at an intellectual altitude so elevated as to make structuralism or neo-Cartesian linguistics seem positively commonsensical. Just what one might have expected from the Germans; and to make matters worse, some of the participants are in the tradition of the Frankfurt school of sociology : in plain language, they are Marxists steeped in Hegelian logic. It is enough to make any decent empiricist despair; and to judge from some of the contributions to this debate, despair is indeed uppermost among the sentiments with which the disciples of Karl Popper have greeted the new phenomenon.

The roots of course go back to Weimar days, and indeed to the first great *Methodenstreit* around the turn of the century, when Max Weber's sociology was taking shape as part of an attempt to overcome the cleavage between scientific rationalism and romantic intuitionism. But after 1945 it was assumed—among liberals anyway—that the issue had been settled for good. West Germany having purged itself (or having been purged by the Allies) of its demons and having adopted the Enlightenment tenets so long and obstinately spurned by its educated elite, the metaphysical blight cast by Hegel and his successors must surely be seen by all as an aspect of the great catastrophe the country had twice suffered in this century.

But somehow the message did not sound wholly convincing to Germans otherwise disposed to make an entirely fresh start. Marxism-Leninism indeed might be (and was) ignored : it was too rigid, as well as being associated with—to put it mildly— unpopular regimes in Eastern Europe. The ancient conservative ontology descended from Schelling and the Romantics likewise did not suit the new positivist temper and was quietly consigned to the attic. Nietzsche too went unread among postwar students—this was progress indeed—and Heidegger was generally thought to have displayed the cloven hoof too plainly in 1933, when he hailed the Führer in language not usually employed by academic philosophers. But scientific empiricism of the Anglo-American type continued to encounter obstinate resistance even among former emigrants, from the conservative Karl Löwith to the radical Theodor W. Adorno. Indeed it was just these returned exiles who perversely insisted upon the enduring relevance of the great tradition of German idealism—a tradition extending from Kant, via Hegel and his pupils, to Marx.

Having spent long years abroad—for the most part in the United States—these exiles had acquired a profounder understanding of the democratic process, a circumstance that facilitated their reintegration within the new society of postwar Germany. The old arrogance which counterposed German *Kultur* to Western *Zivilisation* was gone—it had indeed been discredited among Germans generally. But neither gratitude for hospitality received nor admiration for democratic folkways unknown in Central Europe had blotted out the unshakeable conviction that positivist scientism in all its forms—including those originally evolved in the Vienna of the 1920's—was philosophically sterile.

How is one to account for this perversity? Is there some mysterious entity at the centre of the collective consciousness— a soul, an essence, a spiritual trait securely anchored in the very structure of the German language that resists the beneficent effects of an Anglo-American environment? Yet Central Europe too has produced radical critics of traditional speculative thought: indeed the most radical of them all, Wittgenstein, was a native of Vienna. Or is there perhaps an obscure link between Wittgenstein's unexampled analytical rigour and his unmistakable yearning for veritable insight into the nature of ultimate reality? The final message of the *Tractatus* after all is that science tells us nothing we really want to know. In another context and employing different language, Weber made a similar point some years earlier, when he said there was no bridge between science and faith (*Wissenschaft als Beruf*). To Weber this was a true but tragic insight into the condition of modern man. In general, German thinkers, including those who have stoically accepted the dissociation of thinking from being, do not seem able to endure the resulting disillusionment with anything like the composure to which the denizens of more fortunate lands have become accustomed.

This can be illustrated by considering Adorno's posthumously published collection of essays issued by Suhrkamp under the title *Stichworte*, only a few weeks after his sudden death in August 1969, with an author's preface dated "June, 1969"—a philosophical testament if ever there was one. There is a sense in which Adorno, like the Frankfurt school in general, stood for a specifically modern kind of rationalism: that represented by

T. H. Green's dictum that "every form of the question why the world as a whole should be what it is . . . is unanswerable". This is to make short work of an entire mode of thought ultimately rooted in the pre-Socratics, dominant in European philosophy until the eighteenth century, and influential in Germany down to our days—witness the sensational success of Heidegger's *Sein und Zeit* in the 1920's. It is to acknowledge that questions of this sort are not, properly speaking, a theme for rational discourse at all.

To that extent the logical positivism of the original Vienna Circle—of which Wittgenstein was not, in the strict sense, a member—did not conflict with the basic assumptions of those Hegelian Marxists who in the 1930's grouped themselves around the *Zeitschrift für Sozialforschung*. Where then lay the crucial difference, and why do we now have before us a volume of essays labelled *Der Positivismusstreit,* with a lengthy polemical introduction by Adorno, an important contribution by Sir Karl Popper, and a fascinating dispute between Professor Hans Albert and Professor Jürgen Habermas? Principally, it seems, because the kind of rationalism to which Adorno and his colleagues were committed had never cut its connection with the tradition of German idealism. That is to say, it aimed at something over and above the *Wissenschaftstheorie* of logical positivism without for that reason yielding an inch of ground to ontology. The case is best stated in Adorno's own words:

> With Kant, thinking . . . makes its appearance under the term of spontaneity. Reasoning is *prima facie* an activity of the sort registered by the naive consciousness when it distinguishes the sensations, the impressions apparently made available to the individual without any exertion on his part, from the experience of laborious activity inseparable from thought. However, Kant's greatness . . . manifests itself not least in the fact that . . . he does not simply identify the spontaneity which, according to him, constitutes thought with conscious activity. For him, the basic constitutive operations of thinking were not the same as acts of reasoning within a world already constituted. [They] are barely

> noticeable to self-awareness. . . . *The Critique of Pure Reason* is already a phenomenology of Mind in the sense of Hegel's analysis of consciousness which later bore that title. . . .

Implicitly Adorno, and with him the Frankfurt school in general, adheres to the Kantian distinction between a sensible world of appearances and an intelligible world that lies open to rational knowledge. On this assumption the empirical sciences deal with mere appearance while philosophy has to do with *Wesen* (Being), that is to say, with transempirical reality. *Wesen* is not to be understood as a supersensible realm of being in the traditional metaphysical sense. The distinction between reality and appearance relates solely to the circumstance that philosophy transcends the horizon of the sciences, in as much as it is not bound by the instrumentalist character of the scientific process. The latter presupposes a particular way of investigating an object whose existence science takes for granted. The philosopher for his part subjects this object-world, and its scientific correlative, to a critical investigation whose standards are indeed meta-scientific, or ontological. They are "critical" in the twofold sense of being descended both from Kant's *Critique* and from its materialist antipode: the "critical theory" of Marxism.

This appropriation of the Kantian heritage by the Marxist Adorno is mediated by the fundamental presupposition of the entire Frankfurt school: Marxism is rooted in German idealism— not in the trivial biographical sense familiar to every student of the subject, but in the sense that Marx's "materialist" inversion of Hegel conserved the problematic enshrined in Hegel's earlier critique of Kant. The thesis is briefly expounded in Alfred Schmidt's preface to the volume of studies he has edited for Suhrkamp: *Beiträge zur marxistischen Erkenntnistheorie*:

> The specific epistemological approach of dialectical materialism arises from the fact that Marx and Engels accept Hegel's critique of Kant without being able to accept

its speculative foundation. With Hegel they affirm the cognoscibility of being [des Wesens der Erscheinungen]; with Kant (albeit without invoking the *Critique of Pure Reason*) they insist upon the non-identity of form and matter, subject and object of cognition.

Another contributor to the same volume, Jindrich Zeleny, makes a related point :

> Marx proceeds critically from the theorizing about the ontological structure of reality which German transcendental philosophy, notably Hegel, had worked out in opposition to the scientism of Galileo-Descartes and their conception of movement and causality. The starting point is the materialist interpretation of Hegel's concept of Spirit.

Albrecht Wellmer, who suspects Marx of positivism, none the less comes to similar conclusions concerning his relationship to Hegel in his *Kritische Gesellschaftstheorie und Positivismus*.

It is perhaps as well to bear in mind that the distinction between appearance and reality is not as such peculiar to transcendentalists, let along to Hegelians. In a sense it may be said to be as old as science. Certainly the Baconian or Newtonian understanding of scientific method operated with some such contrast, as did Ricardo's analysis of the economic process (a point rightly stressed by Zeleny).

Common sense here inevitably prompts one to ask the irritable question : "Why then all this fuss about Hegel ?" Because (replies the Frankfurt school) positivism and Marxism differ about the meaning to be imputed to the notion of reality or *Wesen*. Ever since Comte began to extrapolate the method of the natural sciences, sociology has been in search of invariant structures underlying the surface play of historic change. The latest and most ambitious attempt in this direction is associated with the structural anthropology of Claude Lévi-Strauss and its various offshoots— including the quasi-Marxism of Louis Althusser, for whom a genuinely scientific theory of society remains to be worked out after the unfortunate Hegelian heritage has been shed.

Anyone who imagines that this standpoint is compatible with

Marx's own interpretation of historical materialism is advised to read Alfred Schmidt's essay "Der strukturalistische Angriff auf die Geschichte" in *Beiträge zur marxistischen Erkenntnistheorie* (which ought to be translated for the benefit of British and American students of the subject who in their enthusiasm for Lévi-Strauss may have missed Sartre's and Lefebvre's devastating attacks on Althusser and his school). What we have here is a discussion whose significance far transcends the silly dispute between Western empiricists and Soviet Marxists : a quarrel which has now gone on long enough and should be quietly terminated before the audience dies of fatigue.

To avoid a possible misunderstanding which may easily creep in at this point : in the context of the recent German *Positivismusstreit* the "positivism" of Comte and his school is not particularly relevant, except that the heirs of logical positivism frequently tend to be positivists (in the nineteenth-century sense of the term), in matters political as well. Whether this is purely fortuitous is perhaps open to doubt. Equally one may suspect that the prevalence of empiricist and pragmatist ways of thought among contemporary Anglo-American liberals is more than a coincidence, even though empiricists are notably reluctant to flaunt a political banner in public. Anyone who has attended a gathering of Continental European philosophers will have noticed that whereas Marxists and Thomists make no bones about their respective political orientation, it is remarkably difficult to get their empiricist critics to take a stand on political principles. Somehow or other they are not anxious to advertise their faith in New Frontiers, Great Societies, Alliances for Progress, and similar slogans of the Kennedy-Johnson era. Even when the debate ranges over strictly academic topics—say, the uses and misuses of sociology—they can rarely be induced to abandon the security of their methodological shelter.

Can we at last confront this latest *Methodenstreit*? Alas, not yet. We still have to surmount one more preliminary hurdle : Albrecht Wellmer's onslaught on the Vienna Circle and its heritage. But perhaps "preliminary" is not quite the word, *Kritische Gesellschaftstheorie und Positivismus* appeared in 1969 : twelve years after Adorno had opened the debate with a lecture titled "Soziologie und empirische Forschung" at the Frankfurt Institut für Sozialforschung; eight years after Karl Popper had restated his well-known doctrines at a Tübingen session of the Deutsche Gesellschaft für Soziologie in October, 1961; and six years after Jürgen Habermas, in an essay titled "Analytische Wissenschaftstheorie und Dialektik" (now reprinted in the *Positivismusstreit* volume) had unlimbered the heaviest artillery at the disposal of the Frankfurt school. Perhaps Wellmer's little volume should rather be regarded as a postscript to a controversy which has now raged for more than a decade. It is, however, an extremely learned postscript, and for good measure it carries a punch that lifts the debate well beyond the range of polite academic disputation. A brief quotation will suffice :

> In contrast to the belated liberal Popper, Carnap represents unreservedly the technocratic consciousness of his age. One might even say that he has carried the language-critical approach of the youthful Wittgenstein to as radical a conclusion as Wittgenstein himself. If the late Wittgenstein deciphers the meaning of language in its practical functioning, Carnap rejects as senseless any language which does not function properly; if Wittgenstein affirms the unity of language and existence, Carnap apprehends the residual difference between them; his aim is to eliminate it.

Wellmer, it must be added, is a pupil of Habermas.

To the battlefield then. *Allons marcher aux canons.* After all this distant gunfire the reader is entitled to an account of the actual slaughter. But of course no one was killed or even seriously injured. When the smoke had lifted, all the contending parties were seen to be securely in possession of their ground. The great contest had ended in a draw : or perhaps one should say the rival armies never really came to grips. In the end they did not perhaps have enough in common to make a genuine engagement possible. Certainly Professor Albert's "Kleines verwundertes Nachwort zu einer grossen Einleitung" gives the impression that its author was somewhat put off not merely by the excessive length of Adorno's introduction to the volume (more than seventy pages), but also by its philosophical sweep. The positivist has some trouble with the Hegelian who *will* insist on talking about everything at once, as though it was still possible to carry on in the ancient holistic manner. And it is undeniable that Adorno's reckless cavalry charge across the entire field of debate, from metaphysics to linguistics, carried its own dangers. Albert is not alone in feeling that the grand manner is no substitute for the kind of rigorous analytical reasoning which became the hallmark of the Frankfurt school once younger men —Habermas above all, closely followed by Schmidt and Wellmer —had taken over from the veterans Horkheimer and Adorno. All the same, if someone had to meet Popper head on, Adorno was not a bad choice : the more so since in the 1920's both men inhabited that specifically Viennese intellectual world from which logical positivism, psychoanalysis, musicology, linguistics and neo-Marxism were shortly to radiate outwards.

Yes, but what is *Der Positivismusstreit in der deutschen Soziologie* finally about? Well, to put it as briefly and unfairly as possible, it is "about" the ancient quarrel between the disciples of Marx and those of Max Weber. Of course this is not quite how it was put (except when Albert and Habermas briefly lost their tempers and clashed over a corner of the field recently brought into prominence by the neo-Marxist revisionism of Leszek Kolakowski whose earlier work Habermas had already criticized in his 1963 essay collection *Theorie und Praxis*).

For the most part, the contestants avoided political topics and stuck to their methodological guns. Even so, the spectre of Marxism raised its head when Habermas observed : "I am concerned to question . . . the separation of science and ethics." This was followed by a brief reference to "the dialectic" which, to cite Habermas once more, "figures as a scarecrow in the unbuttoned Weltanschauung of certain positivists". These positivists currently employ Popperian language, but no German would dream of denying that the sociologists among them are the spiritual heirs of Weber.

Now it so happens—another coincidence?—that Weber was the most important and consistent theorist of liberal imperialism in Wilhelmine Germany. That is to say he was the intellectual leader of a school which stood for a very definite political orientation. This circumstance carries awkward implications for theorists who insist that sociology to be genuinely scientific must be "value-free": Marxism being unscientific by definition because it makes no secret of its commitment to certain values. But did not Weber espouse a value system of his own? Yes indeed, but he had the honesty to affirm that his beliefs were unrelated to his real work as a scholar. His values, that is to say, were grounded in purely personal decisions not anchored in a speculative philosophy or Weltanschauung. It was just this which to his followers made his approach seem responsible and scientific: his methodological assumptions were divorced from his private desiderata. This radical disjunction of science from ethics was and is the pride of the school. It also represents what its critics regard as a confession of intellectual bankruptcy.

Here then is the link, or a link, between the earlier *Methodenstreit* and its present-day sequel. Now as before the positivist school conceives itself to be defending the autonomy of science against assailants from the Romantic right or the Marxist left, both in the last resort invoking arguments derived from speculative metaphysics. The rationale of this two-front war, whether stated in Weberian or Popperian language, is always the same: science in general, and social science in particular, needs to be *wertfrei* (value-free) so as to perform the task of exact empirical description. In so far as the scientist gives his allegiance to religious, philosophical, political or artistic values, he does so in his personal capacity.

While not disputing the theologian's belief in a divinity, or the artist's right to embrace the Romantic creed—the latter being a kind of metaphysical inflation of the artistic view of the world —the scientific investigator in his professional role eschews these temptations. Likewise he departs from the older positivist tradition associated with Comte, for he does not regard it as his task to prescribe the aims which rational understanding of the world, or the social whole, is destined to serve. Lastly, he abandons

the search for "laws" of historical development, therein following a line of thought inaugurated by Weber's neo-Kantian contemporaries, notably Dilthey and Rickert, and brought to
perfection in our own days by Karl Popper. As far as sociology
is concerned, this restriction of the field results in the detailed
elaboration of formal systems of "social relations" (Tönnies) or
"social action" (Weber, Talcott Parsons). In Weber's system
rational behaviour counts as the "ideal type" of social action,
with the obvious proviso that ideal types are not actually encountered in empirical reality. None the less the course of
Western history, down to and beyond the industrial revolution,
is interpreted in terms of a general theory of social action; as
against the historicism of the Marxists, for whom bourgeois
society represents a transitory phase of societal evolution, to be
succeeded by the "truly rational" order of socialism.

Finally, and this is where the current debate becomes overtly
political, the "technocrats" of the New Right (Hans Freyer,
Arnold Gehlen) have stepped in with a theoretical model of their
own which is no more to the taste of liberals like Popper, Albert,
and Ralf Dahrendorf, than the romantic Rousseauism of Marcuse and the New Left. Technocracy has been described (by
Habermas) as the doctrine that the social order can be consciously adapted to the requirements of contemporary science
and technology. To put it in language familiar to Marxists, the
"superstructure" no longer needs to be reshaped by social revolutions stemming from the familiar contradiction between
"forces of production" and political relations. Instead of these
convulsive eruptions from below—which admittedly still do occur
in the more backward regions of the globe—what we now have
is a deliberate rearrangement of the socio-cultural sphere,
brought about by the managers of the new technology and their
political allies or masters.

This point does not emerge clearly from the *Positivismusstreit*
volume, but then Gehlen's followers—like those of Herbert
Marcuse—were not invited to contribute. The academic establish-

ment in the Federal Republic is indeed split down the middle, but at the professional level the only really significant confrontation opposes the left centre (Habermas) to the Weberian or Popperian liberals (Albert). The extremes are excluded. Freyer and Gehlen were too deeply involved with the Third Reich to be acceptable among liberal or socialist humanists; and the romantic mysticism of the aged Ernst Bloch, with his rather endearing faith in Schelling's *Naturphilosophie,* appeals only to that section of the New Left which is eternally in search of a Weltanschauung to bolster its instinctive rejection of the modern world : a very Germanic treat this, at one time suggestive of fascist tendencies, nowadays fortunately transmuted into a rather harmless kind of anarchism.

From the positivist standpoint the foregoing remarks introduce extraneous considerations having to do with the more or less accidental political positions of some of the participants in the recent German discussion. To the dialectician they are of the essence, and this is just where the debate between Albert and Habermas runs into the sands. Albert explicity subtitles his first section "Dialektik contra Positivismus", thereby incidentally pulling the rug from under certain learned bystanders who dispute the legitimacy of this terminology. For good measure he introduces his critique of the Frankfurt school with a brief retrospective glance at Weber's heritage. This approach has the merit of enabling the reader to grasp the intimate connection between *Wissenschaft* and *Wertfreiheit* in the sense usually given to these terms. Albert, whose *Traktat über Kritische Vernunft* was dedicated to Karl Popper, makes no bones about his dislike of the Hegelianism implicit in the publications of the neo-Marxist school. At the same time he sees clearly enough that the positivist disjunction of technical rationality and normative ethics leaves a gap between theory and practice. His solution of the problem has a neo-Kantian ring :

> It is . . . possible to overcome the positivist resignation in questions of moral philosophy without lapsing into the existentialist cult of *engagement* which replaces rational discussion of such problems by irrational decisions. The

criticism which opens up this possibility before us has . . . itself a moral content. Whoever adopts it thereby commits himself not to an abstract principle without existential significance, but to a way of life. Among the direct ethical consequences of criticism there is the conclusion that the unshakeable faith . . . upheld by some religions is not a virtue but a vice.

In his epistemological study *Erkenntnis und Interesse* Habermas proposes an alternative solution by postulating an inherent union of cognition and interest : likewise at the level of "criticism", but in a sense plainly derived from Hegel and Marx rather than from Kant and Weber. What he terms "Kritik als Einheit von Erkenntnis und Interesse" is not *Erkenntniskritik,* but something a good deal more practical. Both books were written, or at any rate published, after their distinguished authors had fired prolonged salvoes at each other during the debate over the methodology of the social sciences. They help to explain the fundamental standpoints underlying the essays reprinted in the *Positivismusstreit* volume.

However unbridgeable the gulf between Albert's empiricism and the neo-Hegelianism of the Frankfurt school, all concerned express themselves with a clarity and precision not universally common in earlier and stormier days. When Habermas gets down to the business of explaining the difference between the functionalist (Weberian or Parsonian) notion of "system" and the dialectical concept of "totality", even the reader not initiated into the mysteries of Hegelian logic can easily follow his train of thought. With Albert's exposition of Popper's positivism, there is of course no problem at all : the English-speaking world is thoroughly familiar with it.

We are now in a better position to answer the question what the whole argument is "about". As far back as 1963, when Habermas fired the opening shot in his critique of Popper (see "Analytische Wissenschaftstheorie und Dialektik"), he spelt out a number of propositions which, whatever one might think of them, are plainly incompatible with the scientist credo. Dialectical theory, he wrote, "questions whether science is entitled to proceed in regard to the world of men with the indifference successfully practised in the natural sciences". And again, dialectical thinking "overcomes the separation of theory and practice".

In his 1964 rejoinder, Albert described the purpose of the enterprise as a "practically orientated philosophy of history dressed up as a science". By the conventional standards of the academic world this was plain speaking, and there was to be a lot more on both sides. The basic issue emerged almost incidentally when Albert registered astonishment at the sight of a colleague in search of legitimation of practical action. "He [Haberman] looks for an objective legitimation of practical activity through meaning in history, a legitimation which naturally cannot be provided by a scientific sociology bearing a realistic character." Well, at any rate there is no dispute about the normative incompetence of this kind of positivist sociology.

If one adopts the criterion of *praxis,* two rival but interrelated standpoints are automatically excluded : the dogmatic crucifixion of the individual in the name of God, the World Spirit, or Being; and the empiricist conviction that anyone equipped with a normal dose of intelligence can make sense of the world simply by applying ordinary moral criteria. As regards the former there was no dispute among the participants, although matters might have become awkward if the debate had been joined by a theologian. The difference related to the latter, and it did so because empiricists proceed from the nominalist assumption that the social whole is made up of individuals who have to learn rational behaviour, if they are not to get in each other's way.

In a sense this is obvious, but it is the kind of truth that blurs the perception of what is really at stake in this sort of controversy. For a society in which individuals are held together by nothing but their manifest self-interest is precisely the target of critical theorizing on the part of the dialecticians. The latter need not be orthodox Marxists—Habermas at least is a revisionist even by the tolerant standards of the Frankfurt school—but they have inherited the basic insight of the "critical theory" into the whole problematic nature of contemporary society.

What if this society increasingly becomes a deliberate artefact produced by the technocratic managers of the new order? Then a philosophy which in the name of empiricism excludes every kind of transcendence must inevitably turn into an apologia for the status quo.

One may also put it differently: the logical status of value judgments has become a practical problem not just for a few reflective individuals, but for everyone. Weber was able to ignore this circumstance because the society of his age was still autonomous vis-à-vis the state, and because the kind of liberal Protestantism on which he had been brought up was adequate for the educated German middle class to which he belonged: a stratum that has since undergone catastrophic upheavals, and incidentally shown itself helpless, to say the least, when confronted with the monstrosities of the Third Reich. *Der Positivismusstreit* is among others the record of a spiritual crisis brought about by the unprecedented collapse of German liberalism in 1933. It is true and important that enlightened rationalism has now, at long last, become the creed of the German educated world. It is likewise important that the romantic undercurrent, which for so long nourished the politics of the extreme Right, has been diverted leftward by the student movement. But welcome though these changes are, they do not dispose of the dangers arising from the technocratic model—and anyway the new mood cannot validate the empiricism of the positivist school. So far as sociology is concerned, the school appears to be operating with equipment which was already inadequate in Weber's day. Its notion of rational behaviour is too formal to constitute an effective barrier against irrationality.

This is not to say that the debate can be written off as an academic dispute—another *Methodenstreit*. The issues at stake in the Albert-Habermas controversy, and in the antecedent duel between Popper and Adorno, concern us all. It is perhaps worth emphasizing once more that the discussion cuts across the East-West antagonism to which we have all become habituated. In so far as politics enter the matter, they relate to the functioning of a democratic order in a free society. None of the participants would want to be seen in the company of Spanish generals,

Greek colonels, or East European bureaucrats. In short, this is a thoroughly civilized debate between the representative thinkers of a leading European country, now for the first time fully integrated within the general orbit of what is vaguely known as Western civilization. As such it merits attention irrespective of the intricate logical and philosophical topics at the centre of the dispute. In the long run, though, what counts is the core of the argument. It is just conceivable that this generation of German philosophers is going to make up for the misdeeds of its predecessors by helping the rest of us to find a way out of the maze into which the uncontrolled explosion of scientific technology has led us.

In the light of the foregoing remarks we may now conclude with a brief reappraisal of a work which for many years led an underground existence among the homeless Left of the Federal Republic: the joint study of modern culture by Max Horkheimer and Theodor W. Adorno, entitled *Dialektik der Aufklärung*, originally composed by its two distinguished authors during their Californian exile in 1944, first published in 1947 by Querido in Amsterdam, repeatedly pirated, and finally reedited and re-published by S. Fischer in 1969 with a joint preface dated "Frankfurt am Main, April 1969". The book can stand as a monument to the intellectual trajectory described by two eminent representatives of the Old Left during the quartercentury separating one age from another. There is no hyperbole involved in speaking of an "age" dividing the present generation from its fathers; it is only since 1945 that modern society has begun to assimilate the technological upheaval associated with nuclear fission, computerized knowledge, lunar rockets and so on. The concurrent transformation of the socio-political "superstructure", although dimly visible since the day the first atom bomb fell on the unsuspecting inhabitants of Hiroshima, is now sufficiently far advanced to lend point to the gloomy analysis Horkheimer and Adorno placed at the opening of their joint enterprise in 1944:

Historically the Enlightenment, in the most general sense of progressive thinking, has aimed at the goal of delivering men from fear and making them masters of the world. But the wholly enlightened globe radiates triumphant disaster.

The theme has become rather tediously familiar, and signs are not lacking that what was new and original in 1945 is now turning into a litany of cut-price apocalyptics—what the eponymous hero of Saul Bellow's *Herzog* called "the commonplaces of the Wasteland outlook, the cheap mental stimulants of Alienation, the cant and rant of pipsqueaks about Inauthenticity and Forlornness". For all that, the book is still worth reading as an introduction to the peculiar synthesis of Marx, Freud, Nietzsche and Heidegger commonly associated with the name of Herbert Marcuse, and innocently popularized by a rising generation of intellectuals to whom the violent death of the Weimar Republic, and the concurrent collapse of the Old Left, signify no more than a particular bloodstained episode in the recent history of Continental Europe. Few of them are likely to respond favourably to the 1969 preface, with its disillusioned side-glance at "the conflicts of the Third World, the new growth of totalitarianism" as the legitimate prolongation of the age of Hitler and Stalin. "Critical thinking . . . today demands that one should side with the residues of freedom, with tendencies towards real humanism."

Where then is the rising generation to look for guidance? To the ultra-left? But Maoism for practical purposes has a following —in Europe and America anyway—only among the lumpenproletariat and the lumpenintelligentsia, those ancient reservoirs of anarchism. Can one seriously build upon such foundations? The pseudo-intellectuals of today cannot tell the difference between Mao and Marx, or between Freud and Timothy Leary, or between Beethoven and the Beatles. Many believe that the enemy is not the technocratic ruling stratum of the new order, but civilization itself—any civilization. What can one do with such human material? Make a revolution? But the working class loathes the very sight of them, and the cry "kill the pigs" testifies only to the mental sickness of those who utter it. People who invent such slogans are themselves part of the disease they talk of curing.

The *Dialektik der Aufklärung*, then, has itself become an illustration of the dialectical interplay between the critique of "mass culture" and the utilization of this critique by the leaders of a new generation of infuriated telly-watchers who rush into the streets whenever their blood boils over at the sight of yet another massacre in some faraway country of which, alas, we know only too much. It has become a commonplace that the driving force behind this non-stop protest is the cleavage between the omnipotence of the new technology and the felt impotence of the individuals who service it and are served by it. The diagnosis is true and apposite. Its current exemplification in the chaotic politics of the United States—at once the most advanced and the most conservative country in the Western world—bears out the statement that the Enlightenment has turned into its opposite. Only—and this is where the two authors felt obliged in 1969 to modify their original prospectus—this particular dialectic is not confined to the Western world, let alone to the collapsing culture of European bourgeois society. It applies to the "socialist camp" as well. For proof one need only consider the current state of relations between Moscow and Peking.

On dialectical principles this outcome was to be expected. The universality of the crisis testifies to the effective unification of the world by the new technology let loose by the second industrial revolution. The fact that this revolution takes place over great areas of the planet under the banner of socialism or communism is historically significant when viewed from an authentically global standpoint. It then becomes apparent that the dichotomy capitalism/socialism is on the point of losing its former significance. What it portends is no longer a fundamental choice between alternative modes of existence, but a convergence towards a point where both systems disclose their joint descent from principles held in common since the Enlightenment triumphed over its enemies : the defenders of the pre-industrial order. The socio-political cleavage symbolized by the effective partition of Europe in 1945 falls into place as an important but subordinate aspect of the global transformation in progress since that date, and the divergence between the "two camps" loses its relevance in the measure in which both sides in this global contest for preeminence confront the threat of instant annihilation, and the subtler menace of technocracy: the latter signifying the conscious adaptation of the "superstructure" to the new technological "base". Hence the *Methodenstreit* between the heirs of Marx and Max Weber occurs within a dimension of experience where the secret of the new order is at last out in the open: the social structure has become malleable on both sides of the political divide and it has done so because the original Baconian vision is now close to fulfilment: science has become the instrument of total reconstruction. On what principles? In the name of what aims and values? Science as such has no answer to this question. Nor will it ever have one.

The Role of the Intellectuals

An essay on the current social significance of the floating stratum variously known as "the intellectuals" or "the intelligentsia" must at the outset face the obvious problem of coming to terms with its own implied assumptions : notably, the belief that the theme warrants yet another effort at clarification. This could easily turn out to be a piece of self-deception. Intellectuals, after all, are people who specialize in generalities. A writer who assigns an important role to their particular function possibly overrates an activity which by some (unattainable) standard of judgement may not rank quite so high as he supposes. As against this, it is arguable that the intelligentsia has hitherto managed to keep its role concealed : partly from lack of awareness, partly from a justified apprehension of the consequences were it publicly admitted that much of what passes for "cultural life", "informed opinion", "enlightened attitudes", etc.—not to mention "spiritual values"—could easily be subsumed under some such unfeeling label as "intelligentsia thinking". So far from inflating its own importance, the intelligentsia, it might be said, pretends that it does not carry much weight, and on occasions even protests that it does not really exist.

The assumption here made, however, is that the intelligentsia exists and it matters, though perhaps not quite in the way most of its members commonly think. Moreover, we take it for granted that anyone who reflects on the part played by the social stratum to which he himself belongs cannot help believing that it is a significant one.

As everyone knows, or ought to know, the intelligentsia is a modern, that is to say, a post-medieval phenomenon, its distant forerunners being the humanists of the fifteenth and sixteenth centuries. If one wants to push the date further back, one may conceivably include among the precursors the wandering scholars, vagrant ex-students, and unfrocked priests and monks of the later Middle Ages; not, however, the clergy, since they formed a close corporation, possessed all the attributes of an "estate", and derived both their income and their influence from sources other than those commonly at the disposal of professional intellectuals. If these distinctions were to be challenged—possibly on the grounds that the medieval clergy were simply intellectuals who in a theocratic society had a corporate monopoly of information, and consequently of power—one might redefine the terms so as to draw a sharper line of division between the medieval and the modern "intelligentsia". Such redefinition, however, would not affect the argument that the stratum currently called the intelligentsia has in fact arisen from these non-clerical groups who first make their appearance in the later Middle Ages (characteristically as an element subversive of the established order). By the eighteenth century, the churches and the intellectuals are already so clearly distinguished—at any rate in Western Europe—as to exclude the possibility of lumping them together under the same label.

The intelligentsia, then, is a product of the secularization of society. With the spread of this phenomenon from Western to Eastern Europe, and latterly to Asia and Africa, it has become plain that the process has a certain regularity which does not depend on local conditions, though from a different aspect each historical situation is unique. Thus the Russian intelligentsia of the nineteenth century, and the modern intellectual proletariat of the so-called "underdeveloped" (i.e., pre-industrial) regions, react differently to socio-political stresses; and their reactions differ even more strikingly from those of their Western predecessors who grew up in a stabler environment with a slower tempo of change. But to the sociologist or the historian of culture they look alike, not least in respect of their hostile attitude to the "medieval" (i.e., religious) integration of the pre-modern age.

Now for a brief glance at the varying fortunes of the intelligentsia in the liberal, or bourgeois, age which lies behind us. In its political role we encounter the new stratum on the threshold, so to speak, of modernity : at the onset of the French Revolution. This is the first great upheaval in which intellectuals not merely provide general ideas, but actually hold power, or at least share it for a time with political leaders who have been indoctrinated with the new beliefs. Later the division of function between politicians and intellectuals tends to run parallel with the growing cleavage between bourgeois conservatism and intelligentsia radicalism : the intellectual vanguard becomes critical of the society it helped bring into being, and its plebeian stratum proceeds to get the socialist movement under way. Indeed, from one aspect socialism is the creation of the proletarianized intelligentsia—chiefly in France—between 1830 and 1870. The members of this group not merely formulate the general principles of the new movement, but are decisive in shaping its basic attitudes : hostility to the propertied class, to the state, to the church—in short, to everything that blocks complete fulfilment of the Enlightenment at the climax of the great revolution in 1793–94. Some, though not all, of the same intelligentsia values later find a new embodiment in Marxism, but in the main they are carried forward by various "national" schools of French socialism, whose rebellious activity comes to a disastrous climax in the Paris Commune of 1871. Since these ideas are profoundly marked by romanticism—another current manifestation of the intelligentsia's hostility to bourgeois society—they tend to assume utopian and impractical shapes, and frequently come into conflict with the soberer and less violent aspirations of the real labour movement. The latter gradually emancipates itself from the influence of intelligentsia radicalism and—by a somewhat paradoxical development—adopts Marxism as a more scientific and less utopian version of the socialist faith. This is not altogether a misunderstanding, as the history of German socialism is to show, but it contains an element of misapprehension which becomes manifest in the Russian Revolution. Hence the 1917 upheaval revives both the typical utopianism of the romantic age and the key role of the intelligentsia—at any rate until the moment when the intelligentsia is once more expelled from the political stage and forced to take up the role of the "critical consciousness".

These developments, which can only be sketched out here, naturally have their counterpart on the other side of the political fence. With the decline of classical nineteenth century conservatism and liberalism (which continue to lead a spectral existence in the pages of academic journals, but no longer shape the most active minds among the intelligentsia) the inevitable polarization of thinking and feeling that accompanies every major social crisis promotes a new alignment among all groups which are in principle hostile to bourgeois society, but differ over ways of combating it, and on the question of what should take its place. Fascism, like socialism and communism, is an intelligentsia movement, and moreover just as hostile to the bourgeois integration as are its competitors, from whom it differs, however, in its romantic irrationalism and elite-worship. This actually becomes the principal factor in its eventual defeat, since irrationalism in philosophy is incompatible with a rational choice of means in politics, while the open repudiation of democracy does away with the principal check upon uncontrolled personal despotism. The fascist crisis signifies nevertheless that liberal society, at any rate in Europe, is on the point of giving up the ghost, its dominant class having lost the will and the capacity to rule. The trend continues after 1945, notwithstanding the defeat of fascism.

What currently passes for bourgeois society in the principal Western countries—even those that escaped the fascist crisis—no longer fits the old categories. The new, partly planned and socialized, industrial society is not yet post-capitalist, but it is certainly post-bourgeois, in the sense that its basic institutions are no longer held together by a class of independent property-owners, but rather controlled by a hierarchy of planners, managers, bureaucrats, and technicians, who are about to evolve a new ethos as well as new forms of political and social life. Together with the bourgeoisie, the proletariat also tends to disappear. Both are "sublated", i.e., transformed and partly preserved in a new state. Their common ground—the market economy of liberal capitalism—suffers a slow erosion and they are being "socialized" by an impersonal process which they do not altogether welcome, but which nonetheless exerts its influence over them. Since the new society is bound together by a different *modus operandi,* the class struggle in its nineteenth century form comes to an end, and with it the ability of the intelligentsia to act the part of revolutionary "vanguard". In the stratified society of post-bourgeois industrialism—whether described as "socialism", "modern capitalism", "managerialism", or by some other term—the intelligentsia can no longer play the same role as in the "open society" of nineteenth century capitalism. It settles down, forgets its "vanguard" ideology, becomes status-conscious, and at last even acquires something like a theoretical awareness of its own existence.

If under present-day conditions the intelligentsia tends to fade out of the political struggle, is this equivalent to saying that the intellectual content of politics is bound to evaporate? To anyone brought up in the tradition of intelligentsia politics the question must appear almost meaningless. But it would not have appeared meaningless in the early nineteenth century, or at the height of the Victorian epoch. A coherent ruling class makes use of intellectuals, but does not identify the content of politics with the changing opinions of a stratum that happens to specialize in general ideas. The notion of "class", however, implies a kind of stability which belongs to the nineteenth century rather than to our own age. It suggests a combination of traits—ownership, hereditary status, shared outlook—which still retains something of the permanence at one time assigned (in principle anyhow) to the medieval estates. A class in this sense, even though not fixed and privileged like an estate, is able to establish traditions which can be shared with newcomers and passed on to rising social strata. It is a truism that this transmission has become increasingly difficult because ideas and values nowadays lose currency much more rapidly than in the past. Yet at the same time, social patterns tend rather to grow more rigid and hierarchical. This appears above all in the almost universal rise of bureaucratic power, as a result of which the frontier between "state" and "society", so sharply defined in the last century, is increasingly blurred.

The consequent loss of personal freedom is at the heart of the mental and emotional corrosion which has overtaken classical liberalism. It may in the long run have an equally depressing effect on the democratic socialist movement. When one remembers that it was possible for Shaw to distribute his enthusiasm impartially between Marx, Ibsen, and Wagner, one realizes with a start how much that was intrinsically romantic and "bourgeois", i.e., individualist and libertarian, even anarchistic, was involved in the old socialist ethos. With the moderns, whose disillusionment is adequately portrayed by Silone and Orwell, socialism becomes stoical and gloomy. It renounces the hope of bringing communal existence into conformity with the human essence ("realizing the aims of philosophy", in Marx's phrase) and contents itself with a rearguard action against what it conceives to be a hopelessly corrupt civilization.

Disillusionment always occurs at the point where a movement has "seen through" its own limitations. The latter in turn become visible only when an attempt has been made to transcend them. Such transcendence is involved in the strained effort to realize the original aims of the movement, conceived under circumstances different from those which attend their actual fulfilment. Realization remains incomplete, not only because conditions have changed in the meantime, but because the programme was from the start shot through with metapolitical ideas and anticipations. In the history of liberalism, the French Revolution marks the watershed between the naive utopianism of the Enlightenment and the commonplace outlook of the Western middle class around 1850. By that time the radical intellectuals were already becoming disillusioned with the achievements of liberalism, and critical of its guiding notions, but the bulk of the class from which they stemmed—and to which in effect they belonged—

had not caught up with them and still regarded the ideas of 1776 and 1789 as the ultimate standards of judgment. Yet when the same ideas were first formulated, they were considerably ahead of what was then thought possible by the majority of "sensible" people—i.e., non-intellectuals—and in fact appeared utopian.

The factor of time lag, however, is not the only one in this recurrent cleavage. The intellectuals not only run ahead of the general movement: they also experience in a much higher degree the desire to see ultimate aims translated into reality, whereas the bulk of their following is content with an approximation. Once parliamentary government and free trade had been secured, the middle class was satisfied, and left the radical intellectuals to agitate for full democracy. Similarly, the long-range and short-range goals envisaged in socialism appear quite differently to the socialist intelligentsia and to the industrial working class: the two strata which together make up the modern labour-socialist movement. They have enough in common to co-operate in the political field, but their interests do not necessarily coincide in all respects, and the resulting tension can be dangerous to their morale. In other ways too it is apparent that the present situation differs from the characteristic problem of middle-class liberalism a century ago: there is today less fear of democracy as a potential threat to social privilege. This fear is the common theme of mid-Victorianism, and the almost hysterical form it then took has no parallel today, unless Western nervousness in the face of the emerging peoples of Asia and Africa be regarded as the modern counterpart of bourgeois alarm over the menace of popular rule a century ago. The corroding effect of this alarm upon the morale of the propertied class—not to mention the aristocratic governing caste which still monopolized office but had already lost control of legislation—can be studied in the writings of the Victorians who set the tone around the time of the American Civil War and the second Reform Act of 1867. Here the contrast between Macaulay (who died in 1859) and Bagehot is instructive. Macaulay, for whom the first Reform Act of 1832 was the formative event of his life, still displays the unbroken self-confidence of an older generation of liberals, to whom full democracy was not so much a threat as a self-evident absurdity. Indeed he disclaims the very title of liberalism, preferring to describe himself (quite accurately) as a Whig, i.e., a middle-class supporter of that oligarchy whose principles might be summed up under the three headings of Protestantism, patriotism, and parliamentary government (with a narrow franchise). "You can call me a Liberal", he observes in one of his letters, "but I don't know that in these days I deserve the name . . . I am in favour of war, hanging, and Church Establishments". Here is the authentic voice of the eighteenth century, specifically of the Whig tradition, whose last great representative in British politics was Winston Churchill.

There is not a trace of such naive brutality in Bagehot, who already represents a much more modern type : cynical, neurotic, and "realistic" in the manner of a privileged class with an uneasy conscience. Yet the careers of both men overlap, with the important difference that Bagehot witnessed the breakthrough of democracy in the 1860's, when Gladstone moved away from Whiggery and founded the Liberal party, to cope with the newly enfranchised industrial masses; while across the ocean democracy found an embodiment in Lincoln (whom Bagehot characteristically described as "a village lawyer"). Where Macaulay despised democracy, Bagehot had learned to fear it, and he did much to implant this fear in the cultivated upper-middle class. Bagehot, as any student of his writings perceives at first glance, is far more sophisticated than Macaulay, but he altogether lacks the older man's self-confidence and his belief in the validity of his principles. Where Macaulay is complacent, forthright, and occasionally brutal, Bagehot sounds unpleasantly timorous, cynical, and evasive, thus betraying a sense that reality may be dangerous to his values. The difference in tone between the two men is not merely stylistic : it heralds the disintegration of liberalism as a political philosophy relevant to an industrial age. Bagehot's personal neurosis, to which his recent biographers have drawn attention, foreshadows the growth of nervous instability in the cultivated upper class, a change of mood which lays that important stratum open to irrational fears and narrows the gap between it and the intelligentsia. Thus in various ways he typifies the beginning of the process which eventually culminates in the general crisis of liberal civilization.[1]

The important point to note here is that in an "open society" of the nineteenth century type the professional intelligentsia's ability to play a political role is linked to its relative freedom of movement as a floating stratum which can attach itself, wholly or in part, to social classes other than the one which originally gave birth to it. From the standpoint of those committed to the existing order, such shifting from class to class is treachery, and it explains the wariness with which the intelligentsia has been regarded ever since its dangerous instability was first perceived or suspected. The decisive change occurs with the French Revolution. Burke's denunciation of pettifogging attorneys and rattle-brained journalists, who presume to legislate for mankind, inaugurates a chorus of woe which is later taken up by liberals frightened into conservatism by the advance of radical democracy. After 1830, and in particular after 1848—when the "revolution of the intellectuals" triggers a premature proletarian insurrection in Paris—the intelligentsia splits into warring camps. Its plebeian ranks rally to democracy and even socialism, while the patrician upper layer turns conservative: albeit in the nineteenth century sense of the term (i.e., without any special fondness for monarchy, aristocracy, or the church, but with a great concern for "law and order"—meaning unconditional defence of property against the threatening onslaught of the "masses").

This anti-democratic frame of mind carries over into, and thoroughly confuses, the discussion of socialism, since in actual fact the industrial proletariat—once it appears on the scene as organized labour—is no threat to civilization but rather its chief bulwark against the irrational tendencies emanating from the crisis of the established order. Here we have a reversal of roles which reaches its culmination under fascism, where the déclassé *Lumpenbourgeoisie* and its ideologists continue to clamour for "order", and to fulminate against the "masses", in the very act of themselves destroying the foundations of civilized existence. Neo-conservatism, with its glorification of a non-existent golden age of pre-industrial harmony and contentment, is a feeble-witted and correspondingly harmless form of the same mental aberration. At the opposite end of the political spectrum, the rationalist drive towards total reorganization of society according to a predetermined plan finds a new embodiment in communism. These rival movements feed on each other, mobilize social forces rendered desperate by the collapse of the liberal integration, and finally exhaust each other. Their conflict terminates only with the disappearance of the common framework supporting the edifice of bourgeois civilization.

Although the state of affairs just described is commonly in the minds of people who say that we live in a post-revolutionary age, they do not always perceive that it really signifies the end of an era in which class conflicts had major political significance. Where status wrangles, or sectional disputes among interest groups, take the place of struggles over the form of society, politics loses its ideological (in every sense) flavour, and intellectuals no longer find much to interest them in the rivalry of parties operating within a common framework of ideas and institutions. As in eighteenth century England, the party game becomes an affair of "ins" and "outs", from which revolutionary ideas and passions are effectively excluded. In this perspective the antagonism between liberals and socialists—defined as supporters or opponents of the market economy and individualism —gives way to a new alignment dividing centralizers and autonomists, authoritarians and libertarians, believers in over-all state control and supporters of regional decentralization, functional autonomy, corporate self-government, etc. The issue, one might say, is no longer "liberty", but "liberties", in the traditional sense of corporate privileges (e.g., for universities and other autonomous corporations). If these disputes are going to shape the specifically modern situation, the intelligentsia may come into its own again : though only in the event that it manages to acquire or forge collective instruments which are not themselves subject to bureaucratic control.

But what is the precise role of the intellectuals, individually and as a group, under the new circumstances? The question is difficult to answer because of the dual nature of the intellectual, as someone whose ideas are supposed to be—and occasionally are—valid for his age, and as a member of a specialized stratum which produces its own kind of ideology, i.e., "false consciousness". Moreover the two functions merge in practice, so that genuine insights and ideological distortions are not simply jumbled together externally, but frequently appear as different aspects of the same body of thought. J. S. Mill's doctrine of representative government, or Marx's theory of class conflict, to take two notable examples, are so constructed that they cannot be neatly divided into empirical and philosophical, or scientific and utopian, constituents. After a sufficient lapse of time it is indeed usually possible to distinguish what is valid from what is merely speculative in a theoretical construction; but one must not overlook the fact that the "merely speculative" element, though of no interest to the practitioners of politics, may conserve insights of long-range importance for a later age. Again, it does not follow that because parts of the structure are scientifically unsound, they are "ideological" in the sense of reflecting a distorted group interest or prejudice. They may reflect nothing at all save the personal bias of the theorist; on the other hand, ideas that do conform to group attitudes may nonetheless be quite sound.

For all that, however, one must still try to distinguish intellectual creations from intelligentsia opinions, though the former commonly have their source in the latter, and conversely help in turn to shape the outlook of the entire stratum within which every kind of intellectual activity—scientific, artistic, philosophical, etc.—occurs. The term "stratum", incidentally, commits one to a certain view of society, inasmuch as it dispenses both with the romantic notion of the intellectual as a solitary individual floating in a vacuum, and with the currently fashionable vagueness which causes people of similar antecedents or occupations to be lumped together into the same "class". A stratum, as distinct from a class, has no direct relation to what Marx called "the production and reproduction of material life", though its members may form an important section of one of the major classes. The assumption here, of course, is that classes are defined in relation to "means of production". Anyone is free to choose a different nomenclature, on condition of making it plain what sort of criterion has been adopted. This clearly is easier if one has no axe to grind, but axe-grinding is not confined to conservatives and defenders of the established order; it is just as frequent among radicals[2]. The fact that the radical intelligentsia, which for over a century spearheaded all major revolutionary movements in the West, showed so little interest in the sociological approach to radical politics, is itself revealing. In principle it ought to be plain that one cannot analyse intellectual constructions without coming upon intelligentsia attitudes; but plain or not, the idea has never commended itself to a majority of those engaged in "social criticism".

Here we touch upon what is commonly described as the politicization of culture. In our part of the world this is still regarded as a problem peculiar to the Soviet orbit, but—quite apart from the experience with fascism—the West cannot be said to be altogether innocent of its own politicizing of culture. It is not even certain that innocence is commendable, if it encourages helplessness in the face of unrestrained commercialism decked out as "consumer sovereignty". The scandal of the mass media is there to show what happens when society fails to establish generally accepted standards in a domain where the "satisfaction of needs" is by no means synonymous with "progress". (Not to mention the fact that needs can be artificially created or inflated.) As the repository of society's cultural traditions, the intelligentsia has a responsibility which cannot be adequately discharged by any other group, and intellectuals cannot therefore compromise their own standards without doing harm to the body politic.

If this statement is not compatible with a certain simplified notion of democracy as the "consumer sovereignty" of everyone capable of reading a newspaper or an advertisement, so much the worse for those who cling to such notions. For the present and the immediate future it remains true that standards will either be set by the intellectual elite or by those interested in reducing the general level to the lowest common denominator. But to say this is also to imply that the intelligentsia—if it wants to play a definite part in the new society—cannot simply content itself with affirming a faith in democracy. It must work out political concepts which harmonize the democratic idea with an understanding of its own role under conditions where the major questions are no longer left to the free play of market forces, but are increasingly determined by centralized decision-makers of one kind or another. Failing greater awareness of this, the standing temptation to back some kind of totalitarianism will not be easily avoided.

Thus far we have been dealing with the negative side of the matter. Positively, it may perhaps be affirmed that there are opportunities inherent in the growth of organization : simply because this trend involves the conscious reshaping of social patterns which in the past grew up spontaneously and without much thought. The crux here is the importance assumed by the intellectual function under conditions where society becomes increasingly dependent both upon specialization in the various departments of social life, and upon integration at a higher level. Up to now the failure has lain at the second stage. The increasing rationalization of the most varied and extensive spheres of existence has not led to a commensurate growth of rationality at the top level where the key decisions are taken. On the contrary, rational choice of means has proved compatible with extreme irrationality in the (conscious and unconscious) selection of ends. Germany under Hitler was a particularly disastrous instance, but a similar contrast is apparent in the Soviet orbit, notwithstanding the doctrinaire rationalism of the official ideology, which serves to integrate the various sectors of public life and interpret them to each other. Here the element of irrationality—after being solemnly expunged from the official consciousness and driven into limbo—reasserts itself in the Manichaean division of the world into redeemed (communist) and unredeemed (non-communist) parts : a caricature of the older religious faith, but with (literally) explosive power behind it. Nor is the West altogether free from such mental aberrations, in which the unresolved conflict between scientific methods and ideological goals find bizarre and potentially dangerous expression.

Whatever ground for optimism nonetheless exists must be sought in long range considerations. At least it may be said that *in principle* the transition to a more highly organized form of existence implies a superior level of rationality and consequently a larger social role for the intellect. If the argument sounds question-begging—there is after all no guarantee that the transition is actually going to be made : we may blow ourselves up instead—it can still be said that the past half century gives no encouragement to the advocates of irrational behaviour. Romanticism in politics has faded out, *et pour cause!* It may also be suspected that the fascist rebellion was in the nature of a rearguard action, as it was certainly in conflict with the relentless march of global forces hostile to worshippers of the "will to power" and "thinking with the blood". If the liberal integration collapsed at one decisive moment, the rational principle in the end asserted is supremacy.

There is further ground for cautious optimism in the reflection that the choice has currently been narrowed down to a simple question of survival, and that this dramatic confrontation occurred *after,* and not before, the extreme proponents of destructive, death-worshipping romanticism had been eliminated. Lastly, the social revolution which—as on previous occasions— accompanied and speeded a decisive step forward in the control of nature, may already be over, at least so far as the West is concerned. There are still a number of countries where social change will come via class conflict, but in the West class conflict is fading out. What takes its place is the evolution of a new directing stratum and the struggle to determine its orientation. That is why all contemporary politics not concerned with the problem of the growth of organization and central planning are so trivial and boring. The mechanism continues to revolve, but the spirit has departed. This is as true of democratic electioneering in the West as of totalitarian phrasemongering in the East. The death of outstanding personalities is illustrative of the stalemate. The great figures of the revolutionary age now about to end—Churchill, de Gaulle, Stalin, Roosevelt—are already beginning to look somewhat archaic. What succeeds them is the confusion and mediocrity inseparable from the reaction to a prolonged and exhausting crisis. Nor are we better off for theorists of the first magnitude. It will take time for the new integration to establish itself. Mean-

while one may note such signs of change as are already beginning
to declare themselves.

Are there such signs? It is at any rate possible to think that
we are in for a new era of rationalism. For reasons which
should now have become a little clearer, a new rationalist ethos,
if it should prevail, is likely to run parallel with a considerable
growth in the socio-political weight of the intellectual stratum.
Alternatively, if one prefers the simplified version of historical
materialism popular in some quarters, one may invert this
statement and say that the growing importance of the technical
and scientific intelligentsia is going to reduce the area of mischief
still open to political movements of a more primitive type. Either
way we get a perspective that is slightly more comforting than
the currently fashionable existentialist prophecy of doom. Given
the assumption that the world can turn the nuclear corner without total disaster, there seems to be some ground for supposing
that rational integration will at last penetrate to the areas of
decisive choice. Without being a hopeless visionary one can even
now foresee circumstances in which—to take merely one example
—the inhabitants of some particular human plague-spot will
publicly express a preference for being governed by the United
Nations Secretariat rather than by homegrown fanatics, be they
military dictators, political rabble-rousers, or just plain bunglers.
If that happened, it would constitute what might be called
rationalization in politics, and everyone who has the good of the
world at heart ought to hope that the first such instance will
occur in the coming decade. Politics of course is not everything,
but an outbreak of common sense in this sphere would be an
important step forward.

More generally, we may perhaps surmise that the trend toward
greater organizational complexity, and its corollary, central planning, cannot fail to enhance the significance (and the responsibility) of the stratum which does the thinking for the rest of
society. If one is right in believing that social evolution will
henceforth proceed, if at all, by means of rational organization,
then it cannot be a matter of indifference that the chief vehicle
of the process should in recent decades have become more clearly
identifiable. When one has said the worst that can be said about

the intelligentsia, it remains a fact that this stratum carries within itself the main potentiality of evolution still open to mankind. Or if that sounds too portentous, one can rephrase it by saying that we have here at least an identifiable organ of societal development whose spontaneous tendencies are in tune with the requirements of the next historical phase. The latter formulation would seem to do justice to an observable trend, while skirting the danger of "historicism", i.e., policy-making in the guise of prophecy. It is not a question of trying to divine the predetermined course of history, but rather of indicating where the future still appears to lie open. For of course there is no guarantee— at least from our limited standpoint—that the experiment will come off; in other words: that the transition to a wholly rational, scientifically controlled, planetary order will be made without disaster or relapse into totalitarian fantasy. One can only suggest that progress, if it occurs at all, is going to depend on the survival and further perfection of the stratum which incorporates the main evolutionary tendency. That this is not the proletariat may distress some surviving romanticists, but need not upset any followers of Marx who have taken his method rather than his system to heart. The issue transcends such 19th-century quarrels (on both sides: for liberals will have to get out of the habit of playing Mill off against Marx). It is an aspect of a situation in which, as was remarked before, the rival classes are being "sublated", and there is consequently nothing further to be hoped (or feared) from the class struggle.

The tentative conclusion which emerges, then, is that social evolution is increasingly going to depend on mind, and consequently on the quantitative and qualitative growth of the stratum which embodies the capacity of the intellect to introduce order into the environment. The "open conspiracy" to effect the same purpose—proclaimed by a few writers half a century ago—may be regarded as an imaginative foreshadowing of a situation which has actually come to pass in our days, with the exhaustion of traditional passions and the disappearance of the class structure inherited from the 19th century. It is this structural transformation which has made it possible to envisage coming social changes in terms of conflicts within the new directing stratum which is about to evolve out of the non-specialized (or omni-specialized) section of the old 19th century intelligentsia. Where liberalism and socialism are now seen to have erred was in supposing that the whole development was bound to remain a party matter. Actually it is the result of the end of the social conflict as the principal vehicle of change, and the emergence of a type of society in which the major transformations increasingly result from conscious decision-making. By comparison with the liberal century—which may be said to have opened in 1830 and run its course by 1930—the new situation represents, among other things, a shift in the balance between state and society such as to make the state the dominant partner. In its opening phase this was one of the preconditions of totalitarianism, and of revolutionary intelligentsia politics in general. The long-run tendency toward greater complexity of organization, central planning, and conscious control need not, however, be identified with the political turmoil of the transition period which, for the West, has come to an end. The tendency persists in its own right and thereby makes possible the conversion of the intelligentsia into the directing stratum of industrial society.

Social evolution, in the measure that it takes place, is likely to be directed from now on by the "brain" of the body politic, as distinct from the hit-or-miss mechanism of class conflict characteristic of the preceding age. Societies which remain permanently below this level of advance are not due to disappear: they simply cease to participate in the general movement. The same applies to political sects, or schools of thought, which continue to repeat slogans appropriate to an earlier phase. If the foregoing all sounds decidedly unromantic, there may be some consolation in the thought that it represents merely the abstract outline of a process which is certain to generate its own heat as it goes along. The new society, like the old, will have its problems, and the discovery that some of them are insoluble can be relied upon to keep the presses fed with blueprints for utopia.

But what is the justification for supposing that society will develop both a degree of rationality and an institutional mechanism adequate for the task of planetary organization? The question had better be rephrased: what are the criteria for judging that some such development is actually under way? For there is of course no guarantee that the requisite level will be reached without disaster. What is required is a kind of social mutation, if that expression may be permitted. Reference has already been made to evolution being carried forward by a stratum which represents, as it were, the "brain" of the social organism. How far can one push these analogies without lapsing into absurdity? The answer, it would seem, depends on whether it is possible to identify an actual phenomenon of growth in the directing stratum of society which can be described in terms appropriate to natural and social science alike. Is there such a phenomenon? We know at any rate that in nature no organism of great complexity can function without a central mechanism capable of processing a great deal of information: in other words, a brain. We also know that increasing complexity of organization has historically been linked to greater mental convergence, meaning thereby a tendency for central mechanisms—biological, social, cultural—to take shape, and ultimately to take command of the situation.[3] On this rather trite, but perhaps not altogether useless, analogy it can at least be suggested that there may be a link between the drive for global organization and the growing importance of the social stratum which incorporates the rational principle. The connection is not perhaps immediately obvious, but "the banal fact of the earth's roundness"[4] is clearly responsible for a great deal of our present trouble, just as in the past it may have been behind the particular form taken by evolution over much lengthier spans of time. In any case it would seem evident that the nuclear threat could not have occurred in an "unlimited environment" leaving ample room for migration to "safe" portions of the globe. The same might be said of the growing pressure upon the more highly civilized nations arising from the "population explosion" in backward countries. The resulting web of circumstances is really not amenable to political guidance of the old-fashioned hit-or-miss kind typified by the familiar cycle of war-revolution-distintegration, with the replacement of one historic class by another serving as a mechanism of adaptation. This is not to say that the old familiar process no longer operates—it does, but plainly at the risk of blowing us all into the stratosphere. Also there is the simple fact that social evolution by way of historic conflict between one class and another—or one social order and another, or one group of nations and another—is not merely an extremely clumsy and dangerous mode of adaptation, but much too slow and haphazard to keep up with the fantastic rate of technological change.

To pursue our analogy : the increasing centralization of public life—which is really what one means in saying that the individualist era is closed—is at the same time a process whereby decision-making is located in a directing stratum, or "brain". Historically, the social group which embodies the tendency toward centralization stems from the intelligentsia of bourgeois society, although it is not identical with it. The growth of this stratum in all its aspects—from the managerial and technocratic to the genuinely intellectual—is the specific mode of evolution open to a society which has become fully industrialized, i.e., fully subject to the rule of technical-scientific rationality. Increasing complexity and growing rationality are two sides of the same coin. The stratum within which the dual advance manifests itself —not passively, but as a *willed,* consciously intended, process— is *ipso facto* the only one capable of getting the whole movement under control. By the same token it incorporates the rational principle itself (and probably mankind's only chance of survival). The growth of the intelligentsia—now that it has finally emerged from the chrysalis of the bourgeois epoch, with its antagonistic classes and its increasingly irrational political upheavals—is the precondition of orderly progress, though not in itself a sufficient guarantee that further evolution will in fact take place. That "progress" in this sense does signify "evolution" appears from the simple consideration that what we are witnessing is an instance of that mental "convergence" toward a directing centre which has been operative as far back as natural and social history can be traced. However speculative such ideas may sound, it will at any rate be conceded that the sudden appearance at the same time of a new type of society, a new pattern of global organization, and an unexampled threat to life itself, cannot be *merely* due to a set of coincidences. Unless all these tendencies operate so as to bring about a social mutation of the type here sketched out, it is going to be very difficult to make sense of the simultaneous convergence of so many novel and unprecedented factors. At the risk of sounding both unduly speculative and irritatingly dogmatic, one may therefore conclude that what the entire crisis has been building up to is a change which is going to locate the mechanism of further evolutionary advance in the stratum which represents the "brain" of the social organism. That this stratum has, in part at least, grown out of the old intelligentsia which fought and lost so many battles to make society more rational, may perhaps serve as some consolation to the less dispirited among its survivors.

Is this all? Probably not, but it will not do to push the analogy too far. One may note, however, that the evolutionary pattern is repeated in the tendency for new directing organs to take shape in response to pressures which evoke an intellectual effort that is at the same time an attempt to control the environment. As we have tried to suggest, these pressures arise at the circumference of the field and press back upon the centre, thereby calling attention to the need for control over forces that threaten to get out of hand. It is a pattern that appears to have a lengthy evolutionary record behind it. Whether one says that mind is generated in the process, or that the brain responds by synthesizing the information brought to its attention, makes little difference. The relevant point is that it has now become a life-and-death matter for society to respond to the emergence of new material forces in such a manner as not to let a wholesale catastrophe occur. This situation is new; it has evidently been brought about—as everyone says—by the fantastic discrepancy between the rate of scientific-technological advance and the failure of social evolution to keep step. But there is considerable reluctance to admit that the eventual response is likely to involve some qualitative change in our mental habits. The bare idea of dispensing with "politics" in the traditional sense strikes people as bizarre, though in practice the integration of scientific and political decision-making is already far advanced (mostly with the aim of blowing the planet to bits). It will take some further time for the notion to sink in that control of nature involves a far-reaching social reorganization, and that in future this kind of decision can no longer be left to the accidents of political upheavals or the "successful" outcome of wars.

Of course none of the foregoing is altogether new: H. G. Wells had a premonition of it many years ago. The strange thing is that we are now actually on the threshold of its happening, while the politicians go on drooling about stone-age issues, and most intellectuals are sunk in despair because the particular sect they fancy has not converted a majority of the electorate. If the remarks set forth here have indicated an alternative approach to the problem of what is going on around us, they will at any rate not have been entirely useless. The great trouble is that we find it extremely difficult, with our limited perspective, to visualize the kind of "convergent integration" that will be needed to get the whole planetary movement under control. All that the biological parallel really tells us is that there has to be a rational focus *somewhere*. For clearly rationalization, to be effective, must have a centre. Or to put it differently, consciousness must come to "a point at which all the impressions and experiences knit themselves together and fuse into a unity that is conscious of its own organization".[5] This, however, is not simply a postulate; it is inherent in the process, reflection being "the power acquired by a consciousness to turn in upon itself, to take possession of itself. . . ."[6] If the case were otherwise, psycho-social evolution would never have got to the present point. Whether it goes on would seem to depend on the outcome of the current race between potentially destructive and rationalizing tendencies, the latter coming to a focus in the various modern attempts—of which Communism is certainly one—to formulate something like a planetary consciousness. All this can perhaps be made palatable to empiricists by saying that after all the whole drive is merely the counterpart of the actual unification of the globe which is going on under our eyes. The Russians, with their own lunar expeditions, should be the last to protest at such an explanation, which incidentally pays due tribute to their recent scientific achievements. And the rest of us? In any event, we may suppose that the last word has not yet been spoken.

NOTES

1. See H. Stuart Hughes, *Consciousness and Society* (1958), *passim*, for the continuation of this process after 1890.

2. See C. Wright Mills, *The Sociological Imagination* (Oxford University Press: 1959), *passim*.

3. Compare Julian Huxley's preface to *The Phenomenon of Man*, by Teilhard de Chardin (1959).

4. Huxley, *ibid.*, 17.

5. Chardin, *op. cit.*, 165.

6. *Ibid.*

Index

Index